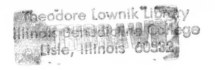
PREPARE FOR ARMAGEDDON

SURVIVAL IN THE NUCLEAR AGE

*Dr. Lydia R. Strother
& Claude L. Strother*

Box 1065
Gardena, CA 90249

LEE PRESS

Glendale, California

First Edition 1968.

Second Edition 1969.
Second Printing 1973.

Dedicated to the stouthearted everywhere "who refuse to be swallowed by the whale."

If a man speaks or acts with an evil thought,
Pain follows him;
As the wheel follows the foot of the ox
That draws the carriage.

If a man speaks or acts with a pure thought,
Happines follows him like a shadow
That never leaves him.

The Buddha

PREFACE

In writing this book an alternate title, *The Survivability Gap*, was considered. The scope of a book with this title might logically have started with Chapter Five, "Vietnam." Although the last eleven chapters alone would have provided a meaningful volume, this approach, it seemed, would have omitted an essential section generally included in the discussion of a serious subject — the background. With inclusion of the background in Chapters One through Four the scope of the book warranted a more relevant title.

The central message of this book is survivability. Available sources of information on preparations for survival in the Red World are reviewed and basic information on applicable techniques are summarized in a simplified manner. As long as certain problems are considered *as unthinkable* in the United States, and in the rest of the Free World, the Communists have a marked advantage — because inside the Iron and Bamboo Curtains these matters are handled on an unemotional basis.

The basic objective in writing this book is that of "sounding the alarm" and, at the same time, providing some constructive suggestion for positive action while there is yet a little time left. But, failing this, there is even a further objective — of providing documentation of the final period of a Great Nation. Of course, it is presumptuous to attempt to look beyond an armageddon, or The Armageddon, but a life's work based on scholarly procedure cannot be easily laid aside so that in this survey the treatment was organized in a way which might be useful to a future research — picking through the rubble, as it were.

A translator is sometimes called a traitor. Conveying exact shades of meaning by paraphrasing is even more difficult than translating; therefore, frequent use is made of quotations to provide as vivid a presentation as possible of the viewpoints presented. For example, who but an experienced reporter could have so vividly described the cold dread that gripped the entire world before the one-week war in June 1967, as the following appraisal by Joe Alex Morris Jr. in his report in the May 28, 1967, *Los Angeles Times:*

"Although the two superpowers find themselves in classic cold war positions, although they hold the cards which would provide the ultimate answer in any Middle East war, the fuses and the matches are in the hands of the Arabs and the Jews."

Lydia and Claude Strother   November 1969.

ADDENDUM 1973

It is apparent that the march of world events toward a nuclear Armageddon is closely following the course anticipated in the last printing of this book. A revision has not been required, only typographical errors have been corrected.

When the second edition was published in 1969 it was uncertain whether President Nixon would fulfill the promises made in his 1968 campaign: to *clean out* the State Department, to adopt a firm and positive posture against the swiftly progressing international Red tide, and to uphold *traditional* American interests. However, it develops that Richard Nixon is resorting to world-wide appeasment of the Red Powers. As the military is withdrawing U.S. troops from key overseas bases, the State Department is preparing plans for rebuilding North Vietnam and for massive trade and credits for all of the rest of the Red World.

As a result, it may be expected that within a few years the bamboo curtain will quietly be drawn around South Korea, South Vietnam and all of Indochina, the Philippines and probably Japan. The Free Chinese on Formosa may make a "deal" with the Russians to enter the Soviet bloc. In Europe, it may be expected that the economic union will fall under Russian control and Europe will be Findlandized, as U.S. troops are returned home and NATO is dismantled.

It still is possible—in an industrial sense—for a revitalized America to undermine the Red world's limited production capabilities by means of *economic warfare*, as well as to regain its position as *the* leading military power by; *introducing satellite weapons, establishing a nationwide shelter system, shielding our cities with a full scale anti ballistic missile (ABM) system, protecting other free world countries against the Red missle threat with sea-based ABM's building a nuclear merchant marine fleet, and the launching of an all-nuclear Navy.* However, we are convinced that the Red influence in Washington is too strong to consider such a course as forseeable.

It is, therefore, apparent that the discerning individual, although continuing to do everything possible to support a return to national independence, must begin to make such preparations as he can, or may care to make, for his personal survival through a world-wide nuclear holocaust. However, such national destruction should not be expected as a result of direct confrontation with the United States— which can be expected to buckle under to future demands presented by our Communist enemies—but from *secondary involvement in a Sino-Soviet confrontation,* arising from territorial disputes of those two factions in the struggle for world domination. A probable trigger issue can be expected in the Middle East, as the Egyptians and the guerrillas turn to Red China for support.

The Authors   February, 1973.

CONTENTS

PART I

THE BEGINNING OF THE END?

background

CHAPTER 1

PROLOGUE

In 221 BC, a ruthless despot, Shih Huang Ti, the Tiger of Ch'in, had conquered all of the provinces of modern China and decided to build the Great Wall of China — partially to reduce the constant Mongol threat, but also to crush internal dissent against his rule. To this latter end most scholars, artisans, and other politically dissident groups were conscripted into the vast hordes of coolie labor required in the construction work.

All libraries were destroyed, in an effort to achieve a complete break with the traditions of the past, to make history begin with Shih Huang Ti, and to prevent the use of the past to discredit the present.[1]

In a very few years, by 207 BC, the historical order was re-established, and people resumed their centuries-old tradition of looking into the past as they progressed forward. However, their vision of ancient times was now always more limited, and one might imagine their onward steps on the Tao, or path, a little less sure. After a few generations, recovery was more or less complete, but dating from the purge of the scholars and the libraries, the windows to the past must always be shrouded by a somewhat legendary mist.

In China, as elsewhere, the history of revolutionary social changes — generally effected by the use of force — has not been impressive. Even the moderate change, introduced in 170 BC by introduction of old age pensions[2], is not recorded as being a major milestone in Chinese history.

At the present moment in history we are experiencing another attempt to purge historic cultural, religious and governmental traditions. As evidenced in Russia, one of the essential requirements in building the society-of-the-proletariat is the development of an entirely new set of cultures — free from bourgeois elements. Further, in support of the Communist objectives, activist groups in the Western bloc, and

3

especially in the United States, are working frantically to erase the religious-cultural heritage of the past three or four thousand years.

These elements do not hesitate to make use of any group they can penetrate, or otherwise use. If none suitable is available, a new one will be formed. But wherever possible, taking over existing groups by penetration and corruption of objectives seems to be the preferred expedient. For example, it would appear that the National Council of Churches has to some extent been subverted or pulled off course to this end. Consider, for example, the following quotation taken from one of their recent publications.

> Our culture declares that all sexual activity within marriage is legal, proper and good, while any such activity outside marriage is illegal, sinful and wrong. This is to ignore the personal dimensions of life, to seek to force everyone under one massive legal umbrella. You know and I know perfectly well that there are many marriages that are simply matters of convenience that such sex as goes on within them is selfish, exploitative, and evil.
>
> We know further, that there is sexual contact between unmarried couples that is motivated by love and which is pure and on occasions beautiful.[3]

The writer of these lines was surely not aware of the true beauty of a proper Christian marriage and the peaceful bliss available to those individuals who are so fortunate as to spend their entire life "in grace," never having been led away from fundamental standards. (Of course, purge of improper experience is possible — certainly forgiveness is fundamental — but this is generally not an easy process.) Also, he was apparently not aware of the uplifting effect of a religious outlook in a home, in correcting or preventing elements of inharmony, discord, etc. In short, he was blind to the great spiritual truth that the source of inharmony, unhappiness, etc. arises from an improper spiritual outlook.

Returning to the quotation above, by this and many similar techniques, these activists work toward the elimination of all of the aspects of our society which tend to develop strong character, uprightness and independent thinking — characteristics of our Judeo-Christian heritage.

But a fundamental precept within this heritage is (in common with the Chinese concept of Tao) the assurance of heavenly protection for the faithful from the influence of evil and the threat of danger from enemies. How is it that we can be threatened with loss of our spiritual-cultural heritage and traditions by iconaclastic elements within our society; that we have been involved in two World Wars in this century; and that we are now continually faced with a cataclysmic danger — the threat of a thermonuclear war? Bishop Ivan Lee has commented:

> We started on the way to hell two generations ago. The intellectual leaders lost faith in God. They still held on to their ethical convictions. With faith gone there came another generation which surrendered even ethical convictions. The descent continued until we reached the Concentration Camp at Dachau. We blame German Nazis for Dachau, but it would have come at the hands of others because European feet were set decades ago on the path that led to hell. Let America watch the way she goes.[4]

Let us try to consider if we have been unjustly exploited, or rather, have we, by improper or un-wise action, ourselves effected the resulting chain of events? To explore this possibility, it will be informative to review some of the historical highlights of this century, giving special attention to the entrance of the United States into World War I and II. And in this review, the special influence of the Chief Executive in controlling the course of events will be emphasized.

CHAPTER 2

'HE KEPT US OUT OF WAR'

Woodrow Wilson, the Democratic candidate for the Presidency in 1912, had been nominated at the Democratic Convention on the 47th ballot, after a failure in getting the two-thirds majority required (at that time) for the generally favored candidate, Champ Clark. Wilson had entered politics only two years previously. He successfully ran for governor of New Jersey, after leaving his post as President of Princeton University — where his stubborn leadership caused bitter controversies in that institution.[1] He campaigned for the Governorship as a conservative Democrat, but when in office quickly shifted to a liberal position. His campaign for the Presidency in 1912 introduced a *social benefits* type of mass appeal, then called the New Freedom.

Nevertheless, Wilson would have had no chance of winning the election had not the former President, "Teddy" Roosevelt, become restless in retirement and decided to run against incumbent President Taft (Roosevelt's own selection for his successor in 1908), thereby splitting the Republican vote. As a result, Wilson was elected with only 43 per cent of the total vote.

At the outset of World War I, in August 1914, Mr. Wilson urged America to remain neutral in deed and spirit. His Secretary of State was William Jennings Bryan, who was widely recognized both as an outstanding national figure (having himself run for the Presidency three times) and as a prominent Christian leader. But from the first week, the American press was biased in favor of the Allied cause: partially because of the common language with England, the debt to France in the Revolution, the news stories unfavorable to their cause seemed to get lost in the British-controlled cable service,[2] and Mr. Roosevelt declared that he was impressed by, "the very friendly feeling of this country towards England" and that he had a "genuine apprehension of German designs."[3]

6

Despite Bryan's efforts to follow Mr. Wilson's neutral sentiments, the U.S. quickly became involved commercially by sale of goods and munitions. Since the Allies declared a blockade of Germany and the Central Powers (an acceptable method of warfare according to international law at that time), only the Allies were to benefit from this trade.

As a result of this situation, Germany announced, on February 4, 1915, a submarine blockade of the British Isles with the warning that even neutral shipping would be in danger because of the use of neutral flags by British ships.[4, 5]

The German Embassy published a warning to all American passengers in the New York Times not to sail on the British merchant ship, Lusitania;[6] but the U.S. State Department would not forbid American travel on belligerent vessels, holding that un-armed merchant and passenger ships should not be subject to attack. The Lusitania sailed from New York on May 1, and on May 7 was attacked by the German Submarine, U-20, causing the loss of 1200 lives — including 128 Americans. Recent photographs by an American skindiver indicate that the rapid sinking (approximately 18 minutes) was effected by a massive internal explosion, either from detonation of munitions carried as cargo or from a boiler explosion.[7]

In the ensuing exchange of communications between the United States and Germany over this issue, Secretary of State Bryan resigned because of his view that Mr. Wilson was being partial to the British. Bryan also maintained that Britain's violation of international law was as extensive as that of the Germans! After some time, Germany agreed to restrict attack on unarmed belligerent shipping.

American aid to the Allies mounted and special private loans were arranged by banking interests to finance this assistance, with the approval of the State Department — because not to allow these loans would have been unneutral.

Bryan was succeeded as Secretary of State by Robert Lansing, to whom we are indebted for the following assessment of Mr. Wilson's ways in working with others:

> When one comes to consider Mr. Wilson's mental process, there is the feeling that intuition rather than reason played the chief part in the way in which he reached conclusions and judgements. In fact, arguments, however soundly reasoned, did not appeal to him if they were opposed to his feeling of what was the right thing to do. Even established facts were ignored if they did not fit in with this intuitive sense, this semi-divine power to select the right. Such an attitude of mind is essentially feminine. In the

case of Mr Wilson, it explains many things in his public career, which otherwise are very perplexing.

In the first place it gave superior place to his own judgement. With him it was a matter of conviction formed without weighing evidence and without going through the process of rational deduction. His judgements were always right in his own mind, because he knew they were right. How did he know they were right? Why he knew it and that was the best reason in the world. No other reason was necessary.[8]

Lansing's position was also supplemented to some extent by Col. Edward M. House, who acted as a special assistant to Wilson and traveled frequently to Europe to talk directly with both sides.

In Jul 1915, Mr. Wilson asked for extensive preparedness plans and in November the resulting defense program was presented to Congress. By autumn 1916 this program was fairly well accomplished, despite the widespread objections raised by pacifist groups.

After the sinking of the Lusitania, Germany agreed to avoid attacking un-armed merchant ships (some had been hastily armed by installing small gun turrets) with the U-boats. On March 24, 1916, however, the unarmed French channel liner, Sussex, was sunk, and on April 10, Germany admitted to sinking what they thought was a warship at the same place and time. On April 19, 1916, Mr. Wilson, pressured by his wife, Lansing and House,[9] issued an ultimatum against attacks on un-armed shipping, threatening a severance of diplomatic relations. On May 4, a German reply agreed to observe the rule of visit and search before sinking merchant vessels, both within and without the war zone. The German note also reserved the right to change this position unless the United States would compel the British to observe international law.

When the Congress convened in December 1914, a flood of legislation was introduced to embargo the sale of munitions, but too many orders had already been taken. And the British loudly declared that any "change in rules" during a war would be unneutral (of course, they changed their rules as it suited them). In this matter, Mr. Wilson missed a valuable opportunity to insure neutrality since there was nothing in international law which would have forbidden a munitions embargo from applying equally to all belligerents.[10] Also, Mr. Wilson was insistent on upholding the safety of Americans when traveling on belligerent merchant ships. To this end he used his control of patronage to defeat the Gore-McLenmore bill which would have warned Americans against traveling in armed belligerent ships. Otherwise, this bill would have easily passed both houses of Congress, although it was opposed by much of the press. It represented a challenge to the Wilson foreign policy by the Congress — which Mr. Wilson was barely able to counter.[11]

Following up on a suggestion from the British, that the Allies might be willing to negotiate a reasonable settlement of the war if the United States were prepared to join a post-war League of Nations to insure lasting peace, President Wilson sent Col. House to Europe, in December 1915. Before his departure, House had broached the cunning scheme of secretly conspiring with the Allies to arrange for the President to issue a manifesto for peace. Should the war then not be stopped, the United States would enter this war on the side of the Allies.[12] After spending four days in Germany and several weeks in England, House returned to Washington in March 1916, with a draft memorandum, now known as the House-Greg Memorandum of February 1916. The text is as follows:

Colonel House told me that President Wilson was ready, on hearing from France and England that the moment was opportune to propose that a conference should be summoned to put an end to the war. Should the Allies accept this proposal, and should Germany refuse it, the United States would probably enter the war against Germany.

Colonel House expressed the opinion that, if such a conference met, it would secure peace on terms not unfavourable to the Allies; and, if it failed to secure peace, the United States would leave the conference as a belligerent on the side of the Allies, if Germany was unreasonable. Colonel House expressed an opinion decidedly favourable to the restoration of Belgium, the transfer of Alsace and Lorraine to France, and the acquisition by Russia of an outlet to the sea, though he thought that the loss of territory incurred by Germany in one place would have to be compensated to her by concessions to her in other places outside Europe. If the Allies delayed accepting the offer of President Wilson, and if, later on, the course of the war was so unfavourable to them that the intervention of the United States would not be effective, the United States would probably disinterest themselves in Europe and look to their own protection in their own way.

I said that . . . I must inform the Prir 'linister and my colleagues; but that I could say nothing until (the matter) had received their consideration. The British Government could, under no circumstances, accept or make any proposal except in consultation and agreement with the Allies.

This draft was presented to Mr. Wilson by House at his

return to Washington on March 6, 1916. Mr. Wilson's only change in accepting the memorandum of understanding was to add one more "probably": "The United States would *probably* leave the conference as a belligerent."[13]

Nine years later Col. House was to realize the naivete of this course, that a free hand in settling peace terms could not very well be obtained by agreeing to enter the war on the side of the Allies, on their terms.[14]

In 1916, the Republican Party was again united on a single candidate, Charles Evan Hughes, Associate Justice of the Supreme Court. However, this campaign was seriously handicapped by Teddy Roosevelt's barnstorming around the country calling for vigorous action against the Germans, while ostensibly campaigning for Hughes. This allowed Wilson to run as a "peace" candidate and to charge that the Republicans were a war party. By implication, Wilson promised to keep the U.S. out of the war by saying, "I am not expecting this country to get into war " (assuming he was re-elected). The Democratic campaign slogan was "with honor, he kept us out of war," although the phrase, "with honor," was generally not used.

Wilson was re-elected, receiving 9,129,606 votes against 8,538,221 for Hughes. The newly organized labor vote went largely to Wilson as did the defection of some 300,000 votes from the Socialist Party.

Despite the fact that at the time of his election, Mr. Wilson had acknowledged his lack of experience in foreign affairs,[15] he had made various overtures to the belligerents for a "peace without victor or vanquished" and actually produced much embarrassment to both sides by calling for statements of "war aims", and observing that the causes of this war "were not at all clear" (both sides were intending to obtain substantial territorial gains, but this could never be openly stated, of course.)

In the spring of '16, the German Verdun offensive failed, and in the following fall the Allied Somme offensive was not successful. As a result, both sides resorted to desperate measures. The British published a blacklist of some 87 American and 350 Latin American firms with whom British subjects were not allowed to do business. Also, they devised a coal bunkering agreement which neutral nations were required to sign in order to obtain coal at any British port throughout the world. The Germans stepped up their submarine warfare.

On January 31, 1917, the German government announced that all ships, belligerent and neutral, found in a zone around Great Britain, France and Italy and in the Eastern Mediterranean would be sunk without warning. One American passenger ship, traveling in a defined route, and clearly marked, would be allowed per week. The German communication further stated that: "This decision had been made in the certain consciousness that the commencement of an unrestricted U-boat warfare would be inevitably followed by war with America."[16]

Both Lansing and House urged a break in relations accompanied with a ringing denouncement of German "barbarism." But Mr. Wilson, in an address to a joint session of the Congress on February 3, issued an announcement of the break in relations with regret, and expressed hope of avoiding hostile conflict. Military readiness plans were intensified, *but American ships were not restricted from entering the danger zone,* nor were Naval convoys for shipping provided — as some urged. It was obvious though, that allowing American merchant shipping to enter the danger zone directly invited war. President Wilson had continued to talk neutrality, while the shipments of commodities and munitions had continued to grow each month, producing a boom economy in the United States.

Had Mr. Wilson above all wanted the United States to remain out of the war, he could have simply announced that the U.S. had not, in effect, been following a neutral course, but that, since his efforts to get the belligerents to announce their war aims had been unsuccessful, henceforth the U.S. would trade with the belligerents on a "delivered-in-U.S.-ports-only" basis. Another alternative would have been to have asked Congress to provide funds for loans to the British Government for leasing or purchasing American ships needed for transport. But most importantly, he could have restricted the travel of U.S. citizens abroad on American and Allied merchant ships.

Now there was strong support for Mr. Wilson's upholding for "unrestricted rights" by the press, from political leaders such as Senator Henry Cabot Lodge and Teddy Roosevelt, and by the public-at-large, but the majority of the American people were still firmly for peace as late as April 1, 1917 — shown by the thousands of letters and telegrams received at the White House.[17]

The public concern was greatly intensified by Mr. Wilson's release on March 1, of a secret message from the German

Government to the Mexican Government, intercepted by the British, offering substantial aid to Mexico in an attack on the United States in the event that the latter should enter the European war on the side of the Allies.

In considering the possible alternatives from the favorable position in time, one may conclude that what was needed most in this situation was the cool courage of President Grover Cleveland when he told the Congress (which was under great pressure from the yellow journalism of that day) to go ahead and declare war against Spain (over Cuba), but that he was Commander-in-Chief and that he would keep the army in the continental United States.

On March 18, three U.S. merchant ships were sunk without warning. Congress was not in session, but in response to Mr. Wilson's call, it re-assembled and on April 2, the President asked, in a stirring message, that we *"intervene to make the world safe for democracy."* Four days later Congress responded by declaring war on Germany and the Central powers.

While the U.S. attention was focused on the U-boat crisis, a revolution had occured in Russia, and in March 12-16, 1917, various revolting groups established what was soon to become the Kerensky provisional Government. The replacement of the Imperial Russian Government by a democratic one aided the cause of the interventionist bloc in the U.S., since the "war for democracy" theme could now be pushed. In the first few weeks the Mensheviks and Socialist revolutionaries cooperated with the new Russian Provisional government, in accordance with the wishes of their leader, Kamenev.[18]

At this time, Vladimir Ilyich Lenin was in exile in Switzerland — the Tsar's Government having recognized his dangerous nature. After the establishment of the provisional government his banishment was no longer necessary, except for the matter of transportation across enemy territory. To foment further trouble in Russia, Germany secretly transported Lenin and other exiles across Germany in a sealed railway car. They started in Switzerland on April 8, 1917, and arrived in Petrograd, Russia on April 16.

One cannot positively conclude that Germany would have left Lenin isolated in Switzerland, had the U.S. not declared war a few days previously. One of the basic thoughts of this book is that if there is one lesson in history, it is the relationship of action and re-action. History is repetitive because people are unfamiliar with history. As Disraeli said,

"Man is not the creation of circumstance; circumstance is the creation of man." But in the Western World people are so accustomed to taking positive courses of action, that the fact is overlooked that frequently a more resolute course is simply to restrain from ny action whatsoever. The appreciation for the merit of action and non-action is best obtained in the Oriental literature, such as the Bhagavad-Gita, for example. But perhaps the Prophet Isaiah is the most cogent, "For thus saith the Lord God, the Holy one of Israel; in returning and rest shall ye be saved; in quietness and in confidence shall be your strength: and ye would not." (Isaiah 30:15)

After Lenin's arrival in Russia, he quickly displaced Kamenev and started attacking the provisional Government, as a first step for the bloody revolution soon to follow. Lenin's activity was financed by a contribution of 80,000,000 gold marks from Germany,[19] among other sources.

Now the German Government knew the sort that Lenin was; and could well visualize that they may very well have been opening a Pandora's box of future trouble — but this was an expedient which would give immediate aid. The realization of this is perhaps reflected in subsequent attempts to defend this action. General Ludendorff said:

In having sent Lenin to Russia, our Government took on itself a special responsibility. From the military point of view his journey was justified; Russia had to fall.[20]

And General Hoffman wrote:

Just as I launch grenades at the enemy trenches, just as I release poison gasses against them, so I have the right to make use of the means of propaganda against the opposed force.[21]

In November 1917, the Russians, now in the throes of the Red revolution led by Lenin, sued for peace. Forty German divisions were now hurriedly transferred to the Western front,[22] to support the unsuccessful offensive in the spring of 1918.

In January 1918, Mr. Wilson issued his famous fourteen points as a basis of ending the "war for democracy." Chief among these were: open treaties of peace, to supplant secret alliances; freedom of the seas; removal of trade barriers; reduction of armaments; more liberty for the nationalities of Austria-Hungary; and an association of nations to afford guarantees of rights and peace for all nations large and small.

The American armies and supplies arriving in France transformed the Allied position. On November 11, 1918, Germany agreed to an Armistice on the basis of Mr. Wilson's "neither victor nor vanquished" concepts as reflected in his fourteen points.

Despite widespread opposition in the United States to his doing so, Mr. Wilson decided to personally attend the peace conferences and sailed for England on December 4, 1918. Europe had, until now, viewed the President as a philosopher-statesman. As the treaty negotiations dragged through winter and spring of 1919, this impression of Wilson changed, to that of a "hard-shelled" fundamentalist, spouting moralistic platitudes — who was unable to make use of his supporting staff, thereby being easily outmaneuvered by England's perceptive Lloyd George and France's wiley Clemenceau.[23]

The resulting Treaty of Versailles, reflecting Lloyd George's objective of reparations and Clemenceau's preoccupation with a Carthaginian settlement on Germany, fastened war guilt on Germany, forbade the maintenance of significant armed forces, took from her all her colonies and sizeable parts of the national territory, appropriated all foreign investments, and imposed a crushing indemnity — the amount of which was never defined.

All of this was later to provide grist for Hitler's mill. In fact, the inequity involved was so apparent at the time that the noted British economist, John Maynard Keynes, wrote two books on the need for remission of the treaty and said, in part:

> . . . It has not been understood in England or in America how deep a wound has been inflicted on Germany's self-respect by compelling her, not merely to perform acts, but to subscribe to beliefs which she did not in fact accept. It is not usual in civilized countries to use force to compel wrongdoers to confess even when we are convinced of their guilt; it is still more barbarous to use force, after the fashion of inquisitors, to compel adherence to an article of belief because we ourselves believe it. Yet toward Germany, the Allies had appeared to adopt this base and injurious practice, and had enforced on this people at the point of a bayonet the final humiliation of reciting, through the mouths of their representation, what they believed to be untrue.[24]

> . . . Alas for the wickedness of the world! It is not in international affairs that we can secure the sentimental satisfactions which we all love. For only individuals are good, and all nations are dishonorable, cruel and designing.[25]

It should be noted though, that Mr. Wilson was able to exert a moderating influence in working out the terms at Versailles. Otherwise the settlement would have been far more harsh.[26] Also, he resisted the wishes of the other Allies to set up the League of Nations by separate treaty, insisting that it be established in the peace treaty formally ending the war.

Although no doubt painfully aware of the imperfection and the compromise of the Treaty, as he sailed back to America at the end of June 1919, Mr. Wilson gave no indication of this in his remarks to the Senate. Rather than frankly admitting to extensive compromise with the other powers, his recommendation asked for complete acceptance of the Treaty, as a charter for a new and idyllic world order.

Because of widespread skepticism about the treaty in the Senate, coupled with partisan opposition, Mr. Wilson decided to go to the people. Disregarding the advice of his doctors, he undertook a nationwide trip — delivering one or two speeches every day. After (personally) composing and delivering forty different, visionary speeches relating to a dream world and treaty,[27] Mr. Wilson suffered a stroke following a speech at Pueblo, Colorado on September 25, 1919. He returned to the White House, where he remained an invalid for the rest of his term. Only limited communication with him was allowed, through Mrs. Wilson or others in attendance. It was suspected in effect that Mrs. Wilson was actually running the country as a regent.[28]

On November 19, 1919, the Senate defeated the Treaty. Subsequently it proposed a separate treaty with Germany, which Mr. Wilson vetoed. He remained adamant to the end about the treaty, hoping that the election of 1920 would serve as a "great and solemn referendum" by which the masses of the people would rise up and vindicate his efforts. When this support failed to materialize, the new Republican President, Mr. Harding, signed a separate peace treaty with Germany. America did not join the League of Nations but did cooperate with other powers in regulating military capabilities.

CHAPTER 3

DAWN AT PEARL HARBOR

By 1935, the "revisionist" view of American participation in World War I had become the majority view.[1] According to this perspective there had been guilt on both sides; the United States had unhappily been drawn into the war by British propaganda, abetted by commercial interests. In April 1937, a Gallup poll on the question, "Do you think it was a mistake for the United States to enter the World War" drew a "yes" from 71 percent of those polled. In response to apprehension by the public about events in Europe, the Congress passed the Neutrality Act in 1935, and President Roosevelt reluctantly approved the act. The State Department viewed this legislation with disfavor, since they preferred to be free to follow along with the British policy.[2] This legislation forbade the sale of munitions or commodities to either belligerent in a recognized war.

As the Fascist nations started committing various acts of aggression, President Roosevelt at Chicago in October 1937, gave what was to become known as the "Quarantine Speech," in which he stated that the moral consciousness of the world must be aroused ... to put an end to the acts of aggression.

In this period, the British policy was to encourage Germany to view Russia as the potential enemy and to otherwise buy time (e.g. Munich) for construction of planes and development of a new secret defense equipment now called radar. But in 1939, as Germany and Russia moved to divide Poland (thus establishing an extended common frontier — as would be essential for a war between Germany and Russia), England elected to support Poland. On this developing crisis we have from the Forrestal Diaries:

> Joseph B. Kennedy, Roosevelt's ambassador to Great Britain, said that Prime Minister Chamberlain's position in 1938 was that England had nothing with which to fight and that she could

16

not risk going to war with Hitler. But his, Kennedy's, view was that Hitler would have fought Russia without any latter conflict with England if it had not been for Bullitt's (William C. Bullitt, then U.S. Ambassador to France) urging on Roosevelt in the summer of 1939 that the Germans must be faced down about Poland; neither the French nor the British would have made Poland a cause for war if it had not been for the constant needling from Washington. Bullitt, he said, kept telling Roosevelt that the Germans wouldn't fight — Kennedy, that they would, and that they would over run Europe.[3]

But, regardless of the many contributing causes to the outbreak of WWII, on looking back, it should be recognized that the advent of this struggle was presaged by "limited" wars in Ethiopia, Spain and China. And in these "little" wars the Communist and Fascist, anti-Communist forces were involved in varying degrees.

In January 1939, President Roosevelt called for a heavy increase in American armament — which Congress granted. After the outbreak of World War II, on September 1, 1939, the President asked the Congress for an amendment to the Neutrality Act to allow sale of munitions to the British and French. This was granted.

During the early part of the war, while Chamberlain still remained Prime Minister of England, President Roosevelt took steps to set up secret coded cables with Winston Churchill, then in command of the Admiralty. This procedure was unprecedented in American diplomatic history. Most of the more than 1,700 messages still remain secret.[4]

In June 1940, the President, in a cabinet shake-up, replaced his (Democratic) isolationist Secretaries of Navy and War, with Frank Knox and Henry Stimpson respectively (both were Republicans, and ardently pro-British).[5]

In 1940, Roosevelt ran for the unprecedented third term on a "peace" platform. However, on September 3, 1940, just before the presidential campaign got under way, Mr. Roosevelt informed the Congress that by executive act he had obtained lease rights to military bases in British Guiana, the British West Indies and Newfoundland. In exchange for which Britain received fifty of our "over-age" destroyers (a violation of the then tottering international law — which the Axis powers ignored completely).

The Republican candidate, Wendell Wilkie, although not directly criticizing the Roosevelt foreign policy, made a strong issue of staying out of war. Roosevelt was moved on October 30 (just a few days before the election and one day after the first peace-time draft-numbers were selected) to address the nation by radio in his characteristically compelling voice:

> . . . And while I am talking to you mothers and fathers, I give you one more assurance. I have said this before, but I shall say it again, and again, and again. Your boys are not going to be sent into any foreign wars. They are going into training to form a force so strong that, by its very existence it will keep the threat of war away from our shores. The purpose of our defense is defense.

Although these "high-sounding" words were devoid of any meaningful commitment on the Rooseveltian foreign policy, the emotional impact of the speech was enough to smooth over any widespread apprehension about our going too far in supporting England or the French (exile) government.

Roosevelt's defeat of the relatively unknown Wilkie, despite the third-term handicap, was apparently due, in addition to the fact that he was widely known as the President of eight years, to the appeal of the New Deal welfare program (coupled with the lingering depression), to the don't change horses factor, and to the glamor of his stirring radio speeches.

After his re-election, Mr. Roosevelt presented to Congress, in January 1941, the Lend-Lease bill – which would allow the President to sell or give commodities or armaments to any government in support of United States national interest. And Mr. Roosevelt announced his intention to support nations at war with Hitler and Mussolini with "ever-increasing numbers of ships, planes, tanks and guns." (Under established international law – which, as previously noted, was beginning to crumble away – this too was an act of war.)

During the latter half of 1941, "limited" encounters developed in the Atlantic between the American Navy and the German submarines. But these "engagements" were not sufficient to provide a justification for a declaration of war by either participant. However, the Tripartite Treaty of September 1940, between Germany, Italy and Japan was to provide the "opening" for the United States to enter the war.

On June 22, 1941, Hitler invaded Russia, and England – without waiting to consult with the new "ally" – immediately pledged, over the radio, to join with Russia against the common enemy.

On July 31, Mr. Roosevelt discussed in Washington with visiting Russian officials the forthcoming massive Lend-Lease support – just as Harry Hopkins (who was something of a counterpart to President Wilson's Col. House) was visiting

Stalin in Moscow for similar discussions. At this time, the former President, Herbert Hoover, was motivated to warn America against "a gargantian jest . . . joining in a war alongside Stalin to impose freedom is a travesty."[6] Charles A. Lindberg sorrowfully projected and predicted the future of the planned support for Stalin . . . "a Europe half enslaved and barbarized, an Asia corroded by hatred, an America bled and drained of its resources for at least a decade, perhaps two."[7]

And several prominent Americans including Robert M. Hutchins, Herbert Hoover, and Alf M. Landon issued the following statement on August 5, 1941:

> The American people should insistently demand that Congress put a stop to step-by-step projection of the United States into the undeclared war . . . Exceeding its expressed purpose, the Lend-Lease bill has been followed by naval action, by military occupation of bases outside the Western Hemisphere, by promise of unauthorized aid to Russia and by other belligerent moves. . . . We have gone as far as is consistent either with law, with sentiment or with security . . . it (the war) is not purely a world conflict between tyranny and freedom. The Anglo-Russian alliance has dissipated that illusion . . . Few people honestly believe that the Axis is now, or ever will be in the future, be in a position to threaten the independence of any part of this hemisphere if our defenses are properly prepared. Freedom in America does not depend on the outcome of struggles for material power between other nations.

Further, following Hitler's attack on Russia, Senator Harry S. Truman offered the following pithy wisdom:

> If we see Germany is winning, we ought to help Russia and if we see Russia is winning, we ought to help Germany, and in that way let them kill as many as possible, although I wouldn't want to see Hitler victorious under any circumstances. Neither of them think anything of their pledged word.[8]

Since 1937, Japan had been involved in a costly and not too successful war with China. Since the war was not "declared," the United States had not recognized the state of war and had continued to trade with both Japan and China. As a result of this trade, Japan was dependent on the United States for oil and various raw materials needed to keep her war machine going.

In response to a request to evaluate the effect of a trade embargo against Japan by the United States, the Navy Department reported to President Roosevelt on July 22, 1941, that an oil embargo would probably result in a fairly early attack by Japan on Malaya and the Netherland East Indies and perhaps include an attack on the Philippines.[9] On July

25, the United States, Great Britain and the Netherlands, acting together, in response to Japan's seizure of French Indo-China, froze Japanese assets and stopped all trade with Japan.

In the complex series of negotiations that then ensued between the United States and Japan, the United States was to have the unique advantage of full and immediate knowledge of Japanese communications, because the United States had broken the Japanese diplomatic codes used in transmitting encrypted messages. For example, on August 16, when the Japanese Ambassador in Washington wired Tokyo that the British believe that a Japanese-American war was the key to the United States entering the European war,[10] this message could be decrypted and interpreted with little more delay than that incurred by the Japanese.

During this period, the U.S. was so fortunate as to be represented in Japan by the very able Joseph C. Grew. Ambassador Grew repeatedly urged the importance of reaching some degree of understanding with the Konoye government. He felt that Japan was willing to make concessions and that failing some agreement, a further government shake-up would bring into power a more military element.[11]

As it became apparent that the price the U.S. desired for restoration of trade was more or less equivalent to the withdrawal of Japan from China, the Konoye cabinet fell nd General Hideki Tojo established a military dictatorship.

The seriousness of the situation was fully appreciated by President Roosevelt and his cabinet, as we have learned from Secretary of War, Henry L. Stimson, about the "war council" meeting of November 26, 1941:

> The President brought up the event that we were likely to be attacked (perhaps as soon as next Monday) for the Japanese are notorious for making an attack without warning, and the question was what we should do. The question was how we should maneuver them into the position of firing the first shot without allowing too much danger to ourselves. It was a difficult proposition . . . [12]

In the rapid series of coded messages between the Japanese government and the Japanese ambassador in Washington, it became apparent that some type of formal break in relations was coming at once, since Japanese embassies throughout the world were instructed to destroy files and all codes except one. Knowledge of these instructions was, of course, at once available to Mr. Roosevelt, as it was to the British and to the American forces in the Philippines, who also had the capability of decrypting the coded messages.

However, there was no knowledge of this ominous situation in the Hawaiian Islands, as they were not equipped to intercept the Japanese communications – nor were they advised of the threatening turn of events.[13]

On December 6, the Japanese sent the first 13 parts of what was announced to be a 14 part message to be prepared in proper form for delivery to the U.S. Government. By 7:30 a.m. Sunday, December 7, the 14th part of this communication had been received and decoded by the U.S. military staff in Washington. It concluded with:

> . . . The Japanese government regrets to have to notify the American government that in view of the attitude of the American government it cannot but consider that it is impossible to reach an agreement through further negotiations.[14]

Also following were instructions to destroy the one remaining cypher machine, all remaining codes and secret documents, and to deliver the fourteen-part note to the U.S. Secretary of State at 1:00 P.M.

The significance of the 1:00 p.m. hour, Washington time, was at once apparent since it would then be dawn at Pearl Harbor, Hawaii.

The Chief of Naval Operations. Admiral Stark, was not to arrive in his office until 9:25 a.m. He was immediately shown the 14th part of the message. However, he refused to follow the recommendation of subordinates, to immediately alert the Pacific Fleet at Pearl Harbor, but preferred to wait until General Marshall, the Army Chief of Staff, could be reached. By 11:30 Sunday, General Marshall arrived, and after carefully reading the entire message remarked that, "Something was going to happen at 1:00 p.m." After all officers concurred in urging that all U.S. bases from Panama to the Philippines be notified, Marshall wrote:

> The Japanese are presenting at 1:00 p.m., EST today what amounts to an ultimatum, also they are under orders to destroy their code machinery immediately. Just what significance the hour sent may have we do not know, but be on alert accordingly.[15]

The message was sent at 11:50, by the time-consuming coded process, with first priority to the Phillines, despite the fact that the Phillipine command had a separate facility for decrypting the Japanese communication. Although a simple telephone call could have alerted Pearl Harbor in a few minutes, there would have been little time to have dispersed the fleet. However, antiaircraft artillery and fighter aircraft could have been readied – thus brunting the attack and greatly reducing damage.

From these events, and many others (discussed in the references cited) not possible to include in this brief account, the United States was involved in a three-sided war. Further, the war did not allow a clear grouping of issues and war aims. Nevertheless, the Communist issue was mostly suppressed.

After the war a Joint Senate House Committee investigating the events leading to Pearl Harbor summarized in part:

From the Majority Report:

... Secret diplomacy was at the root of the tragedy. The United States had warned Japan that an advance into Malaya and the Dutch East Indies would mean war with this nation. The President gave Great Britain assurance of our armed support in such an event. What Japan and Britain knew, our commanders in the field and our own people did not know. Washington feared that the national unity could not be attained unless Japan committed the first overt act. Accordingly, the army in Hawaii was put on anti-sabotage alert, a defensive posture containing the least possible risk of incident in Hawaii which Japan might claim was an overt act by the United States. The mobilization of American public opinion in support of an offensive by the Pacific Fleet against Japan was to be accomplished, if at all, by a message to Congress at the last stage of our relations relating to actual hostilities . . . [16]

And from the Minority Report:

In the future the people and their Congress must know how close American diplomacy is moving to war so that they may check its advance if imprudent and support its position if sound. A diplomacy which relies on the enemies' first overt act to insure effective popular support for the nations formal war decision is both outmoded and dangerous in this atomic age. To prevent any future Pearl Harbor more tragic and damaging than that of December 7, 1941, there must be constant close coordination between American public opinion and American diplomacy.

Eternal vigilance is the price of liberty and in the atomic era . . . no war comes in a moment. War is the sum of many minor decisions and some that are major. [16]

The matter of the breaking of the Japanese codes is discussed in detail in *The Broken Seal.*[17] In *Perpetual War For Perpetual Peace*[18] several authors analyze and review the events leading up to the tragedy at Pearl. However, in reflecting on the course of history in this period, the basic nature of fascism and communism should also be considered. A brief discussion of the similarity of these two forces is included in Chapter 14.

CHAPTER 4

THEY CAN ONLY BE STOPPED

The review of recent history is frequently painful, as past mistakes stand out with sufficient background known to project alternate courses of action, which might have rectified certain dire courses of events. On the other hand, in the study of "ancient" events, say a hundred years or more in the past, the individual is sufficiently removed from the times, and the historical detail so smoothed over, that little feeling is aroused. Likewise, in this account of some of the important history following the entrance of the United States into World War II, the emotional impact will increase.

All too frequently some of the current issues coming to public attention are dismissed as incredible because of the unpleasant nature of the issue. The truth of this observation was borne out on the occasion of the retirement of President Harry S. Truman. Despite the fact that Mr. Truman had announced the explosion of the first Soviet atomic test, "Joe One," in September 1949 a few days after his retirement, on January 20, 1953, he said:

I am not convinced the Russians have achieved the know-how to put the complicated mechanism together to make an A-bomb work. I am not convinced they have the bomb.[1]

Of course, Mr. Truman referred to a "bomb," as opposed to a non-transportable "device" — but this sort of disclaimer can only be considered as wishful thinking.

The account in this Chapter will be, to some, disturbing, but nevertheless factual and concise. Surrender terms, casualties and atrocities will not be discussed; this will also apply to operation "Keelhaul" and the famine in India, in 1943.

After the attack on Pearl Harbor and the entrance of the United States into the Second World War, the country was quickly mobilized and opposition to the involvement collapsed. The public response and rapidity of mobilization was perhaps a bit slower than in 1917, but now the issues were more

23

complex — as was the industrial structure, and the weapons to be turned out. Following the division of Poland between Hitler and Stalin, anti-Communist propaganda in the United States had been intensified, but after Germany had attacked Russia this abated. After the United States was in the war, a pro-Russian propaganda campaign was launched, as a part of the war effort.

Typical of this effort was a book by former Ambassador to the Soviet Union (1937-38), Joseph E. Davis, entitled *Mission to Moscow*. A film based on the book followed. Also Mr. Davis made many speeches throughout the country in which his theme was, "By the testimony of performance and in my opinion the word and honor of the Soviet government is as safe as the Bible."

Now, President Roosevelt knew the nature of the Communist state; he had been so incensed by Stalin's aggression against Finland that he had influenced the expulsion of the Soviet Union from the League of Nations. But as the fury of the war intensified, the tendency to be "victimized" by the prevailing propaganda increased.

After the war, this situation was reviewed by the former Ambassador to the U.S.S.R. and France, William C. Bullitt. He noted that President Roosevelt was guided in formulating his policy toward the U.S.S.R. by Harry Hopkins, who considered Stalin appeasable. The President and Hopkins even worked out a plan to transform the Soviet imperialism into peaceful international cooperation:[2]

- Give Russia all the aid requested during the war, without exacting concessions.
- Use of the wartime power to influence public opinion in the United States to effect a favorable view of the U.S.S.R.
- To meet with Stalin and *persuade him to accept Christian ways and democratic principles.*

The President implemented this policy in an open manner, personally approving the issuance of the statement, "Mr. Roosevelt, gambling for stakes as enormous as any statesman ever played for, has been betting that the Soviet Union needs peace and is willing to pay for it by collaborating with the West."

At the time, Mr. Bullitt submitted to the President a memorandum objecting to the proposed policy with the U.S.S.R. At the end of a three-hour discussion of the memorandum, the President remarked:

Bill, I don't dispute your facts, they are accurate. I don't dispute the logic of your reasoning. I just have a hunch that Stalin is not that kind of man. Harry says he's not and that he doesn't want anything but security for his country, and I think that if I give him everything I possibly can and ask nothing from him in return, *noblesse oblige,* he won't try to annex anything and will work with me for a world of democracy and peace.[2]

The strategy employed by the United States was to follow these three points; and in implementing the effort, the Foreign Service and State Department officials who were knowledgeable and patriotic were moved to unimportant posts. Opportunistic personnel, ready to say that "Stalin had changed," were quickly brought up to positions of high responsibility. Security barriers were lowered and Soviet partisans poured into the Treasury and State Departments as well as into many of the specially created wartime agencies. The War Department admitted fellow travelers, and known Communists were allowed to serve as officers with access to Confidential information.[3]

As former Communist Louis Budenz described the situation in the Roosevelt Administration in the middle forties, "Practically the entire official family of the President was being advised technically by Communist agents or those working with Communists."[4] In the State Department there was Alger Hiss, in the Treasury there was Harry Dexter White, chief assistant to Secretary Harry Morgenthau, Jr., and in the Presidential offices was Harry L. Hopkins who "illustrates how valuable to the Soviet fifth column are confused 'Liberals,' and whose counsel on Poland and the rest of East Europe was all in the Soviet direction." Also in the White House staff was Laughlin Currie, who was able to influence other key appointments such as that of Owen Lattimore as advisor to Chiang Kai-shek (Lattimore, although never identified as a Communist agent, was later found by a Senate committee to be a "conscious articulate instrument in the Soviet conspiracy.")

Throughout the course of the war, the British Prime Minister, Winston Churchill, showed recognition of the three-sided nature of the struggle and consistently advocated policies which supported the Anglo-American interests involved. It was to be a great misfortune that the United States could not benefit more from the astute judgement of this European statesman.

In December 1941 and January 1942, a global planning conference called Arcida was held in Washington. Tentative plans for crossing the English Channel to establish a second front sometime in 1943 were established. But by April 1942, General George C. Marshall, Chief of Staff, was proposing a cross-channel operation for the latter part of that year, in an operation called Sledgehammer. Although Mr. Roosevelt preferred following the original plan of invading North Africa first, and Churchill was most insistent that this course be followed, it fell to General Mark Clark, the Commander of American troops in England, to point out that a cross-channel invasion would necessarily be, in the main, an English effort – with troops evacuated from Dunkirk. There were only a limited number of American troops available.[5]

It was not possible to mount the cross-channel attack in 1943, but during this year plans were established for the second front to be launched in 1944. The need for a diversionary third front was apparent. The two candidate areas were southern France and Yugoslavia, where a beachhead of sorts was already established by General Mihailovic's Serbian forces and Tito's partisan (Communist) forces. In the definitive discussions at the Teheran Conference, November 28 to December 1, 1943, the projected invasion of southern France decided on was code named Anvil. Churchill held inflexibly to "slit this soft under-belly of the Axis" by the attack across the Adriatic into Yugoslavia – and on into Vienna, Budapest, and Prague. But Stalin, according to General Clark:

> Knew exactly what he wanted in a political as a military way; and the thing he wanted most was to keep us out of the Balkans, which he had staked out for the Red Army.[6]

Inasmuch as Mr. Roosevelt depended on Marshall in military affairs, and since Marshall supported Stalin's position – despite the negation of much of the Italian campaign by Anvil – the third front was fixed in southern France.*

This decision, far more than subsequent conferences and events, sealed the fate of East Europe, and extinguished the hope of the Polish people for their freedom – over which,

---

*The usual apology for this decision was, that unless Stalin's demands were substantially met he would make a separate peace with Hitler. This was clearly Communist propaganda. While it is true that one nation can start a war, it takes two to make a peace. Hitler knew that no meaningful peace treaty could be signed between himself and Stalin, after the viscious attack in June, 1941.

The only outcome of an attempt by Stalin to make a separate peace with Hitler would have benefited Hitler by allowing him to have informed the British and the Americans and to propose a separate peace with them.

the war had been started. Further, it might be observed that, from this point on, the Russians were the obvious winner in the three-sided war. That this victory was not as complete for them, as it might have been was to result from the forthright nature of the succeeding President, Harry S. Truman. However, it was not to be possible for Mr. Truman, on the basis of the Teheran agreements, to restore the freedom of Eastern Europe. He was barely able to keep Western Europe out of the hands of the Communists.

The Allied forces launched the second front at Normandy, on the French coast, on June 6, 1944. Two months later the third front was established in southern France. By the spring of 1945, the Allied forces were ready to cross the Rhine.

As Teheran spread the Red Shadow over Eastern Europe, so did the Yalta Conference in the Far East. Stalin, Churchill and Roosevelt met at Yalta in the Crimea on Feb. 4, 1945 (Stalin refused to travel further). Generalissmo Chaing Kai-shek did not attend, as Russia had not entered the war with Japan.

On October 30, 1943, Stalin had stated to Secretary of State Cordell Hull, that as soon as Germany was defeated the Soviet Union would join in the defeat of Japan.[7] One month later, in November 1943, Roosevelt and Churchill, while conferring with Chiang Kai-shek in Cairo, had signed and published an agreement to guarantee to China the territories taken from her by the Japanese, such as Manchuria, Formosa and the Pescadores.

But at Yalta, Mr. Roosevelt, behind the back of China, pledged to the Soviet Union in a secret agreement: detachment of Outer Mongolia from China, vital strategic interests in Manchuria, possession of Port Arthur and control of the railroad cutting across Manchuria to Dairen and Port Arthur. *This action was later to give the Russians and the Red Chinese the base from which the defeat of the Free Chinese was to be accomplished.*

It should be said that President Roosevelt's health was failing at this time. He had difficulty in concentrating and greater difficulty in expressing himself coherently.[8] But most importantly, one of Mr. Roosevelt's assistants at this conference was Alger Hiss, later to be identified as a Communist spy by Whittaker Chambers in the infamous Pumpkin-Papers case.

The role that Hiss played at Yalta, was suggested to a

Congressional committee which inquired if he had contributed to the drafting of the Yalta agreement. Hiss replied, "I think it is an accurate and not immodest statement to say that I did, to some extent, yes."[9]

Having supplied this background, it may be noted that the President made these concessions on Chinese territory in response to Stalin's demand, as the price of Russia's entering the war against Japan following the defeat of Germany — this despite Stalin's prior pledge to enter the war in the Far East, and the obvious advantages accruing to the Communists by doing so.

In 1948, while the Free Chinese were still holding out on the mainland, Bill Bullitt reviewed the Yalta conference:

> But Stalin had already promised Cordell Hull — for nothing — that "when the Allies succeeded in defeating Germany, the Soviet Union would then join in defeating Japan." And anyone who understood the depth of Stalin's desire to seize Manchuria and Korea and to Communize China, knew that no power on earth could have prevented him from declaring war on Japan at the last minute, when she was about to go down for the count under our blows. It was not only unnecessary to pay Stalin a price for making war on Japan, but it would have been greatly to our political advantage to have prevented him from doing so. If Stalin had not invaded Manchuria, we and China together could have brought a rapid and just peace to the Far East. But we paid Stalin the railroads and ports of Manchuria to do just the thing which was most contrary to our vital interests.[10]

On April 12, 1945, just two months following the Yalta conference, Mr. Roosevelt died and was succeeded by Vice President Harry S. Truman. Mr. Roosevelt never realized the course of history to result from his policies. In reviewing the war years in his memoirs, Sir Anthony Eden observed:

> Roosevelt was familiar with the history and geography of Europe. Perhaps his hobby of stamp collecting had helped him to this knowledge but the academic yet sweeping opinions which he built upon it were alarming in their cheerful fecklessness.
>
> He seemed to see himself disposing of the fate of many lands, allied no less than enemy . . . He did all this with so much grace that it was not easy to dissent. Yet it was too like a conjurer skillfully juggling with balls of dynamite whose nature he failed to understand.[11]

Also Sir Anthony strongly criticized Mr. Roosevelt for his handling of the Yalta conference, especially the secret negotiations on the Far East in which neither the British nor the Chinese were consulted. Bill Bullitt's reflections were not dissimilar:

The President had lost his gamble "for stakes as enormous as any statesman had ever played for." In truth, there had never been a gamble. There was never the slightest possibility of converting Stalin from the creed which calls for the installation of Communist dictatorship in all countries of the world. *Stalin, like Hitler, would not stop. He could only be stopped.* Roosevelt had not gambled. He had been gulled.[12]

As the American and English drove east toward the Rhine, in the spring of 1945, it was obvious that the German collapse was imminent. They could have easily occupied Berlin. Despite Churchill's urging on the matter to do so, President Truman followed the advice given him to let the Red army capture Berlin.[13] VE day was proclaimed as May 8, 1945.

On July 17, 1945, the Potsdam conference was held to formulate post-war policies in Europe and especially for defeated Germany and Italy. Both President Truman and Stalin attended. Churchill was replaced as Prime Minister by Clement Atlee midway through the sessions, as a result of the first national elections held in Great Britain since 1935.

Mr. Truman had just taken over three months previously, and had not had opportunity to arrive at definitive positions from which to negotiate. There was the Morganthau post-war plan, designed to reduce Germany to an 18th century agricultural economy. This plan had been proposed by Secretary of Treasury, Henry Morgenthau, Jr., whose assistant was Harry D. White, later identified as a Communist spy — so there is little reason to doubt that this was actually the Stalin plan for Germany.[14] The plan called for complete dismantling of all German industry, within six months, and flooding of the Ruhr mines.

Although Mr. Roosevelt had accepted the Morganthau plan, and the British had approved, after having been offered several billion dollars of aid for reconstruction of war damage in England, Mr. Truman accepted the plan with variable reservations, relating to the limit of industries that were to be dismantled and shipped to Russia. Using these reservations later on, Mr. Truman was able to halt the total destruction of German industry, and avert the establishment of a serf-like status for the peoples of Western Europe. At Potsdam also, the terms for the Japanese surrender were discussed.

General Douglas MacArthur's forces had landed in the Philippines and defeated the Japanese in Manila by March 1945. By this time Japan was nearly defeated, her merchant marine had been largely sunk, and it was apparent that the same massive air force which had been used to defeat Germany could be shifted to the Far East. The military strategist Hanson Baldwin, in reviewing the war noted:

> At the time of Yalta, Japan was already beaten — not by the atomic bomb which had not yet been perfected, not by conventional bombing then just starting, but by attrition and blockade.[15]

The significance of the Japanese situation at this time was its relation to two subsequent events: (1) The dropping of the first atomic bomb on Hiroshima on August 6, 1945, and on Nagasaki on August 9. (2) The entrance of the Russians into the conflict by attacking the Japanese forces on the mainland of Asia on August 9, a few hours before the second atomic bomb was used.

As previously noted, the entrance of the Russians was indeed unfortunate. As to the dropping of the atomic bombs — probably those responsible for the decision did not fully appreciate the significance of the act. Intelligence estimates showed that Japan would collapse in a matter of a few weeks,[16] but some reviews of the event defend the decision for use of the bombs.[17] General Eisenhower has stated he had urged Secretary of War, Henry L. Stimson at Potsdam not to use the bombs,[18] but Marshall was the chief military tactitian at the time. On the other hand, Dr. J. Robert Oppenheimer, Director of the Los Alamos facility which produced the weapons, favored dropping the first bomb without warning.[19]

On August 10, Japan offered to surrender, providing the Emperor was allowed to retain his traditional civil position. This was allowed, and the capitulation was formalized with General MacArthur's forces on September 2, 1945. It was learned that the Emperor had to resist die-hard efforts of the military to stage a last-ditch defense.

General MacArthur remained to assist with the post-war recovery which transformed Japan to an economic status not conceivable for a country with such limited resources by economists and political scientists in the 1930-50 era.

At the Yalta Conference, Mr. Roosevelt had agreed to Soviet occupation of Eastern Europe, with the understanding that free elections were to be held. Clearly, elections are meaningless in a territory occupied by the Russian army. Mr. Truman did not elect to press the matter of elections, but he did maintain U.S. forces in Western Europe. The Morganthau plan had called for immediate withdrawal of American forces from Germany after surrender, with Russian occupation of the whole of Germany.[20]

Unfortunately, before the falsity of the wartime propaganda about the Communists was realized, most of the great American Armed Force was demobilized. Fantastic amounts of munitions, arms and equipment were destroyed. Contrariwise, all of the remaining lend-lease and captured enemy equipment which the Communists could collect was carefully stored for subsequent use. One of the contributing factors to the rapid American demobilization was the widespread publicity given to the newly founded United Nations organization.

In a way, the United Nations was a delayed product of World War I. At the Versailles Conference in 1919, it was apparent to Col. Edward M. House that the League of Nations established by the Treaty would never support the fulfillment of the visionary dreams of perpetual peace enforced by a single, super-world government. On May 19, 1919, Col. House called together a group of young English and American intellectuals to consider the formation of an organization "for the study of international affairs," Among the Americans present were John Foster and Allan Dulles, Christian A. Herter, and Tasker H. Bliss.

The Americans came home from the Conference and formed an organization which they named the Council on Foreign Relations (CFR). It was incorporated as a non-profit institution in 1921. In the period between the two wars the organization slowly and steadily built up its standing, primarily through the vehicle of its prestigious publication, *Foreign Affairs.* This publication was organized as a source of information for professionals in the diplomatic and business world and for the university set of instructors and students. By 1927, the CFR had picked up substantial support from the Rockefeller foundation and later the Carnegie and Ford foundations also began to support the Council.

By 1941, the CFR was able to exert a marked influence in the State Department, and after America's entrance into WW-II it naturally supported the *one-world* thesis widely discussed in the public media. The flourishing growth of the CFR following WW-II is discussed in a provocative treatment by Dan Smoot, in *The Invisible Government.*[21] In this book Smoot maintains that the CFR and splinter organizations, in effect, produce a continuous policy in the conduct of foreign, and many domestic affairs, regardless of changes in the political party in power.

Returning to the formation of the United Nations, the

basic argument for the organization was the failure of the
League of Nations to prevent World War II. Had the League
been set up with *supra-national* power, it was held, it could
have stopped the first small aggressions of the Axis nations
and prevented, thereby, the outbreak of the second World
War. It was axiomatic from this reasoning, that the proposed
United Nations organization should have supra-national power. Author Smoot describes the role of the CFR in the
organization of the United Nations at the San Francisco
Conference, April 25 to June 26, 1945, in part:

> The crowning moment of achievement for the Council came
> at San Francisco in 1945, when over 40 members of the United
> States Delegation to the organizational meeting of the United
> Nations (where the United Nations Charter was written) were
> members of the Council. Among them: Alger Hiss, Secretary of
> State Edward R. Stettinius, Leo Pasvolosky, John Foster Dulles,
> John J. McCloy, Julis C. Holmes, Nelson A. Rockefeller, Adlai
> Stevenson, Joseph E. Thompson, Ralph J. Bunche, Clark M.
> Eichelberger, and Thomas K. Finletter . . .

> By 1945, the Council on Foreign Relations and various
> foundations and other organizations interlocked with it, had vir-
> tually taken over the U.S. State Department.

> Some CFR members were later identified as Soviet espion-
> age agents: For example, Alger Hiss and Laughlin Currie.[22]

The United Nations was formally established on October
24, 1945. The first session of the U.N. Assembly met in London on January 10, 1946, and in the following year the Sperry
Plant at Lake Success, Long Island was used as a temporary
headquarters until the permanent home was established in
New York. In selecting the site the Russian choice was accepted. First Stalin stated a preference for a location anywhere in
the U.S., and then changed it to anywhere on the East
Coast.*[23]

During the Korean War, by chance, a New York grand
jury discovered evidence of Communist agents among the
American members of the U.S. Staff. A Senate Committee
became interested and began to investigate. Approximately
200 Americans employed by the U.N. resigned, apparently
to avoid testifying.[24]

---

*From an American view, the ideal location would have been Moscow,
as this would have allowed U.N. discussions to "spill over" to the Russian public. The Americans made no suggestion as to location. The
Europeans were generally disappointed with the decision for the U.S.
location.

At the Potsdam Conference, an Allied Control Council had been set up to deal with the immediate post war problems in Europe. During the first year of operation of this group hardly anything was accomplished, because of the repeated Russian, *niet*. By September 1946, the new Secretary of State, James F. Byrnes declared, "that the United States would no longer accept the responsibility the needless aggravation of economic distress." The rem of the Morganthau plan was abandoned and relief measu being handled by lend-lease and the American-financed United Nations Relief and Rehabilitation Administration (.R.R.A.), were stepped up. The Cold War was under way March 5, 1946 Winston Churchill had declared in his ic Fulton, Mo. speech:

> Nobody knows what Soviet Russia and its Communist international organization intend to do in the immediate future or where are the limits, if any, to their expansive and proselyting tendencies . . .
> From Stettin in the Baltic, to Trieste in the Adriatic, an iron curtain has descended across the Continent . . .
> This is not the liberated Europe we fought to build up, nor is it one which contains the essentials of a permanent peace.[25]

British forces had liberated Greece at the end of the war. By February 1947, they w forced to announce an evacuation due to the Communis "war of liberation" being waged from Russian controlled Bulgaria. President Truman then responded with the now fa ous Truman Doctrine* to supply military and economic aid to Greece and Turkey (since Turkey was also scheduled for Russian take-over). Thanks to the forthright action by the President, the Communists were stopped cold in both countries.

Continuing in this spirit, on June 5, 1947, General Marshall, then Secretary of State, proposed in a speech that European nations work out detailed plans for their national recovery and that the United States supply the necessary funds to implement the plan. The response from the free countries in Europe was "instant" approval; four years later western Europe was well on its way to recovery, and a policy for limited egalitarianism effected by world-wide aid programs was established. Although Russia and the East European satellites had been tentatively included in the initial pro-

---

*Actually this might have been called the Truman-Forrestal plan, after the first Secretary of Defense, James V. Forrestal whose support was instrumental in the establishment of the plan.

posal, the Soviets refused to allow any of their captive nations to participate.

In February 1948, the Communists seized Czechoslovakia by a coup. Foreign Minister Jan Masaryk was liquidated by the classic method of defenestration. The Iron Curtain had clanked shut on another free country.

On June 24, 1948, following the establishment of the West German government, under Anglo-American sponsorship, Stalin ordered the Berlin Blockade. For 321 days the American and British were compelled to "crawl-through-the-air" with enough supplies to sustain the population and military units there. On May 12, 1949, the Berlin Blockade was ended, likely as a result of the completion of the Red Chinese conquest in the Far East. But before discussing this area, the formation of the North Atlantic Treaty Organization (NATO) should be mentioned. As a result of the cold war tensions, the Senate passed the Vandenberg resolution in 1949, which sanctioned the formation of peacetime regional defense alliances outside the Western Hemisphere. This allowed the formation of NATO, which included: the United Kingdom, France, the Benelux countries, Norway, Denmark, Italy, Iceland, Portugal, Canada and the United States. Two years later Greece and Turkey were included. General Eisenhower became Supreme Commander of the NATO forces in 1950. Communism was contained — by unified military power, in Europe.

As the Berlin Blockade was lifted in May 1949, a hollow victory was proclaimed by the Free World participants. *The larger Cold War issue had been in the American election and in the Far East, but this had not been noticed.* For the Americans did not, as a whole, understand the "mysterious" Orient with its many strange languages, different mannerisms, and countless millions of peoples. But the Russians understood the Orient, and especially the Chinese geography, all too well. As the veteran Far Eastern Commander, General Claire Chennault, commented:

> If China remains friendly to the United States, the Russians will not dare move deeper into Europe, leaving their vitals exposed on their Asiatic flank. If the Asiatic flank is secure and American airpower is pushed out beyond critical range, then the way will be open for new and more powerful ventures in Europe.[26]

During World War II, the role of the Chinese Communists, led by Mao Te-tung, was largely that of a "hand-sitting" operation while they waited for the Japanese to wear down the Kuomintang, led by Chiang Kai-shek.

The American forces in the China-Burma-India (CBI)

theater were charged with the responsibility of supplying Chiang's forces by air, over the Himalayan Hump, and giving air support to the Chinese. The American Commander was General "Vinegar Joe" Stilwell. On Stilwell's staff as State Department advisors were John Patton Davies, John Stewart Service, and Raymond P. Ludden. Also there, as an officer, was Dean Rusk, who rose rapidly to become Stilwell's Deputy Chief of Staff.

Stilwell proposed that he train and equip a force of one million Chinese Communist troops. This proposal eventually caused such a furor that in September 1944, Chiang demanded Stilwell's recall.

General Albert C. Wedemeyer relieved Stilwell and soon became so concerned over the Communist Chinese that he recommended priority for the occupation of Manchuria and the Chinese seaports over the Japanese occupation. This was to prevent the Communist or Red Chinese from taking over China. This was not done; rather, the opposite policy of quick withdrawal of all American forces from the Asiatic mainland was employed. Over three million troops were returned from the Pacific area between September 1945 and March 1946 — as Stalin was arming Red Chinese with captured Japanese weapons.

General Patrick Hurley had also been sent to China, following the recall of Stilwell, to handle the diplomatic problems, largely between the Kuomintang and the Red Chinese. Within a year, he returned to Washington and resigned, charging:

> That his work had been hampered by Communists and fellow travelers in the Department of State and the Foreign Service. To quiet the National scandal which ensued, President Truman asked General Marshall, who had retired, to go to China as his personal representative.[27]

In December 1945, Mr. Truman sent General Marshall to China on an ill-fated attempt to mediate between the Nationalistic-Kuomintang forces and the Communist Chinese. Marshall forced a temporary cease-fire between the two groups, by threatening to withold the supply of badly needed arms and supplies from the Nationalists. However, the civil war between the two factions resumed before his recall to Washington on January 7, 1947, to become Secretary of State.

Commenting on his role in controlling the fate of the Chinese, Marshall stated, "As Chief of Staff I armed 39 anti-Communist divisions (of Chiang's); now with a stroke of the

pen I disarm them." During the next two years Marshall, as
Secretary of State, was able to lobby against arms appropriations by the Congress and even block the shipment of the
relatively small amount of supplies to Chiang's forces authorized by the Congress over State Department objections. The
Nationalist troops had tanks, trucks and guns, but no gasoline,
tires and spare parts or ammunition. The Red Chinese were
well supplied by the U.S.S.R. About this situation, Bill
Bullitt stated:

> In the field of aviation General Marshall's actions were even
> more damaging to China and the U.S. In September 1946, he
> deliberately broke the contract of the American government to
> deliver to the Chinese government planes to maintain "eight and
> one-third air groups" for three years, and spare parts to cover
> replacements, and ammunition, and materials needed for ground
> services during the same period. From September 1946 to March
> of this year, not a single combat or bombing plane was delivered
> to China under this agreement. The conduct of the American
> government in this matter was strictly dishonorable. General
> Marshall was responsible for that conduct.[28]

By 1948, the Nationalist forces were near collapse, and
Governor Thomas E. Dewey, the Republican Presidential
candidate, had decided to implement a crash aid program for
the Free Chinese, if he were elected. However, his stand-pat
campaign fizzled and Mr. Truman was reelected. By the Spring
of 1949, Chiang's forces were in serious difficulty. As there
was no aid in sight, they suffered from mass defections to the
Communists. *But during this critical period, the attention of
most Americans was focused on the dramatic air lift for
beleagured Berlin — an area which they knew and could
understand . . . As the forthcoming victory of Mao's Red
Chinese forces became apparent, Stalin stopped the Berlin
Blockade on May 12, 1949.*

The whole story of the loss of the Chinese mainland was
such a tragic epoch of Chinese-American history, that the late
John F. Kennedy was moved to give an address reviewing the
matter, which was later read into the Congressional Record by
the Honorable George J. Bates. The foregoing material has
been largely supplementary to this address.

CHINA — STATEMENT OF HON. JOHN F. KENNEDY OF MASSACHUSETTS

**Mr. Bates of Massachusetts. Mr. Speaker, under leave to ex-
tend my remarks in the RECORD, I wish to include the timely
and interesting address delivered in Salem, Mass., on January 30,
by my colleague, Hon. JOHN F. KENNEDY, of Boston, on the
tragic story of China:**

Over these past few days we have learned the extent of the disasters befalling China and the United States. Our relationship with China since the end of the Second World War has been a tragic one, and it is of the utmost importance that we search out and spotlight those who must bear the responsibility for our present predicament.

When we look at the ease with which the Communists have overthrown the National Government of Chiang Kai-shek, it comes as somewhat of a shock to remember that on November 22, 1941, our Secretary of State, Cordell Hull, handed Ambassador Namura an ultimatum to the effect that: (1) Government of Japan will withdraw all military, naval, air, and police forces from China and Indochina; (2) the United States and Japan will not support militarily, politically, economically, any government or regime in China other than the National Government of the Republic of China.

It was clearly enunciated that the independence of China and the stability of the National Government was the fundamental object of our far eastern policy.

That this and other statements of our policies in the Far East led directly to the attack on Pearl Harbor is well known. And it might be said that we almost knowingly entered into combat with Japan to preserve the independence of China and the countries to the south of it. Contrast this policy which reached its height in 1943 when the United States and Britain agreed at Cairo to liberate China and return to that country at the end of the war Manchuria and all Japanese-held areas, to the confused and vacillating policy which we have followed since that day.

In 1944 Gen. "Vinegar Joe" Stilwell presented a plan to arm 1,000,000 Chinese Communists, who had been carefully building their resources in preparation for a post-war seizure of power, and with them to capture Shanghai and clear the Yangtze. This plan was supported by some State Department officials, including Ambassador Clarence Gauss. Chiang Kai-shek refused to cooperate with this plan, which would have presented the Chinese Communists with an easy coup. Chiang requested that Stilwell be recalled, which caused such bitter comment in this country; and Gauss resigned. From this date on our relations with the National Government declined.

At the Yalta Conference in 1945 a sick Roosevelt, with the advice of General Marshall and other Chiefs of Staff, gave the Kurile Islands as well as the control of various strategic Chinese ports, such as Port Arthur and Darien, to the Soviet Union.

According to former Ambassador Bullitt, in Life magazine in 1948, "Whatever share of the responsibility was Roosevelt's and whatever share was Marshall's the vital interest of the United States in the independent integrity of China was sacrificed, and the foundation was laid for the present tragic situation in the Far East."

When the armies of Soviet Russia withdrew from Manchuria they left Chinese Communists in control of this area and in possession of great masses of Japanese war material.

During this period began the great split in the minds of our diplomats over whether to support the government of Chiang Kai-shek, or force Chiang Kai-shek as the price of our assistance to bring Chinese Communists into his government to form a coalition.

When Ambassador Patrick Hurley resigned in 1945 he stated, "Professional diplomats continuously advised the Chinese Communists that my efforts in preventing the collapse of the national government did not represent the policy of the United States. The chief opposition to the accomplishment of our mission came from American career diplomats, the embassy at Chungking, and the Chinese Far Eastern divisions of the State Department."

With the troubled situation in China beginning to loom large in the United States, General Marshall was sent at the request of President Truman as special emissary to China to effect a compromise and to bring about a coalition government.

In Ambassador Bullitt's article in Life, he states, and I quote: "In early summer of 1946 in order to force Chiang Kai-shek to take Communists into the Chinese Government, General Marshall had the Department of State refuse to give licenses for export of ammunition to China. Thus from the summer of 1946 to February 1948 not a single shell or a single cartridge was delivered to China for use in its American armament. And in the aviation field Marshall likewise blundered, and as a result of his breaking the American Government's contract to deliver to China planes to maintain eight and one-third air groups, for 3 years no combat or bombing planes were delivered to China — from September 1946 to March 1948. As Marshall himself confessed in February 1948 to the House Committee on Foreign Affairs, this "was in effect an embargo on military supplies."

In 1948 we appropriated $468,000,000 for China, only a fraction of what we were sending to Europe, and out of this $468,000,000 only $125,000,000 was for military purposes. The end was drawing near; the assistance was too little and too late; and the nationalist government was engaged in a death struggle with the on-rushing Communist armies.

On November 20, 1948, former Senator D. Worth Clark, who had been sent on a special mission to China by the Senate Committee on Appropriations, in his report to that committee said, "Piecemeal aid will no longer save failing China from communism. It is now an all-out program or none, a fish or cut bait proposition."

Clark said this conclusion was confirmed by Ambassador J. Leighton Stuart and top American Army officers in China.

On November 25, 1948, 3 years too late, the New York

Times said: "Secretary of State George Marshall said today the United States Government was considering what assistance it could properly give to the Chinese Government in the present critical situation."

On December 21 a Times headline was: "ECA Administrator Hoffman, after seeing Truman, discloses freezing of $70,000,000 program in China in view of uncertain war situation."

The indifference, if not the contempt, with which the State Department and the President, treated the wife of the head of the nationalist government, who was then fighting for a free China – Madame Chiang Kai-shek – was the final chapter in this tragic story.

Our policy in China has reaped the whirlwind. The continued insistence that aid would not be forthcoming unless a coalition government with the Communists was formed, was a crippling blow to the national government. So concerned were our diplomats and their advisers, the Lattimores and the Fairbanks, with the imperfections of the diplomatic system in China after 20 years of war, and the tales of corruption in high places, that they lost sight of our tremendous stake in a non-Communist China.

There were those who claimed, and still claim, that Chinese communism was not really communism at all but merely an advanced agrarian movement which did not take directions from Moscow.

Listen to the words of the Bolton report: "Its doctrines follow those of Lenin and Stalin. Its leaders are Moscow-trained (of 35 leading Chinese Communist political leaders listed in the report, over a half either spent some time or studied in Moscow). Its policies and actions, its strategy and tactics are Communist. The Chinese Communists have followed faithfully every zigzag of the Kremlin's line for a generation."

This is the tragic story of China whose freedom we once fought to preserve. What our young men had saved, our diplomats and our President have frittered away.[29]

On September 21, 1949, Mao Tse-tung formally announced the establishment of the People's Republic of China. The Nationalist Chinese were retreating into southern China. By March 1950, Chiang Kai-shek's remaining forces had completed their evacuation of the Mainland to Formosa and Hainan, but the latter was lost to the Communists by June of that year.

Thus it is clearly shown, that responsibility for the establishment of the Red Dictatorship on the Chinese mainland rested with the Department of State. In the course of time, this has generally become to be recognized to some extent by historians, as shown by the following excerpt from Vinacke's, *A History of the Far East in Modern Times:*

Secretary of State Acheson's covering letter to the *China White Paper*, released in the summer of 1949, put the seal on official American acceptance of the view of the Kuomintang leadership as corrupt and inefficient, and unworthy of support. But its gradual formulation and expression previously in one form or another was one factor in undermining Kuomintang morale in China and establishing a basis for acceptance among Chinese intellectuals of the view that it had ceased to be a satisfactory instrument of government. Thus the dissemination of the point of view had the ultimate effect of serving to make it one on which it was necessary to base action.[30]

This responsibility of the State Department for the enslavement of the mainland Chinese was even obliquely admitted in the *Chinese White Paper;* if civil war broke out, it was argued:

. . . the Communists would inevitably win . . . because the foreign powers, including the United States, which would support the Government, could not feasably supply enough aid to compensate for the organic weaknesses of the Government.

In this unhappy dilemma, the United States should attempt to prevent the disaster of civil war through the adjustment of the new alignment of power in China by peaceful processes. The desirable means to this end is to encourage the reform and revitalization of the Kuomintang so that it may survive as a significant force in a coalition government. If this fails, we must limit our involvement with the Kuomintang and must commence some cooperation with the Communists, *the force destined to control China,* in an effort to influence them further into an independent position friendly to the United States.[31]

But General Wedemeyer writes more directly:

First and foremost we should realize that had not the time-honored U.S. policy of United States-China friendly cooperation been reversed by the State Department in the Acheson era, China would not now (1948) equal or surpass her master and ally, the U.S.S.R., as a menace to American security. The State Department, *"wait and see,"* or *"let the dust settle,"* China policy rendered inevitable the Communist conquest of China. The Chinese people are realists. They became so disheartened and demoralized by our attitude they finally ceased to resist the Communists. What reason could there be for continuing to oppose them if even America wanted China to come to terms with them? What other alternative was there for the great majority of the Chinese people than to submit to the Communist conquest, since even the United States demanded they do so as the *sine quo non* of American aid?[32]

Finally, it should be noted that from the outset the State Department had actually, openly, encouraged the Chinese Communists — which, of course, gave them a tremendous boost in morale. Louis Budenz reports on a wartime conference:

> At this conference Mr. Wells assured Browder that the government of the United States "desires Chinese unity and depreciates civil strife in China." He stated that the United States would not favor Chiang Kai-shek against the Chinese Communists in order to aid "unity" in China. This decision, promptly communicated to the Chinese Communists, gave them a terrific boost.[33]

During the critical years of the ascendency of the Red Chinese, 1946-49, General Marshall was responsible for the U.S. policy on China – first, on his one-year mission to China, and then immediately on his return, as Secretary of State. It should be noted that six weeks after assuming his duties as Secretary of State, Marshall requested Dean Rusk to return to the State Department to take the desk vacated by Alger Hiss. The limited insight of Rusk at that time is described by Freda Utley in the following way:

> Dean Rusk may be wholly free of any Communist sympathies, but he has proved that he must be classed among the dupes of the Chinese Communists. Not even Mao Tse-tung or Stalin ever ventured to give such a clean bill of health to the Chinese Communists as he. On June 14, 1950, Dean Rusk told the World Affairs Council Conference of the University of Pennsylvania, that the Chinese "Revolution" is "not Russian in essence" and "does not aim at dictatorship," He went further than almost any other State Department official in his desire to represent the Chinese Communists as good liberals who follow the American ideal. For he said that the "revolution in China" is comparable "to the American revolt against the British."[34]

The entire tragedy of the loss of the Chinese Mainland is well documented in: *How the Far East Was Lost*,[35] *The China Story*,[36] and *While You Slept*.[37] It will suffice here to add some additional background as to why the American people could remain passive at the time and allow, what amounted to a gift of the Mainland to the Communists – by sympathetic elements in their government.

In 1951 and 1952, after the outbreak of the Korean war, the Senate Internal Security Subcommittee (SISS) undertook an investigation of the betrayal of China. They found that an internationalist organization called the Institute of Pacific Relations (IPR) had been primarily responsible in propagandizing the public and "educating"State Department personnel. The IPR was made up of an *international body*, including those nations interested in Pacific affairs. There was a sort of a branch *national* chapter in each of the member countries.

Insofar as the Free World was concerned, the individuals participating in the international organization and the national branches were in no way connected with their governments, in an official capacity. The constituent nations were: United States, United Kingdom, Soviet Russia, China, Australia, Canada, New Zealand, Netherland—Netherlands East Indies, Philippine Islands and France. The international ruling body was called the Pacific Council and the U.S. branch was called the American Council.

The active head of the international organization was the Secretary General, Edward C. Carter; however, he was generally influenced by the aforementioned Owen Lattimore. The American Council membership varied, but generally included a variety of names of responsible citizens, many actually of a conservative nature. The nature of the operation was not apparent to these leading citizens who gave a cloak of responsibility by use of their names. The pretentious publications of the parent international organization, *Pacific Affairs*, and the *Far Eastern Survey* put out by the American Council were suave and deceptive. Owen Lattimore was the editor of *Pacific Affairs*, and Lawrence E. Sailsbury was the editor of *Far Eastern Survey* for many years. The people who influenced the policies of the American branch were Edward C. Carter, Frederick Vanderbilt Field, Harriet Lucy More and Owen Lattimore; the most prominent was the "Millionaire Communist" Field, who was able to use part of the Vanderbilt inheritance to underwrite the organization.[38]

Because of the language barrier for Americans in the use of Oriental publications, the IPR was able to introduce its "journals" into governmental and academic usage. From this and other contacts they were able to bring into their membership, and then influence, young men who were later to hold positions within the government. At the present time, some hold responsible positions and have, in recent years, provided valuable service to the IPR. For example, the veteran newswriter and author, Frank Kluckhohn, has noted:

> During the hearings of the Senate Internal Security Sub-committee, startling facts about Rusk's influential support and close cooperation with the IPR came to light: Dean Rusk has recommended that U.S. Military Intelligence use IPR publications; as late as 1950 — when IPR was under serious attack as a Communist operation and the Senate subcommittee was gearing to investigate it — Dean Rusk asked the Rockefeller Foundation for almost two million dollars to support the IPR; and also in 1950, Dean Rusk asked the Ford Foundation for a

large grant for the IPR. In addition, documents inserted into the hearing records show that Dean Rusk was on intimate terms with the highest eschelons of the IPR; that Dean Rusk was the State Department official to whom IPR officers went for financial, moral and diplomatic backing; and that Dean Rusk was asked by IPR officials to select American delegates to the IPR worldwide conference held in Lucknow, India, in October 1950.[39]

Members of the IPR also flooded such popular magazines as *Colliers* and *The Saturday Evening Post* with articles glorifying the Chinese Communists as "agrarian reformers" and other highly biased material favorable to the Communist line.[40] The suave authors were not only prolific writers of magazine articles and books, but many wrote book reviews too. In the period between 1943-1949, there were 29 books listed in the *United States Publishers Catalogue,* which dealt with China. Of these 22 were pro-Communist and only seven were anti-Communist.[41] Needless to say, the pro-Communist books were not reviewed unfavorably, as were the anti-Communist ones.

As the IPR affairs progressed nicely, a "splinter" publication called *Amerasia* was started in 1937. This publication was able to be somewhat more outspoken for Communists causes than those of the IPR. It continued with a small circulation until 1945. In that year some of the staff in General William Donovan's Office of Strategic Services (OSS) recognized an article published in *Amerasia* as a loosely paraphrased version of a classified, Top Secret document. The head of OSS security, Frank B. Bielaski and a group of agents searched the *Amerasia* offices. Author Flynn reports on the results:

> There they found on the desks and in the files an alarming array of documents still bearing the Top-Secret mark of the State and other departments. They were from Military Intelligence, Naval Intelligence, Bureau of Censorship, British Intelligence, Office of Strategic Services and the State Department. The case was turned over to the F.B.I. . . .

> As a result the FBI arrested Philip Jaffe, Kate Louise Mitchell, Mark Gayn, John Stewart Service and Emanuel Larsen, the latter two of the State Department. Also arrested was Andrew Roth, who had been chief researcher for *Amerasia* . . .

> Now, the most startling feature of this case was its climax. The original indictments were quashed. Instead of charges of espionage, the charge of "conspiracy to embezzle" was substituted against Jaffe, Larsen and Roth. Then Jaffe's attorney and the government's attorney got together and agreed on a swift court procedure. The government attorney said little. The case was ex-

plained to the court by Jaffe's counsel. The defendants meant no harm; there was no disloyalty; they were editors − perhaps too zealous in their eagerness to get the facts but also eager that they should make no errors − it was a case of excessive journalistic zeal.[42]

The matter was compounded even further. The government attorney did not elect to tell of Jaffe's Communist connections. As a result of this fantastic "t ..l," Jaffe received only a $2,500 fine, Larsen got off with a $500 fine, and the case against Roth was dismissed, and Service continued on in the State Department − Mitchell and Gayn had not been indicted.

Not only did the IPR operate by inion moulding of public and governmental thinking, it was able to supply personnel to the State Department, the Office of War Information, and the Foreign Economic Administration. It occasionally provided "ladder rungs" to State Department personnel desiring better jobs outside government which would allow them later to return to positions of higher salary and influence.[43]

Commenting on the IPR, Freda Utley says, in part:

Four IPR staff members worked for the China Section of UNRRA. Three were employed as "research" workers on Japanese reconstruction at MacArthur's headquarters. William L. Holland, a prominent IPR official, was appointed to head the Office of War Information in China. Benjamin Kizer, the Spokane lawyer who was Vice President of the IPR, was appointed head of UNRRA in China, where I found him strongly favorable in his view of the Chinese Communists.

The United States Government bought 750,000 IPR pamphlets for distribution in the Pacific and Asiatic theaters of war, thus giving its official blessing to the pro-Communist views of this organization.

Although most Americans have probably never heard of the Institute of Pacific Relations, even their children have been influenced by its propaganda. For over a million copies were sold of its Special Series for youngsters, published jointly by the IPR and the Webster Company of St. Louis. And many an editorial writer, ignorant concerning the Far East, has made use of the material furnished him by the IPR which he has had every reason to trust on account of the eminent names which appear on its masthead . . . [44]

With such cleverly slanted information and mis-information distributed en-masse, it is little wonder that the American public was deceived as to the course of events in the Far East. On June 25, 1950, however, they were sharply alerted by the invasion of South Korea by the Communist North Korean army.

Actually, this attack should not have been unexpected by the careful observer. There had been many warning signals by the State Department, suggesting that here too, as well as with China, America had no intention of making a protectorate of South Korea. Also, at this time, the new Secretary of Defense, Louis A. Johnson (appointed following his successful stint at raising the funds for Truman's '48 campaign), slashed the defense budget — thus greatly weakening the American position in the Far East and throughout the world. Considering the nature of communism, one might conclude that a sizeable reduction of the defense budget would be invariably considered by the Communists as a sign of growing weakness, portending national retrenchment.

Specifically, the position of Syngman Rhee's South Korean government was undermined in the following ways:[45]

- It was denounced in America as reactionary, tyrannical, corrupt and "undemocratic."
- Military supplies were limited to those suitable for internal police work. Tanks and planes were not provided.
- Of $10.5 million military assistance provided by the Congress in 1949, only $200 worth had been delivered by June 25, 1950.
- Owen Lattimore recommended, in July 1949 "Let South Korea fall, but not to let it look as though we pushed it."
- The U.S. troops were withdrawn from Korea in the summer of 1949, and the Korean Aid Bill of February 14, 1950 afforded only economic aid (apparently following the Lattimore suggestion).

President Truman was influenced to announce, on January 5, 1950, that the United States would not support, or aid in, the defense of the Nationalist forces on Formosa — which then seemed to be in imminent danger of being attacked by the Chinese Communists.[46] On January 12, Dean Acheson followed with a speech to the National Press Club, saying:

> . . . For its own security the United States must and shall maintain forces in Japan, the Ryukyu Islands (Okinawa), and the Philippines. But no such line of containment could be drawn in southern and southeast Asia, where the United States had no direct responsibilities and only limited opportunities for action.[47]

And just as if the U.S. were trying to provide re-assurances to the Communists, the Chairman of the Senate Foreign

Policy Relations Committee, Senator Tom Connally, stated in an interview, on May 5, 1950:

QUESTION: "Do you think the suggestion that we abandon South Korea is going to be seriously considered?"

CONNALLY: "I am afraid it is going to be seriously considered because I'm afraid it's going to happen, whether we want it or not. I'm for Korea . . . But South Korea is cut right across by this line — north of it are the Communists, with access to the mainland, and Russia is over there on the mainland. So that whenever she takes a notion she can overrun Korea just like she probably will overrun Formosa when she gets ready to do it. I hope not, of course."

QUESTION: "But isn't Korea an essential part of the defense strategy?"

CONNALLY: "No. Of course, any position like that is of some strategic importance. But I don't think it is very greatly important. It has been testified before us that Japan, Okinawa, and the Philippines make the chain of defense which is absolutely necessary. And of course any additional territory along in that area would be that much more, but it's not absolutely essential."[48]

Prior to the attack on South Korea, U.S. military authorities dismissed South Korean intelligence reports that the North Koreans were preparing for an invasion.[49] However, when the attack on South Korea by the Red Koreans was launched on June 25, President Truman's reaction was intrinsically American. He was able to arrange a sponsorship by the United Nations for the multi-national (largely American) support to the South Koreans.* The "Yo-Yo" movement of the conflict up and down the Korean peninsula may be summarized as follows:

June 25, 1950. Invasion southward over 38th parallel border. The UN Security Council demanded an immediate withdrawal.

June 27. President Truman ordered American support and the UN Security Council called for help from member nations "to restore peace, order and unity to entire Korean Peninsula."

June 30. South Korean capital, Seoul fell, and first U.S. troops landed at Inchon.

---

*At this time the Russians had staged a walkout from the U.N. Security Council, because the U.N. had refused to recognize the Red Chinese in lieu of the Nationalist Government on Formosa. The Communist influence in the U.N. was less at that time, than it came to be in subsequent years. The Russian representative returned to the Security Council in August.

July 18. Gen. Douglas MacArthur appointed overall U.N. Commander.

Sept. 1. American-Korean-U.N. forces driven to Southeast tip of Korea.

Sept. 15. Gen. MacArthur directs amphibious landing behind North Korean lines at Inchon.

Sept. 26. Seoul recaptured.

Sept. 30. MacArthur's Eighth Army advanced to 38th parallel.

Oct. 7. U.N. General Assembly approved drive northward to reunite all Korea.

Oct. 14. MacArthur and Truman meet on Wake Island. MacArthur says there "was very little chance" the Red Chinese would enter the war by crossing the vulnerable Yalu river bridges.*

Nov. 1-20. Front moving north to generally 0 to 50 miles within the Yalu river.

Nov. 25. Red Chinese attack using "human waves" with Russian air cover.[51]

Dec. 15. Eighth Army and U.N. forces retreat below 38th parallel.

Dec. 29. MacArthur receives new directive from JCS to defend all Korea but, no attack on China, or "unleasing" of Chiang from Formosa.

Jan. 5, 1951.   Red Forces retake Seoul.

March 14. Seoul recaptured by Eighth Army and South Korea liberated to a little beyond 38th parallel.

From there on, the war, though heavy in casualties, was a military stalemate. The American command, like Hannibal, was "tethered" by political considerations. This constraint developed gradually with the course of the war, as the State Department was able to influence military policy. For example, on November 6, 1950, word reached the State Department that MacArthur planned to bomb the Yalu River bridges and Manchurian staging areas, since intelligence showed Red Chinese troop concentrations there. But Dean Rusk, then Assistant Secretary of State for Far Eastern affairs, was able to persuade the President that this scheduled action

*The Red Chinese commander, Lin Piao, later stated that he was only able to support the North Koreans because of intelligence leaks, which assured him of the Manchurian sanctuary and secure bridges across the Yalu. (Possibly from the British officials, Burgess and McLean, who later defected to the U.S.S.R.) MacArthur was not appraised of this decision, at the time of the Wake Island meeting.[50]

should be stopped. As Mr. Truman recalled in his memoirs:

> Assistant Secretary of State Rusk pointed out that we had a commitment with the British not to take action which might involve attacks on the Manchurian side of the river without consultation with them . . .
>
> Mr. Rusk also mentioned the danger of involving the Soviets, especially in light of the mutual-assistance treaty between Moscow and Peiping.[52]

As MacArthur's forces drove the Communist troops back into North Korea, the "thinking" within the State Department apparently became more and more restrained. Following an exchange of missives between MacArthur and Washington, the General learned on March 20, that President Truman was preparing to ask for a truce because of the State Department position that Red China was a military colossus.

On March 24, MacArthur released a "bombshell" statement, exploding the colossus myth, stating that Red China had already demonstrated its military insufficiency to cause further loss in position to the Eighth Army, Korean and UN forces. He also included a plan for completely smashing Red China, with the aid of Nationalist Chinese forces, unless Red China withdrew from the conflict.

This violated an earlier Presidential directive imposed on MacArthur against public statements. On April 6, Congressman Joseph Martin released a personal letter from the General stating in part, that Korea was a crucial area in the conflict between the two ideologies, "that here we fight Europe's wars with arms while the diplomats there still fight with words . . . there is no substitute for victory."

General MacArthur was recalled from his command by the President on April 11th.** His return was one of the most dramatic events of the decade, not only because he was a public idol, but also because he had not returned to the United States following World War II, preferring to remain on duty, as it were, supervising the reconstruction of Japan. The high point in the return was an address to both houses of the Congress, which he concluded by quoting an Army ballad, "Old Soldiers Never Die, They Just Fade Away."

---

*This was a bit far-fetched, since the Russians had already armed the Red Chinese "to the teeth" with the best Russian equipment and carefully preserved American lend-lease ordnance. The only addition possible would have been men, which the Chinese hardly needed, and the Soviets had no nuclear weapons deployed then.

**Reportedly, Mr. Truman was persuaded to do this by Dean Rusk.[53]

The ensuing public and Congressional furor stopped the initiation of truce talks by the United States. The remaining period of the conflict has been concisely described by the perceptive writer and commentator, Joseph Alsop:

> In June, 1951, the American and South Korean armies then mounted a powerful offensive which began to achieve brilliant success. Our forces were on the very brink of final breakthrough– of breaking the Chinese and Northern armies in Korea, in fact. Thereupon negotiations were hurriedly proposed, through the Soviets at the United Nations, in fact.
>
> President Truman responded by issuing a standstill order to our forces in Korea. The great chance, so nearly within our grasp, was abruptly thrown away. While the interminable Panmunjom talks began, the enemy brought up supplies and reinforcements. Missing the great chance cost us two more years of hard fighting, countless billions of treasure and 90,000 additional American casualties. [54]

An armistice was finally signed on July 27, 1953, after President Eisenhower quietly threatened, through a number of diplomatic channels, to throw out all geographical and tactical restraints (i.e. suggesting the possibility of the use of nuclear weapons in Manchuria and elsewhere). [55] A formal peace has never been established, however, and there are still frequent border incidents.

The Communists claimed the Korean war as a victory, but no doubt their claims would have been more accentuated had not MacArthur stopped the American proposal for peace talks in March 1951, by his proposed victory plan.

Of course, America was defeated in several ways, but in another the Korean war was a great victory. For a world power like the United States to be even seriously engaged with indigent Communist troops and not thoroughly smash them, was to suffer a defeat. The nuclear capability which the British so generously allowed the Russians could hardly have been in existence then, and the U.S. had been stockpiling atomic bombs for years.

America's victory in the Korean war was on the home front. The unilateral disarmament introduced by Defense Secretary Johnson was stopped cold, and a modern weapons program based on guided missiles was started. This situation is discussed in Chapter 14. Also, the public was alerted, for a time, to the truism, that *Communists would not stop, they could only be stopped.*

Perhaps the biggest defeat was diplomatic, or the demonstration of incapability in that area. The policy of "no interest" in the defense of Formosa was modified to that of a guarantee. That is, while military aid to Chiang's 500,000 man army was resumed, and although it was announced that the U.S. Navy would interdict any attempt to assault Formosa, the Nationalist Chinese government was also requested not to engage in air or sea operations against the mainland. This allowed Mao Tse-tung to redeploy the Red Chinese Armies from positions opposite Formosa to Manchuria for the Korean attack. [56] Also the Red Chinese were now able to purchase additional war materials, as outlined by Freda Utley:

> The effect of President Truman's order concerning Formosa was to enable the Communists to acquire all the war materials which they had hitherto been unable to secure on account of the Chinese Nationalist naval and air blockade of Shanghai and Tientsin. Our British allies in Hong Kong made hay while the sun shone, and such American shipping firms as the Isbrandtsen Line also profited by the United States order to prevent Chinese Nationalist attacks on shipping serving the Communists. Copper, steel, and other war supplies were rushed to Communist Chinese ports by British and American businessmen anxious only to acquire profits, and indifferent to the death and mutilation of British and American soldiers in Korea. Time reported on January 22, 1951, that British traders in Hong Kong, during 1950, had done 400 million dollars' worth of business with Red China, supplying our enemies and theirs with rubber, gasoline, steel, and other strategic materials. [57]

Another tragic aspect of the Korean conflict, which must be noted, taking exception to the no casualties and atrocities rule set up at the first of the Chapter, was the loss of approximately 900 American prisoners abandoned to the Red Chinese prisons.

Just as Communist aggression abroad can only be stopped by positive means, internal subversion also requires constant vigilance and screening to protect sensitive areas. That this course has been too little followed has allowed communism to flourish.

Before the Korean war, criticism of the State Department policies by a few legislators—and some vague public awareness of what was going on in China—brought to the general attention the foolishness of reducing the security controls for Communists in government during WWII. For example, pressure on the State Department by concerned men like Senator Knowland, and Senator Bridges, and Congressmen Judd, Nixon, Mundt, Taber, Dondero, and others, forced a "house-cleaning" in 1946-47. In this operation 112 security risks and 91 homosexuals were fired.[58,59] During this period the Secretary of State was James F. Byrnes. Mr. Byrnes had brought to State, at the suggesion of General Clay and others, the very capable J. Anthony Panuch to head up the administrative and security programs. Panuch was making notable headway with the complex legal problems involved in security, but was fired before his work was well under way. Author William F. Buckley describes this unusual situation in the following way:

> On the 22nd of January, 1947, James Byrnes resigned, and George Marshall assumed office. The following day, after a protracted interview with Dean Acheson, Under Secretary of State and long-time foe of Panuch, Marshall consented to the firing of Panuch, Acheson ordered Panuch out of the Department, at the close of business the same day.
>
> Within a few weeks, every vital member of Panuch's security staff was retired, demoted, transferred to another branch of the Department, or fired. John Peurifoy succeeded Panuch. President Truman's loyalty directive established the inadequate "reasonable grounds" standard in loyalty cases. The State Department security program was now dead in its tracks.[60]

The extent of Communist espionage during WWII was revealed, to some extent, by the public testimony of former spies, Elizabeth Terrill Bentley and David Whittaker Chambers. Both of those individuals had fully re-canted communism and told the full stories of their subversive activities. Chambers' role was that of a courier, and among those he named as agents was Alger Hiss. His testimony was so convincing, that despite the incredibility of the charge, Congressman Richard Nixon persisted with the investigation, causing Chambers to eventually bring forth the famous Pumpkin Papers, in response to a lawsuit by Hiss.*

On February 9, 1950, Senator Joseph McCarthy stated in an address to the Ohio County Women's Republican Club of Wheeling, West Virginia, that there were a number of Communists still working in the State Department. The exact number was never rigorously determined; but whether it was 57, as McCarthy later claimed, or 205 is not really significant. He did produce a list of 81 cases which he said should be *privately* investigated. Rather than taking this objective approach, the Tydings Committee was set up for public hearings. The attempted whitewash of McCarthy's charges by the Committee was evaluated by Senator Lodge, also one of the

---

*The story of this case is well set forth in *Seeds of Treason.*[61]

Committee members, as "superficial and inconclusive." As the events developed, it seemed that McCarthy "stumbled" into the issue of subversion; but, regarless of the nature of his start, he quickly took up the issue with all the vigor of a crusader. When the Korean war broke out in the following June, the issue of subversion in government became a truly vital one. McCarthy's use of the immunity of speeches on the Senate floor made it possible for his critics, with whom the Communists worked overtime, to make McCarthyism an epithet. Freda Utley comments on McCarthy's efforts in the following way:

> The Wisconsin Senator, who had fought with the Marines in World War II, knew that he would be smeared and his aims misrepresented, but went ahead on his frontal assault on the State Department. Those who criticized him for having exaggerated Communist influence in determining American foreign policy were unaware of the reality of the danger he sought to expose. It was probably necessary to paint a terrifying picture on a large canvas without much attention to detail or fine shading, if at long last the American people were to be stirred out of their apathy concerning treason in high places. McCarthy brandished an axe instead of using a scalpel, and his "indelicate" methods were displeasing to many.

> But it cannot be denied that he performed the vitally necessary task of awakening the American people to the clear and present danger to the Republic constituted by the Communist conspiracy in our midst. Until McCarthy started his campaign, Communist sympathizers in government employment had found little difficulty in getting themselves cleared by the Loyalty Review Board, headed by Seth Richardson. [62]

One factor most generally overlooked about the issue of subversion in government, which McCarthy had raised, was its effect on the 1952 election. Commenting on the situation in 1952, historian Morison suggested that McCarthy's charges of subversion were influential in swinging the election to the Republicans that year.*

> . . . thus to win, the Republicans must have a new issue or a glamor-boy like the late Wendell Wilkie, or both. McCarthy supplied the issue, but who could lead the procession?. . . Tom Dewey, twice defeated did not care to try again, but he marshalled delegates to win the nomination for a really glamorous candidate — General Eisenhower. [63]

---

*The measure of public support on the Communist-in-government issue in this period is indicated by a Gallup Poll taken in 1953, which showed that 74% of the people believed that there were still many Communists remaining in government.

And General Eisenhower campaigned on, "Let's Clean Up The Mess In Washington!"

Nearly everyone, except the Communists, agreed that what McCarthy was trying to do was fine, it was his methods that were criticized — but the loudest critics carefully avoided making any suggestions for alternative positive action. McCarthy's basic formula was, "If it walks like a duck, quacks like a duck, and looks like a duck — why it *is* a duck." Perhaps if the press had "let" the Reds-in-government issue be faced, the State Department would have known in advance that Fidel Castro was a Communist.*

---

*The continued deterioration of government security throughout the 1960's promises to effect a trauma in the 1970's. Consider, for example, the following "iceberg tips" which appeared in the news:

● In 1963, the State Department fired 45 homosexual security risks, in 1964, 32 and in 1965, 28. One was a top Foreign Service Officer paid $20,835 per year. Two had been with the State Department for 19 years and two others 17 years. *(U.S. News & World Report,* Sept. 26, 1966.)

● In the early days of the Kennedy Administration a new security official was assigned what he thought was a "clean sweep" in reviewing security risk potential at high levels in the State Department. He found that 20% of the first 100 cases needed re-evaluation (for negative security factors). The investigation was stopped and the too-eager officer was transferred to Guadalajara, Mexico.*(Santa Ana Register,* Jan. 20, 1966.)

● A list of CIA informers in Cuba was routed in the State Department — in two weeks over one half were arrested.*(San Diego Union,* July 27, 1965.)

● Mr. Johnson's Tsar on Vietnam, W. W. Rostow, was twice denied a security clearance by the Eisenhower Administration.*(San Diego Union,* Oct. 24, 1967.)

● Some drug addicts and double agents are tolerated in State and CIA, despite disapproval by the FBI.*(Washington Observer,* Dec. 28, 1967.)

● A foreign Service Officer who admitted to being a homosexual was assigned to a critical post behind the Iron Curtain. *(The Wanderer,* Dec. 28, 1967.)

● The Nixon nominee as Ambassador to Moscow, Jacob D. Beam, was victimized by a Polish Mata Hari, Madam Jerz Michalowski from 1957 to 1961 while he was in Warsaw conducting fruitless negotiations with the Chinese for release of American prisoners, demanding that Radio Free Europe stop its anti-Communist broadcasts in Polish, providing information on CIA dispatches, etc. *(Liberty Letter,* April 1969.)

● Five days before President Nixon took office, the State Department reinstated John Patton Davies, who had been classified as a security risk for 15 years.*(Human Events,* Feb. 8, 1969.)

● On October 13, 1968 in a campaign speech in Dallas, Nixon said, "I want a Secretary of State who will join me in cleaning house in the State Department. . ." Just election oratory?

The problem with the "duck formula" was that it did not discriminate between the dedicated Communist and the imperceptive, well meaning, but not too bright good fellow who, one way or another, allowed himself to be used by Communists. True, from a purely administrative – which is to say, a practical view – this discrimination should be considered as purely academic and not permissible. (Such certainly is the approach taken on the other side of the Iron and Bamboo Curtains.) But allowing for the prevailing Free World tolerance, it must be recognized that many people are not capable of considering the source of their motivations in undertaking a course of action. They may be responding to thoughts implanted from one or several divisive sources – there are certainly too many in this iconoclastic age. In other words, the subversive Communist deliberately acts to further the cause of communism, but a sincere patriot may, through passively following the wrong influences, act in support of Communist causes, although consciously both innocent and generally opposed to communism.

Again, from an administrative view, neither type of individual can be allowed in sensitive governmental or industrial areas. As an alternative discriminant to the "duck formula," the innovation of the term Domestic Lyrical Subliminal Communist or *dolsc* is suggested.

Returning to McCarthy and McCarthyism, the two other major issues he raised were: (1) the question of General Marshall's motivation, first in a Senate speech (June 14, 1951) and later in a book;[64] and (2) the "Who Promoted Peress" TV "trial." The latter did not merit the publicity it received. As to the former, it probably nixed the chance of getting a complete security "house-cleaning" during the Eisenhower Administration. This sort of house-cleaning was badly needed; President Truman had issued an executive order on March 13, 1948, prohibiting access to personnel security files by members of Congress. This had been a vital blow to Congressional investigations, and some relaxation of restrictions in this field was badly needed. Yet, had McCarthy's presentation of the Communist issue been significantly less dramatic, it is possible that Eisenhower would not have been elected in 1952. As it developed, after he became President, not only did Eisenhower discourage investigation of communism in the government during WWII, by Attorney General Herbert Brownell, but on May 17, 1954, he issued an executive order allowing employees of the Executive Branch to refrain from answering questions from Congressional committees. This became known as the "Executive Fifth Amendment." Thus instead of really setting things in order, the new Republican Administration cut off the one remaining source of information to Congressional investigators.

Moving sharply up to a world-wide panoramic view of the two conflicting governmental systems, i.e. Free World and Communist, one can easily hypothesize a five phase evolutionary program. Starting from the Cold War period immediately following WWII, the sequence is: (1) Cold War; (2) Coexistence; (3) Interdependence; (4) East-West condominium; (5) Synthesis.

In the Free World, although there are several indirect advantages accruing to the development of communism from the (eroding) social mores of the peoples, there is one directly contributing factor. This factor is the temporizing politician, who cannot, or will not, see the historic long view, but is merely trying to temporize with short-term expedients to enhance his momentary political position. He is therefore prone to make minor relaxations favorable to communism, in the confrontation of the two political systems, which taken incrementally, are not too significant. However, as these piecewise concessions are integrated over the course of a few decades, the terminal, fifth phase can be easily reached.

Taking this grandiose perspective, the nature of the day-to-day, year-by-year process becomes more apparent. In this country, as in much of the rest of the Free World, prevailing government policies are somewhere in the 2-3 region phase. On the other hand, some of the smaller countries maintain a firm phase-1 status, while others such as Egypt and Algeria are clearly evolving into the phase-5 status. In many countries the Communists refrain from showing the total extent of their present influence, in order not to alarm the Free World.

This policy of concealing influence has been particularly useful in Europe, allowing defection of France from NATO. Although naturally adaptive, the grand scheme seems to involve slow subversion of Europe, assimilation of the Middle East, Southeast Asia and Australia (to be discussed further in a subsequent chapter) and psychological defeat and subversion of the United States. With the latter accomplished, there but remains the task of orderly (?) organization of the Communist system of world government.

Now, having developed this world-panoramic picture of creeping communism, it is possible to drop back and again consider the importance of the proposed acronym *dolsc*.

Since Communists are building communism on a long-range, incremental basis, those in the Free World who desire to oppose this process must have some sense of fixed reference from which to gauge the immediate motion which might be produced by a particular measure, or the effective thrust of a certain candidate. Admitting that all sorts of grey areas and gradations are involved, it is suggested that the term *dolsc* will provide an alerting descriptive which would apply to those generally well-meaning individuals who are, unconsciously, contributing to the upward movement on the phase one-to-five sequence, without inappropriately calling them Communists. With this sort of identification available, key duties can be given only to those whose nature would clearly effect a contrariwise movement on the numerical scale. The individual's sense of judgement must be employed to make this appraisal, thus substituting the somewhat easier evaluation of *direction* for that of *position*. Likewise, on the evaluation of pending legislation, the same measure can be applied: what is this bill leading to, as well as the ostensible objective provided?

This approach is practical. It allows control of the direction of heading, while avoiding hair-splitting on acrimonious tangents of motivation – i.e. *what* a man does is important, not *why* he does it.

Having projected the possibility of a world synthesis, it will be simply stated that this could only be a slightly polished form of communism.

The engagements with the forces of Communism since 1952 have not been included in this chapter because of the general familiarity associated with most recent events, and because of the following detailed discussion of certain developments. In the next chapter the dilemma accruing from World War II and post war policies on China – imposed by subversives, dolscs and naive liberals in the State Department who contrived to prevent arms shipments to the Free Chinese forces – will be discussed. One possible culmination of these policies is projected in Appendix A.

PART II

LET THE DUST SETTLE

problem

CHAPTER 5

VIETNAM

Americans have, in the main, given a courageous support to the Vietnam war, despite the creeping involvement and the complexities of the issues involved. This despite the fact that the *why* of the involvement in Vietnam was not well presented, by the press or the Johnson Administration. Walter Lippman selected the following quotation from the *New York Herald Tribune* as a point of departure for his rebuttal of the role of the U.S. as a world policeman:

We're in Vietnam at the express invitation of the Vietnamese government; we're fighting there for the Vietnamese people.

But we're fighting also for the millions of people in the other threatened lands beyond, people who haven't the power to defend themselves from the (Red) Chinese colossus, and whose lives, safety and freedom depend on the strong arm of the policeman – which only we can provide.[1]

The official position on the U.S. participation is given in a thirty page booklet, *Why Vietnam,*[2] and in testimony by Secretary of State, Dean Rusk, before the Senate Foreign Relations Committee on February 18, 1966.[3]

In the discussion period following, Senator Fullbright remarked that the failures of the peace-efforts to date suggested "something is wrong with our diplomacy." Secretary Rusk cooly replied, "Senator, is it just possible that there is something wrong with theirs?"

General Curtis LeMay, USAF (Ret.) has also commented on the purpose of our efforts in Vietnam saying, "We're swatting flies, when we should go after the manure pile." While it is true that localized trouble spots such as Vietnam and Cuba would not exist without the Red centers in Moscow and Peking, it is helpful to explore the nature of the support for the local aggressions to acquire Red colonies.

But is it possible for the United States to succeed where

the French essentially gave up, after eight years of fighting the Communists? As established during World War II, American soldiers have a friendly directness and interest in the welfare of others, which enables them to mix as equals with peoples all over the world. The effect of this unique characteristic is shown by the following appraisal of American effort in Vietnam by Rev. Maurice Hall, missionary for the Church of Christ:

> I never heard even one (Vietnamese) intimate that the United States was there for any purpose except to help them and to guarantee their continuing freedom.
>
> One lawyer I know contrasted our behavior with that of the French. He said the French and the Vietnamese were always working at cross purposes, but the situation is different when Americans and Vietnamese work together.
>
> Both are interested in defeating and pushing out the Communists.[4]

But, on the other hand, the element of time is also involved, and as will be discussed, this would seem to be on the side of the Communists, assuming the continuation of the "wrist slapping" prosecution of the war.

Ho Chi Minh (meaning the "enlightened" one) was given the name of Nguyen Tat Thank at birth. He was a messenger in the Hanoi rebellion of 1908, thus starting a career of intrigue and violence. In 1920, he helped found the French Communist Party. Later he received training in Moscow. By 1925, he had a position in the Soviet Consulate in Canton, from which he started the nucleus of the Indochina revolutionary movement. Following were seventeen years of Communist activity, periods in jail and occasional disappearances. He emerged in 1941 as head of the Vietminh, short for Vietnam Doc Lap Dong Minh, or League for the Revolution and Independence of Vietnam. Soon thereafter, he was imprisoned again by Chiang Kai-shek, but released in 1942, at the insistence of the U.S. Office of Strategic Services. Ho Chi Minh provided leadership needed to establish Red Vietnam, but left a regime fully able to carry on alone after his death.

Following an abortive attempt in March 1954, to entice the Vietminh into direct combat at Dien Bien Phu, the French sought direct American military support. (The U.S. had supplied three to four billion dollars of economic aid to the French in Indochina following the outbreak of the Korean war.) Secretary of State Dulles consulted with eight leading Congressmen and was told that he had "better go shopping first for allies."[5] The U.S. then undertook the formation of a Southeast Asia Treaty Organization, in advance of the forthcoming Geneva Conference scheduled to seek a political solution for the Indochina region. The American view being, that the establishment of such a group, before the conference, would provide the strongest sort of support to the French during the conference. However, the French were reluctant to meet American conditions, which involved granting full independence to the former colonies — although this had been clearly established as a long range objective by the French — and the establishment of an overall U.S. command.[6] And more importantly, Winston Churchill, then again Prime Minister, wanted to postpone the formation of a Free Southeast Asia bloc until after the planned Geneva conference.[7]

Near the end of the siege at Dien Bien Phu, President Eisenhower consulted Senator Richard Russel, then Chairman of the Senate Armed Services Committee, and Senator Lyndon Johnson, then the Democratic majority leader, regarding immediate air support for the beleaguered French. In response:

> The senators recoiled. "We have no business being out there," they protested. "This is not the time nor the place to fight out there," Senator Johnson declared![8]

The Geneva Conference ended with the establishment of Cambodia, Laos and North and South Vietnam from the former French Indochina empire. The U.S. would not sign the agreement worked out because of the compromises involved.[9] However, the U.S., in effect, picked up the French burden by agreeing to continue aid to the South Vietnamese government-to-be. As a result of this position as the financial supporter, the U.S. was able to influence the choice of Ngo Dinh Diem* as the responsible minister of the new South Vietnam government.[10]

In the book *Vietnam — A Diplomatic Tragedy*, Victor Blator provided a good insight into the 1954 Geneva conference and said of Ngo Dinh Diem:

> There is little doubt that had the Geneva conference failed

---

*Apparently Diem was selected as a result of sponsorship by Supreme Court Justice William Douglas, Senator Mike Mansfield,and the State Department.[10] No doubt, part of the Diem "glamor" came from his brother, Ngo dinh Nhu, who was the leader of an 180,000 member union in Saigon. Later Nhu was to talk of building socialism, but this was never to advance beyond the "back-burner" stage.

and the fight against Ho Chi Minh been carried on, Ngo Dinh Diem would probably have been an admirable war-time leader — Incorruptible, bold, ascetic, an intransigent nationalist, a fanatical anti-communist and finally, the recognized leader of the Catholic North Vietnamese. But, after Geneva, the creation of a unified, cohesive new state needed other qualities which Diem did not possess, among them, flexibility, tolerance, willingness to make conciliatory compromises and skill at political manipulation. Many observers of the Vietnam situation, French and American alike, were convinced that Diem was by his nature unable to adapt himself to this mission. French Prime Minister Edgar Faure, in spite of the restraint that his official position demanded did not refrain from expressing publicly his opinion that Diem was "not equal to his task," that he had little if any popular support.[11]

In the period from 1954 to 1960, Diem consolidated his position with the establishment of a nepotistic, authoritarian administration. His brother Nhu was given the inclusive position of political advisor.

Apparently as a result of his idealism, one of Diem's first undertakings was the elimination of three semi-private armies, which had been quite helpful to the French in the struggle with the Vietminh. Perhaps a more experienced administrator would have sought to gradually integrate these forces into the regular army units. *But most significantly Diem and his American advisors failed to follow one of the most basic strategems of the Orient. Whenever possible, an objective is bought — not worked for.* In the 1954-1956 period the budding Viet Cong* effort might very well have been effectively controlled by the simple expedient of paying an attractive price for Chinese, Russian and (WW-II) Japanese rifles. The private armies would no doubt have proven capable arms "collectors."

American policy of coddling the Diem government with increasing aid continued steadily in the 1954-62 period. Gradually the Viet Cong effort was intensified, until at the end of this period over 15,000 Village Chiefs had been killed, and other widespread atrocities committed — all of which were cleverly intended to subjugate the villagers, whose support was so essential in the guerrilla effort.

Although gifted with a sincere interest in the plight of

---

*The Viet Cong calls itself the Giai Phong Quan. The term Viet Cong means only Vietnamese Communists, which was applied in contempt by the Diem regime.

the people, Diem was reluctant to exploit his frequent trips into the villages by means of news films. Likewise he was reluctant to use the radio network the U.S. had provided, to stimulate the national spirit. He felt that popular support was a duty, and could be expected — as would have been the case in a preceding era. His objective was primarily to provide *proper* government, without departing from the classical formalism of the Mandarin. [12]

No doubt Diem's ascetic life and scholarly background contributed to his popularity with the Americans. Clearly this type individual provided a marked contrast, when compared with that of the heads of state of many of the nations.

On September 23, 1960, the Communist Party of North Vietnam held a meeting in Hanoi in which they decided to launch a full-scale guerrilla war in the south.

As a result of Diem's limitations in establishing a popular government and providing effective control of the Viet Cong, a group of dissident army colonels attempted to stage a coup on November 11, 1960. Diem was able to negotiate, and to agree to a list of reforms: civil liberties, free elections, elimination of the Nhus from the government, more effective measures against the Communists, etc. During the negotiations Diem brought additional troops into Saigon and the coup-effort was quickly suppressed. Not only were the leaders purged and the promised reforms forgotten, but from then on military positions in the army were given first on the basis of loyalty and secondly on the basis of ability. [13]

In December 1960, the Soviets set up an airlift supply of arms and ammunition out of Hanoi to the Communist Pathet Lao forces in Laos. Early in 1961, the Communists were able to launch a major offensive in Laos, with machine guns, artillery, mortars, and armored vehicles.

The SEATO nations in the immediate area, Australia, the Philippines, Pakistan, Thailand, and New Zealand, all favored common action against the Communist attack in Laos — but the British and French were opposed and the U.S. sat on the fence, so nothing was done. [14]

President Kennedy resorted to dramatic warnings, and roving Ambassador W. Averell Harriman entered into a 15-month series of negotiations in Geneva — *establishing, in effect, the access of the Communists to the Ho Chi Minh trail. This trail was an essential supply route for the invasion of South Vietnam.*

Although it is unclear at what time opposition to Diem and the Nhus began to develop in the various branches of the American government involved in administering U.S. aid to Vietnam, very likely the unsuccessful 1960 coup was a turning point. As it developed, the mounting losses to the Viet Cong and increasing international tension caused President Kennedy, in October 1961, to order 12,000 additional men to support the 600 odd American military advisors already stationed in South Vietnam by President Eisenhower.

The 12,000 man commitment obviously represented a second phase of the American effort. James Reston, associate editor of the New Yor' Times, was later to state that President Kennedy had said that he was influenced in making this decision for the additional commitment by discussions with the Russian Premier, Nikita Khruschev, in Vienna, in the preceding spring.[15] In these talks, which came soon after the abortive Bay-of-Pigs affair in Cuba, Khruschev attempted to bully the new American president. After these discussions, a European humorist commented with this dialogue:

N.K., "Give me your watch and your wallet." J.F.K., "No."
N.K., "Allright, let's negotiate, give me your wallet."

On May 8, 1963, a flag-flying crisis developed, in which the Buddhists at Hue ignored a previously recognized ban which permitted only the flying of the National flag, because of the war. (The Roman Catholics had similarly ignored the regulation a few weeks earlier in the same area.) This incident was confounded by a series of growing crises between the Buddhists and the Saigon Government. Moreover, these unfortunate events were magnified by the news services — because of sensationalism, or for other reasons. About this turn of events John Meclin, Public Relations officer for the U.S.I.S. in Vietnam, was to comment on the American correspondents there:

> Still another unlikely aspect of the Buddhist upheaval was the probability that it could not have succeeded without the help of the American press and radio/TV. Expressed more bluntly, American news coverage of the upheaval contributed directly to the destruction of a national U.S. policy of direct importance to the security of the United States, in an area where we have deployed nearly twenty thousand Americans, where we were spending some $500 million a year, at the only point in the world where we were engaged in support of a shooting war against a Communist enemy.[16]

There developed a series of riots and suppressions during which six youths and one elderly monk committed suicide by self-cremation.* These activities were in a large part controlled by one Thich Tri Quang, Secretary General of the United Buddhist Association — a militant organization which is (or was) vitally interested in political action. Quang was reported to have told Marguerite Higgins: "We cannot get an arrangement with the North until we get rid of Diem and Nhu."[17] Later, Quang was imprisoned as a Hanoi agent.

As the news reports of the Buddhist suppression and suicides continued, a major crisis developed in the State Department. Averell Harriman, the Undersecretary of State, and Roger Hillsman, Assistant Secretary for Far Eastern affairs, felt that Diem must go — while on the other hand, the military, including Secretary McNamara, the CIA and Vice President Johnson, wanted to maintain the *status quo*.[18] As a first step the U.S. Ambassador, Frederick E. Nolting Jr., was recalled and Henry Cabot Lodge was sent to Saigon as the replacement.

Late in August some of the aid to the Vietnam government was suspended, although news of this did not reach the public until early in October.[19] In discussing the situation in Vietnam early in September, *Newsweek* reported President Kennedy as saying:

In my opinion, in the last two months the government has gotten out of touch with the people. The trend could be reversed with changes in policy and personnel.

This was a thinly veiled invitation to Diem to dump his chief political advisor, brother Nhu, and Nhu's beautiful but acid-tongued wife, Madame Nhu.**[20]

---

*This unusual practice was sufficiently common, that 25 such deaths had been recorded between the fifth and tenth centuries in China. The first such recorded instance was that of a Bodhisattva named Bhaishajya-Raja in the first century, whose self immolation followed a twelve year period of eating incense and sweet scented substances and scented oils. He wrapped himself in "divine clothes," bathed in perfumed oil and set fire to himself as an offering to the buddha and sutra. It is believed that his body is to continue burning for 12,000 years.

**Madame Nhu was a provocative speaker, but for that matter so was Mrs. Eleanor Roosevelt. At the time the plot was being organized, Madame Nhu was making a speaking tour of Europe and the U.S., and during this time support was mounting for the Diem regime. According to Meclin, a number of prominent Roman Catholic leaders, several political leaders, including Barry Goldwater, columnists like Joseph Alsop, Marguerite Higgins and Walter Lippman and news publications such as the Hearst, Scripps-Howard and *Time-Life* were generating such strong pro-Diem pressures that President Kennedy might have been compelled to capitulate to Diem, in a few more weeks.[23]

By the middle of September, the State Department and Ambassador Lodge were reported as insisting that both Nhu and his wife must go, and some people in State were insisting that Diem should go too.[21] In reviewing the events leading up to the coup that was to occur, David Halberstam, *New York Times* reporter in Vietnam, related, in discussing the event:

The three generals, (Vietnamese Army generals organizing the coup) who had been kept fully informed of Dinh's plans, (General Dinh was in charge of President Diem's troops for the Saigon area — and so must be the key man in the revolt.) now notified the Americans that they were planning a coup. Reportedly they did not deal with the American military, whom they still distrusted, but with Lodge's office. They did not ask for any assistance, but they said that the coup would be pro-American, and asked the mission not to thwart it. In turn, the embassy did not offer any aid, but it did make arrangements to stay in full communication with the rebels.[22]

The coup was staged on November 1, 1963, thus bringing to a tragic end the unfortunate crisis with the murder of both Diem and Nhu.

As any Old China hand can verify, it was never considered wise to directly cross any sort of a Mandarin. Generally, more oblique approaches should have been found, which are much more effective.

On November 22, President Kennedy was shot by a (renegade?) Communist assassin — or perhaps, as some claim, by a number of assassins.

*   *   *

As the coup came to an end, and the echos of the last gunfire faded away in Saigon, organized bands marched to the houses of the most active anti-Communists and burned them. Also the centers of anti-Communism, such as the book shops, libraries and information centers were sacked — even though many of these had had no connection with the Diem government. Although these events were fully photographed by the journalists, the pictures were not presented to the American public by the press.[24]

Seven governments later — and following the burning of nearly the same number of monks — the U.S. government found it necessary to "look away" while the Vietnamese (Ky) government went into Buddhist pagodas and forceably suppressed the militant monks.

In November 1965, earlier reports of a peace feeler

from Hanoi were substantiated by an article published in *Look* magazine by Eric Sevareid. This account covered a long talk the author had with the late UN Ambassador, Adlai E. Stevenson, just prior to his death. As borne out by the State Department, [25] UN Secretary-General, U Thant, had reported in the early autumn of 1964 that North Vietnam was willing to meet the U.S. in Rangoon for peace discussions (but without representation by the South Vietnamese). Inasmuch as the '64 Presidential campaign was then in full swing, it no doubt seemed that the Communists were shopping for "bargain rates." The Administration was able to hold open the possibility of undertaking talks until after the election, but sufficient confidence was not established in the Red Vietnamese position to undertake negotiations. Possibly the Administration was guided by the fact that during the Korean War negotiations were started in July 1951, and continued for two years — during which time there were 90,000 additional casualties.

At the approximate time the Red Vietnamese had made their overtures to U Thant, Candidate Johnson was saying, on September 28:

> Before I start dropping bombs around the country (North Vietnam — this had been suggested by Candidate Goldwater), I would want to think about the consequences of getting American boys into a war with 700 million Chinese . . . We're not going north and drop bombs at this stage of the game, and we're not going south and run out and let the communists take over either.[26]

It should not be considered that this was just election palaver — more likely the President came to learn more of the Communist mettle in the post-election period. However, it was unfortunate that the Vietnam problem was not faced squarely (by the Democrats) during the campaign, as this could have easily been put aside as a non-political matter, had they done so. Barry Goldwater had made a specific point in his acceptance speech of the fact, "We are at war in Vietnam!" Facing the war issue during the campaign would have greatly strengthened the Administration's position afterward, and there is little reason to consider that the result of the election would have been significantly changed. On that matter, the American people are sufficiently conservative that they were reluctant to have a third President in a period of some fifteen months; furthermore, the distortion of the Goldwater campaign by the news media allowed the Democrats to avoid an extended discussion of the Vietnam issue. For example, after his retirement from a long career as a Washington correspondent, Arthur Krock commented:

> Goldwater — I don't know whether he would have rather been right than President, but he certainly felt that he was right on certain things he did that he knew were risky, bold, and turned out to be foolish. Goldwater is anything but a good politician. He does not know the trade, though he has lived it.
>
> Barry Goldwater is bold, but he is not politically wise. *And, of course, he was the victim of very, very brilliant misrepresentation and distortion.*[27] *(Italics added)*

After the '64 election, as the Vietnam issue was at last faced, it became apparent that the U.S. was indeed at war. Material support, as had been provided to Greece, would not suffice; this situation was like Korea — but the geography was much worse. Commenting on the decision for commitment Stewart Alsop said:

> Yet the President made his decision to commit American troops in Vietnam for a good reason. With one exception (Under Secretary of State, George Ball) all of his chief advisors urged him to make the commitment. A partial list would include Secretary of State Rusk, Secretary of Defense McNamara, McGeorge Bundy, all of the members of the National Security Council and all the Joint Chiefs of Staff. . . . Said Senator Richard Russel, 'Go in and win or get the Hell out.' But if the President got out, the Republicans are likely to comment about the chicken-hearted President who wasted thousands of American lives and then ran out on our friends.[28]

However torturous the decision for commitment*, the beneficial "fallout" has been remarkable. First, the Indonesian counter-coup and near retirement of Sukarno must be noted. Then, a gradual shifting toward closer alignment with the U.S. is apparent by free Asian countries from Pakistan to Japan, including the socialist Prime-minister of Singapore, Lee Kuan Yew.[29] The people of Ceylon were heartened enough to actually vote out a pro-Red government and the Indonesia-Malaysia war was quickly ended, following the counter-coup in Indonesia.

The domino theory has been used in discussing the Vietnam issue, but the analogy is hardly appropriate. Vietnam is more in the nature of a keystone to an arch. *Between Singapore on the north and the island of Sumatra*

---

*Undoubtedly the decision was the more difficult because of the financial limitations which were thereby imposed on the "infant" poverty programs being initiated as transitional measures, until full-blown welfarism (e.g., negative income tax, rent subsidies, etc.) could be established.

on the south, lies the 600 mile long Strait of Malacca. This is a gateway between the Pacific and the Indian oceans and is therefore one of the most vital waterways in the world. Over 200 ships a day pass through this strategic sea lane, appoximately 95% of the sea transport into the western Pacific area. Control of this strait by Red China would have given her the means of exerting powerful influence on the government of Japan. For example, 92% of the oil for Japan's industries pass through the Strait of Malacca.

These benefits, resulting from the intensified post-Pleiku efforts started with the bombing of the North on February 7, 1965, have been rather well appreciated by the U.S. public — despite the limited supporting discussion provided during the Johnson Administration. The vitriolic criticism from the Vietniks, dolscs and Communists has been generally recognized for what it is. It is regrettable, however, that so much note is given to such antics by the news services — as this unquestionably adds to the Communist drive.

It should be noted that the college faculty criticism comes primarily from staff members with specialties not requiring detailed knowledge of political science in general, or communism in particular. To explore this matter, Professor Rodger Swearington, Director of the Research Institute on Communist Strategy and Propaganda at the University of California, undertook an analysis of two advertisements objecting to the U.S. role in Vietnam appearing in the May 9, 1965 and the June 5, 1966 *New York Times*. Nearly 800 members of the academic community signed the first appeal, and 6,000 signatures were obtained on the second (three page) advertisement. Although these signatures were obtained from prominent Eastern institutions, in the main noted as centers for training in political science and foreign affairs, the petition signers were overwhelmingly from fields such as psychology, mathematics, physics, biology, theology, bacteriology and romance languages. Only a very small minority were historians, political scientists and the like — but, of those, none was a specialist in Communist ideology.[30]

The really unfortunate thing about the war-protestor movements is the aid and comfort given to the Communists. A typical Communist reaction is the following comment from an editorial in the Peking Peoples' Daily:

> The outbreak of the anti-war struggle of the American people is the outcome of sharpening contradictions between the American people and the U.S. ruling group and a reflection of the rapid aggravation of the class struggle in the U.S.[31]

The editorial goes on to observe that these demonstrations are "unprecedented in scale and duration in American History" and to conclude that internal conflicts in the U.S. will allow an eventual Communist victory in Vietnam.

Although Red China reportedly limited support for North Vietnam to supplies, and of some 200,000 "construction workers" — engaged in the repair of bomb damage and extending transportation facilities — this was more from necessity and strategy than from desire. In 1965 the global strategist, Herman Kahn, in discussing the possibility of massive use of Red Chinese troops in Vietnam said:

> The Chinese are a weak power in that area (Vietnam). There are two areas in the world where the Chinese have readily deployable forces: one is Manchuria, which is next to Korea, and the other is Fukien, which is opposite Formosa.
>
> The Chinese are in a bad way in other areas (Vietnam) even though a simple wall map may not show it. . . .
>
> The Himalayan massif stands in the way. The massif is not as high north of Indochina as it is over India, but it's still there.
>
> There is one decent road and one railroad running from China into Vietnam, and even here the gauges don't match. Basically you can cut both roads and the Chinese would then be reduced to what they can carry on their backs, on bicycles and on mules . . . [32]

However, in the intervening years this outlook has changed radically. The Red Chinese and North Vietnamese established an extensive road and railway expansion program, extending even into Laos and the borders of Thailand. [33] All the while, the McNamara-Rusk-Rostow team conducted the war in a restrained manner—and this despite the Cultural Revolution which immobilized China for two years.

The Communists are serious, mature strategists and integrate military and political strategy to wage *total* war. In February 1968, they launched the Tet offensive — no doubt knowing it would be a military disaster. Which it proved to be, costing them some 45,000 dead plus surviving casualities. However, politically this attack and the two smaller campaigns later on in the year could only be described as politically brilliant. The Tet offensive galvanized the presidential campaign of Sen. Eugene McCarthy, immediately reversed Sen. Robert F. Kennedy's "unalterable" decision not to run for the Presidency and doubtlessly precipitated President Johnson's March 31 decision not to seek re-election. Also, on March 31, Mr. Johnson announced the cessation of the bombing of most of North Vietnam. Thus, the Tet offensive was highly "cost-effective," despite the high loss of life. And further, according to Professor Patrick J. Honey, of the University of London and considered as the world's leading authority on North Vietnam, there had been widespread unrest as a result of the bombing and effective administration was crumbling and the Hanoi leadership was fearful of not being able to continue in power.[34]

Much criticism has been centered on the preoccupation with policies relating to "control of escalation," "graduated deterrence," "limited response" and the like, as actually encouraging Communist wars of "liberation." This criticism certainly is appropriate, taking into account a classic discussion of warfare by T.B. Macaulay in 1828:

> To carry the spirit of peace into war is a weak and cruel policy. When an extreme case calls for that remedy which is in its own nature most violent . . . it is idle to think of mitigating and diluting. Languid war can do nothing which negotiation or submission will not do better; and to act on any other principle is not to save blood and money but to squander them.

Of course, in light of the existence of modern thermonuclear weaponry, the desirability of some formula for restraint seems desirable. Granting this, the question seems to be essentially one of whether an effective campaign could be organized, in a "people's war" such as Vietnam, using limited (non-nuclear) warfare.

Aside from the direct approach of invading North Vietnam – preferably with Free Chinese assistance – the military situation in Vietnam may be examined as an illustration of the role of *measure* and *countermeasure* in limited warfare. Some of the measures which could have been (or, could be) used to effect a military victory – if the news media would have "allowed" (or, would allow) their use – are:

1. Cut the Ho Chi Minh trail in Laos with a Great Wall of Indo China (100,000-250,00 extra troops).
2. Attack of Cambodian based sanctuaries.
3. Unlimited bombing of military targets in Red Vietnam.
4. Establishment of a guerrilla force in the North by Free Vietnamese forces.
5. Mining or blockade of Haiphong and/or destruction of the "giant" dredge used daily for channel clearance.
6. Bomb flood control dikes.

7.   Intensification of psychological warfare.
8.   Use of tribute and bribery.
9.   Initiation of Economic Warfare.
10. Establishment of an effective defense organization of East Asian nations.

Item one, the construction of a Great Wall Of Indo-China across the northern limit of South Vietnam and Laos, extending to Thailand was explored by the news reporter John Randolph. He had one of the American engineering firms estimate the cost of a mile-wide, defoliated, fortified strip serviced by a high-speed military highway. The cost estimate was one billion dollars and the time required for construction was two and one-half years. [35] McNamara, however, elected to spend a $1.6 billion dollar appropriation [36] on an electronic fence made up of miniature sensors, scattered through the jungles from aircraft, to detect troop movements. If the hundreds of thousands of McNamara sensors had ever been distributed their presence would have provided an interesting, but elementary, exercise for the Communist engineers in designing a few electronic jammers to cancel out reception of signals from the low power transmitters in the sensors. *But, the Reds would not have been able to have used a direct counter strategy against a Great Wall of Indo-China, as they must avoid massed conflict because of the superior firepower of American weapons.*

Item two, elimination of Cambodian sancturaries, involves technical violation of neutral territory (as does item one). Naturally, this should be accomplished, at the outset, by the South Vietnamese. The likely Red countermeasure — a massive world-wide propaganda campaign.

Item three, unlimited bombing of North Vietnamese military targets (exclusive of harbor facilities) could have smashed the Red Viet ordnance-supply system, but the prime targets were kept off limits by Mr. Johnson's coterie of war strategists. The only Red countermeasure was the SAM-2 antiaircraft missiles — but the restricted bombing zones allowed the Russian — North Vietnamese team to concentrate these defenses and thereby increase their effectiveness against U.S. planes.

As to item four, the use of guerrilla forces in the North, the Reds were already using the countermeasure involved — the Viet Cong. But the Johnson Administration had no more heart for starting a liberation movement in North Vietnam than does the Burns-Kissinger-Foster cabal, apparently formulating the Nixon Administration strategy. The sensitivity of the North Vietnamese to this type of action has been indicated by their bitter broadcasts denouncing "spies and rangers" — apparently Green Berets — who have made scouting expeditions north.[37] Far Eastern and anti-Communist authorites such as former Congressman **Walter H. Judd**[38] and Senator Thomas J. Dodd[39] have repeatedly called for the establishment of a liberation front formed from the North Vietnamese now in exile in South Vietnam.

Item five, disabling Haiphong by any means whatever, has been the number one suggestion of the Vietnam war critics. This comes more from the high economic value of the missiles, planes, etc. brought in by ships; *the tonnage of supplies into North Vietnam by sea, from all countries, is less than the tonnage by land transport from Red China.* The Russians ship 80% of their aid by sea, because of delays in China. The Red Chinese open all shipments, copy or make notes on new items, and frequently paint over Russian identifications and stamp them "From China With Love."[40] Perhaps the friction between the U.S.S.R. and Red China could be smoothed over to some extent if it were advantageous to do so. Also the shipping into Cambodia could be increased. However, disrupting the commercial shipping into Haiphong by the "Allies" should be worthwhile.

Item six, bombing the flood control dikes, is uniquely immune from counterstrategy. Hanoi is 40 ft. below sea level.

Item seven, psychological warfare, could certainly be stepped up. It is apparent that the Communists have already optimized their use of the world news media, and the dolsc-vietnik camp has the U.S. at a disadvantage with the crocodile-tear street scenes. Massive use of propaganda leaflets and broadcasts directed against Red Vietnam cannot be countered — but would be most effective, if some substantive incentive for sympathetic action were included.

Item eight, tribute, a token form of which was under consideration as a proposal for increased trade with the European satellite nations and the U.S.S.R., was consistent with the long-established policies of the Kennedy-Johnson Administration — as proposed in the Phoenix Papers, discussed in Chapter 14. Historically, for tribute to be effective, it has been necessary for the weaker nation to contribute a sizable fraction of its total output, or gross national product, to the country being appeased.

On the other hand, bribery, which has historically been most effective in the Orient, is a potentially useful measure — but proper use requires old-hand oriental know how for economic application. But, economy is really "out the window" at the present time. Assuming an expense rate of some two billion per month on the Vietnam war, and a Communist personnel loss of 20,000 per month from all causes, the U.S. could afford $100,000 each, in "purchasing" Red defectors. Even as much as $1,000,000 for information leading to the capture of 1,000 troops would represent a "saving" of $99 million. The primary countermeasure would be more name calling and vilification.

Item nine, economic warfare, could be uniquely effective. Here the balance of the initiative rests with the U.S. By stopping trade with the Communist nations, a classic course of non-action would result — and a technique adopted for which there is no effective countermeasure. Of course, such a policy has been adopted already in the case of North Vietnam, North Korea, Red China and Cuba. The policy has been most effective in these areas and should be even more so, if applied universally to the Red World. Not only could the direct trade between the U.S. and the Satellite nations and the U.S.S.R. be curtailed, but imports could be restricted from Free World nations shipping into Haiphong, such as Great Britain.*

Without effective government action in this area, private initiative is called for. *Since such action cannot be carefully tailored, as a government plan could be, the citizens' program (for manufactured goods) can only be — Buy American.* Does this buy American policy seem to be overly harsh? After the U.S. curtailment of trade with Cuba, according to Barry Goldwater:

> British exports to Cuba rose from about $6 million worth in 1963 to a husky $27 million worth last year (1964). Other allies have done just about the same.

---

*In the case of Great Britain, the U.S. has, in effect, subsidized the long term credits for buses to Cuba, by subsequent financial support of the British pound. On the other hand, the British refused to sell the U.S. 2-inch rockets intended for use in Vietnam. [41]

A secret codicil with Canada, on their agreement for sale of wheat to the U.S.S.R., provides that in the event that the Canadian supply is inadequate, U.S. wheat will be supplied on long-term, liberal credit. [42]

France's trade with Cuba jumped from $4 million to $49 million worth in the same period. Canada went from $15 to $57 million, Japan from $3 to $34 million. [43]

The following, hard-to-come-by data lists approximately one-half of the Free World ships arriving in North Vietnam in 1965:[44]

United Kingdom	67	Lebanon	5	Japan	2
Greece	19	Netherlands	3	Malta	1
Norway	18	Cyrprus	3	Panama	1
				total	119

In 1966, Greece stopped shipping to North Vietnam, North Korea, Cuba and Red China.[45] But in 1968, Free World ships unloaded over a million tons of arms and supplies at Haiphong — about one-half of that from the U.S.S.R.

As for the bridge-building with the East European nations, columnist Henry J. Taylor provides a realistic capsulization:

Poland is furnishing Castro thousands of tons of shipping, thanks to our taxpayers' free aid to Poland to construct sheet metal plants. Then Castro sails the ships smack through our Panama Canal to North Vietnam, partly or fully loaded with war materials, and our canal officials usher them through. As this column recently reported, Castro's partly loaded vessels pick up the rest of their deadly cargos in Japan or Red China and then go on to Haiphong.[46]

Commenting on the economy in the U.S.S.R., the Russian authority Eugene Lyons says of the Soviet industrial processes:

The introduction of plastics, synthetic fibers and other chemical products has been made possible to a large extent by equipment and whole factories bought in foreign countries. In fact, the Kremlin should thank its stars that the prophesied doom of capitalism has not come true. It desperately needs lightweight, high strength materials, improved electronic computers, advanced miniaturization and automation equipment from the West. If the capitalistic powers denied these essentials to Moscow, the whole myth of a great self-sustained Soviet industrial power would be shattered.[47]

In reviewing the effect of bridge-building trade with the East European nations, the Senate Judiciary Committee found that:

- No genuine evidence that the satellites are breaking away from the U.S.S.R.
- Breakaway is impossible, as long as Communists rule in the satellite capitals.

- U.S. policy of "rewards" for phony defiance to Moscow inflates puppet prestige and discourages popular resistance. [48-50]

The study goes on to recommend that aid be supplied only in a "swap" for freedom — to wring concessions from both the satellites and the U.S.S.R. Because of military and space overcommitments, coupled with the inefficient Communist production, Russia is in constant economic difficulty. For example, normally the U.S.S.R. produces less cereals per capita than under the Tsar. Control of the Free World grain supply could be used to "encourage" enlargment of private agriculture in the U.S.S.R. — which would in turn diminish the Kremlin's political control and unleash popular movements interested more in consumer goods than in world military dominance. [51]

The list of industrial plants, precision machinery, electronic instruments and plans for detailed manufacturing procedures approved for shipment to the U.S.S.R. in 1966 is simply too massive to include here. [52-54] Review of even the published data is enough to make a soldier's blood boil.

In brief, the North Vietnamese are dependent on the U.S.S.R. and Red China for all sorts of military hardware. This promises to be a long war. A trade wall paralleling the Iron and Bamboo curtains will limit the ordnance delivered to North Vietnam (and Egypt, Cuba, and various points in Africa). Limitation of industrial development in the Communist World will slow down the action in Vietnam and limit the spread of arms throughout the Middle East and other parts of the world, thus minimizing the likelihood of other "limited" wars for "national liberation"

Lastly, in the item-by-item discussion, the strategy of establishing an effective East Asian defense organization stands out as a step which might have been listed first in the order of sequence. Such an organization would be sort of an Oriental NATO (excluding former European colonial powers). However, the establishment of such an organization would be as difficult for the Nixon Administration to establish — despite the fact that the Red World is, in the main, operating on a monolithic basis in respect to the Free World — as it would have been for the Johnson Administration. Both being guided by members of the Council of Foreign Relations, which association tends to induce in the diplomatic and military sectors an effete internationalist outlook devoid of the forthright judgement for decisive, integrated action.

Consider, how could such a diplomatic effort be successful when the U.S. does not stop Allied trade with Hanoi. Or worse, even with the assistance of the huge CIA staff in Vietnam, the Johnson Administration was never able to stop U.S. ships from shipping to Hanoi. As reported by *Der Spiegel* the American ships would dock in Saigon, the cargo would be unloaded into waiting trucks, headed ostensibly to Cambodia or other destinations: but the trucks were then "diverted" to Cambodia, only 70 miles distant, and from there to the Viet Cong and the North Vietnamese. [55] Hopefully, the Nixon Administration will be able to, eventually, put an end to these contrabrand shipments to the Reds, even though it may never assume the decisive stance required to end the Campaign 68 bombing halt and terminate the Paris "negotiations" which only provides a podium for Red propaganda and villification.*

Ho Chi Min's original peace program had four basic points, in addition to the cessation of the bombing of the North: withdrawal of U.S. troops; settlement of South Vietnam's internal affairs by the NLF; reunification of the North and the South; observance of the 1954 Geneva Agreement. However, in January 1967 Ho simplified these demands in a declaration to a group of West German churchmen headed by Martin Niemoeller to a single demand that the U.S. should get out of South Vietnam.

Should this happen, the first sure result would be the slaughter of the one to two million people of South Vietnam responsible for leadership and resistance. Then the dominoes would start to fall: first the rest of Laos, then a coalition government in Cambodia, and following guerrilla action in Malaysia renewed and stepped up in Thailand. The techniques of Ho Chi Minh and his crowd in their drive for conquest are vividly described by columnist Martin L. Gross:

> His methods of warfare are among the cruelest in man's history . . . His terror murder of villagers exceeds the blood lusts of the Nazis . . . Across the entire southeastern Asian complex, he has wrought perhaps a million dead. [56]

---

*The halt of limited bombing in the lower sector of North Vietnam was halted on October 31, five days before the 68 Presidential election and the Paris talks announced for November 2 — despite the refusal of Saigon to participate under the imposed conditions.

Gross also reports that the Arab guerrilla Palestine Liberation Organization (PLO) is sending men to Vietnam for training with the Viet Cong, and concludes:

Simply stated, if Saigon falls, Tel Aviv is in mortal danger of extinction . . . What hopeful annihilator of Israel will then worry about the "paper tiger's" promise to maintain the Jewish nation's integrity? [57]

When the matter of decisive action is again taken up, the wily nature of the oriental should be exploited. The defection of the intermediate level field commanders should be bought, not only for the direct benefit from surrender of troops, ordnance and supplies but mostly for the morale problem it would create in the Communist bloc. However, it would be necessary to heavily "tranquilize" the State Department since they oppose this sort of thing. In 1968, legislation was introduced which would have set up annual stipends and grant permanent residence to Red defectors but the State Department witnesses objected to this measure which would "interfere with the State Department's acknowledged policy of 'building bridges' to communism." [58]

In Vietnam the Communists follow a logical course on their strategy for world conquest. The grand strategy for this conquest is discussed further in the next chapter. For Americans, the lesson in Vietnam is:*The Communist will not stop — they can only be stopped.*

CHAPTER 6

RED POWER

At one time Confucius was considering a visit to the camp of the notorious Brigand Chih, to see if it were possible to introduce some of his teachings on the respect of tradition and moral order. Upon discussing the proposed journey with the older, and quite respectable brother of Chih, Confucius was admonished to give up the visit:

In the present case even such eloquence as yours cannot possibly have the slightest effect. My brother Chih is a remarkable man. His passions, once aroused, leap like a fountain; his calculations are swift as a whirlwind. Not only is he strong enough to defy every foe; he is also clever enough to justify every crime. Humor him, and he is friendly; thwart him and he flies into a rage. On such occasions the language he uses is far from flattering; I certainly advise you not to go near him.[1]

Nevertheless, Confucius persisted, even after being warned away from the encampment by the sentry, who cautioned that the brigand and his men were very busily engrossed in a meal of minced human liver.* Finally, following the relay of some assurances of respect, Confucius was ushered into the presence of the enraged Chih and accomplished his entrance with various rites of obeisance. The brigand chieftain roared with the voice of a tiger, "Come here, Ch'iu!** And remember, if what you say is acceptable to me, you live; if it is not acceptable, you die!" Confucius replied at some length, of which the following is most significant:

---

*Historically, the Chinese brigands have shown something of a propensity for cannibalism; sometimes the relatives of the victims were forced to participate.[2] Six Hong Kong newspapers, including the British-owned *Post-Herald*, reported that on August 27, 1967, arrivals from Canton told of seeing hundreds of the Red Guards participate in this practice, two days earlier. This seemed to result more from the violence of street clashes, rather than from starvation.

**Confucius

But if you will listen to me, I will go as your ambassador to the courts of Wu and Yüeh in the south, of Ch'i and Lu in the north, of Sung and Wei in the east, of Chin and Ch'u in the west, and arrange that a great walled city shall be built for you, several hundred leagues in circumference, with quarters for many hundred thousand inhabitants. You shall be raised to the dignity of a feudal prince, and under your sway the whole world shall begin anew. You will lay down your arms, disband your followers, gather about you brothers old and young, and see to it that they lack nothing; and make due offering to your ancestors. You will thus be behaving like a Sage and Hero and at the same time giving to the world that for which it ardently longs.[3]

To which, the robber chieftain replied:

As to your talk of a great city and a multitude of inhabitants — this is merely an attempt to dazzle me by promises of gain, and is treating me as though I were a common, witless peasant. And even if such success were attainable, how long would it be secured? . . . Some few may live to eighty years, some few to a hundred; but one who lives to sixty has still not died young. And during these sixty years, if we take away the time that is spent in sickness, mourning and trouble, in all this time there will not be more than four or five days in each month when his lips are opened and laughter comes . . . A flash, and it is all over, like a racehorse seen through a crack. He who by the enjoyment of his senses can use this brief moment to the full alone can claim to have found the Way. And all you acclaim, I utterly discard. Be off with you as fast as you can, and never dare to prate to me again! This Way of yours is nothing but noise and babble, humbug and empty fraud, such as could never help any man to perfect the unalloyed that is within him; is in fact not worth a moment's discussion.[3]

It may be assumed that the Brigand Chih allowed Confucius to depart because of some inate fear of the wisdom which he taught.

This fear is also known to Mao Tse-tung, with some variation. It is the wisdom of Confucius and other Sages, giving China over three thousand years of tradition, which Mao would stamp out to build the pure Communist "ant-hill" society. However, there are too many elements in China's rich heritage which uphold the sanctity of the individual. Thus the youth, who had not known capitalism, were formed into the Red Guard and given the task of destroying the *too traditional* communist party leadership.

At the outset of the Great Socialist Cultural Revolution, initiated by Mao and party dogmatists in June 1966, Deputy Prime Minister and Foreign Minister Chen Yi explained that the objective was the elimination of the four olds: the old thought, the old culture, the old customs and the old habits. "This revolution," he stated, "would prevent forever any peaceful evolution toward the recrudescence of capitalism..." Yet the resistance to the Cultural Revolution by the pragmatists has been both persistent and viable.

From the American view, preference for either Mao's dogmatists or the pragmatic forces can not be supported. On the one hand, Mao's group espoused world revolution through the underdeveloped areas, and, on the other hand, the pragmatists favored closer relation with the U.S.S.R. Since Mao's faction did win a qualified victory – by taking a calculated risk in using the Army for civil rule – continued harsh anti-capitalistic policies should be expected. Kenzo Matsumura, an influential senior member of the Japanese Prime Minister, Eisaku Sato's Liberal-Democratic Party, has predicted that whoever succeeds Mao Tse-tung will adopt a policy which is harder toward the United States.[5]

As long as there is *any* type of Communist government in China, undoubtably, the threat to the free countries of Asia, in particular, and the Free World, in general, will continue. It is not impossible that the victory by the Maoist forces will produce such inefficiency in the agricultural-industrial system as to reduce China to a collection of regionalized semistates. But this happy turn of events should not be anticipated, since politicians are generally adept at sensing errors and usually make whatever corrections are necessary to secure the continuation of power. For example, the failure of the so-called Great Leap Forward, in the 1959-61 period, was recognized as such, and a "step backward" taken to circumvent total collapse – although the loss of face which Mao incurred as a result, made it necessary for him to resign as Chairman (President) of the Peoples Republic. On this matter, it is regrettable that the Free Chinese forces on Formosa were not allowed to intervene during this crisis, as some intelligence estimates later showed that they might have liberated the mainland.[6] And although the crisis being produced by the Cultural Revolution may become even more grave than that which developed in the 1960-62 period, the entrenchment of thinking in Washington is more intense now, than in the earlier critical period in 1960-62.

One objective of the Red Chinese has been the development of an intensely anti-Western, anti-capitalist society, as reflected by the following news story on school texts used in Red China:

Books describe how some factories "before liberation" had cages for imprisoning workers and instruments of torture of different kinds. They contained detailed accounts of how workers were "cut with knives or burned with fire, acrid water was poured into their nostrils and bamboo needles were driven into their fingernails."[7]

During the first year of the Cultural Revolution the schools were closed, "reactionary" teachers were purged, and other changes introduced to intensify the purity of the Communist dogma and eliminate remaining elements of the old Chinese c[...][8]

The long-range results accruing from the training in the "pure-Red" dogma will have both social and military impact. Mao's vision of the Communist utopia is based on a uniform distribution of population over the land, where the country-side will be indistinguishable from the cities. The New Communist Man will not only have been freed from selfishness — as envisioned by Karl Marx, once the source of all evil, capitalism, is removed — but will have an equal capacity for both intellectual and manual labor. Bizarre as it may seem, implementation of these concepts is already underway. Sixty million young people have been sent from the cities into the countryside. A graduated program has been started which will, within fifteen years, require that all students above the primary level be employed on a half-time basis. If successful, these plans and preliminary steps would produce a society which, using the terms of a biologist, would "multiply the nerve networks until they become the connective tissue.[9,10,11]

The significance of this type of dispersal in providing immunity to nuclear weapons effects is discussed in Chapters 7 and 11. It should be said that the Red Chinese are far along in planning for a totally dispersed society, although the rate at which they can complete these plans is, of course, limited by their characteristically low efficiency. This planning is shown by the following translation from the Red Chinese military documents captured by Free-Tibetan forces:

For strategic requirements, new barracks, warehouses, and factories must be built in locations far from large- and medium-sized cities, and communication and transportation centers, large manufacturing and mining districts, large reservoirs, and densely populated areas. They should be built near and into hills, on hillsides, and be properly dispersed according to topographic and terrain conditions. Furthermore, they should be properly camouflaged.[12]

As another example of this sort of planning, news reports in 1965 told of movement of major executive offices from Canton to locations 200 miles inland; also travelers into Hong Kong have told of heavy industries being moved 600 miles inland from Canton to the Chungking area.[13] Other reports tell of a long-term policy of "weeding out the cities" and special programs for sending children and old people into the countryside.[14] Further, instructions to the military call for adaption of caves and semi-caves for storage of fuel and weapons.[15] These measures do not represent any new or sudden development of policy as a result of the Vietnam war, but rather are steps in a long-term plan organized following the take over of China from the Nationalists.[16]

There are only some 19 cities in Red China with population over 1 million, and less than 10% of the populace lives in cities of more than 250,000 people.[17] Furthermore, the prominent nuclear physicist, Dr. Ralph E. Lapp, has noted that the scheduled retirement of the B-52 bombers promises to augment Red China's invulnerability to atomic attack.[18] He states that only the 20 megaton weapons, deliverable by B-52s, will create enough fallout to provide a threat to the countryside, where the majority of the people live.* Moreover, the use of intercontinental or sub-launched missiles, as a deterrent against Red China, introduces serious problems. Missiles launched from the United States would have to soar over Russian territory, and even flights of sub-launched missiles could, conceivably, provoke an automatic response from the U.S.S.R. — which would have no way of immediately determining the intended targets.[19]

However, perhaps the most critical aspect of the problem of deterring the Red Chinese, is the attitude of their leaders — which is based on the extent of control they can maintain over the Chinese people. Red Chinese officials, such as Foreign Minister Chen Yi, Chou En-lai, Mao Tse-tung and Mao's appointed heir, Lin Piao, speak impassively about the loss of one-half of their population in a world-holocaust, noting that victory would result afterward and world-wide communism would result from the will of the people. As a result of a superior will, they expect to achieve rapid recovery, and to erase the remaining capitalist rubble in the process of establishing the world-wide socialist order.[20]

---

*The low yield warheads of U.S. ICBMs and sub-launched missiles must be exploded at high altitudes to produce maximum blast, and as a result produce only little fallout. The twenty megaton bombs are most effective at low altitudes and produce fallout over wide areas — which is the only threat to rural areas.

On the other hand, the U.S.S.R., although entirely sympathetic with the cause of world socialism, differs with Red China in matters of strategy — holding that eventually the Communist forces can win through co-existence. The extent of the Sino-Soviet rift, subject to considerable controversy in the Free World, may be more or less superficial and pass with the eventual transition of leadership in China.* In Russia, the death of Stalin unleashed popular demands for more freedom, and the announcement of the Great Leap Forward in 1958 stunned the Eastern European Communists.[21] They were apprehensive of a trend which could bring back the terror of the Stalin period. However, these changes merely illustrate the shifting course of (socialist) history, and point up the possibility of complete alignment of the Sino-Soviet axis in the future through a fusion of the Stalin and Mao Schools.

In the main, Western thinkers would deny the feasibility of the Maoist plans for an "ant-hill" society; however, it should be understood that these plans provide for the establishment of ideal, or pure, socialism, and that any impractical aspects involved would logically seem to result from such imponderables as motivation for developing a "perfect man" in an atheistic society. In other words, what is involved here is the basic nature of man, and his relationship to the Eternal.

One of the best indicators for measurement of the magnitude of the Sino-Soviet rift — from the time it developed in 1956, until the present — is that of trade. The total trade turnover (value of Soviet plus Chinese products) reached a maximum of $2 billion in 1959; by 1962 the total turnover had dropped to 36% of the 1959 figure.[22] However, this decline partially resulted from Red Chinese demands for more sophisticated products and processing plants using more advanced techniques; 70% of the total Red Chinese trade in 1963 was with Western countries and 30% with Communist countries.**[23] In the 1967-68 period the Sino-Soviet trade continued at some $300 million per year. Baring the fortuitous collapse of the Red Chinese Peoples Republic, as a result of

---

*The quick alignment of the Yugoslav dictator, Tito, with the U.S.S.R. during the Arab-Israeli war in June 1967, suggests that the Red World is basically monolithic.

**Japanese trade with Red China has been steadily growing, but in 1964 was only 2.13% of the total Japanese trade — as compared with 28.5% with the United States.[24] In total, some 7% of Japan's trade is with the Communist bloc.[25]

internal revolution, China may very well make the 1970s a Red Decade. The Red Chinese are recognized as a major long-range threat to world peace. Former Secretary of State, Dean Rusk compared Red Chinese strategy to that of Hitler, and there has been no apparent change in the intervening period. Yet proposed neutralization of this threat is not reassuring, as it is based on a 40 year strategy of mollification – hopefully to be effected by the Chinese people's concern for their newly acquired consumer goods, such as refrigerators and washing machines.[26] However, the restraint placed on the Nationalist Chinese on Formosa by the American Government has insulated the Chinese Communists from serious guerrilla threat, while the Red Chinese have built up their industrial capability in a way designed to enhance their military potential. In the period from 1960-66, after the abortive Great Leap Forward was put aside, progress in industrialization was extensive. Some of these developments are reported by Dr. K. Mendelssohn, professor of physics at Oxford University, as he reviewed three visits to Red China, between 1960 and 1966. In this brief period Dr. Mendelssohn noted incredible advances in the industrial process there. For example, in the first visit in 1960, even relatively simple transformers were being assembled by children using crude hand techniques – in Dr. Mendelssohn's graphic words:

> In the open, among horses, ducks and chickens, boys and girls were sitting on the ground, cutting out the transformer housing from sheet metal with a hammer and chisel. Miraculously, in the end the finished transformers appeared, complete with cooling coils, and ready for shipment.
>
> Admittedly, productivity was miserably low, but it had to be remembered that it was greater than no productivity at all, which would have been the case without those small plants in agricultural communes.
>
> More important is the industrial training which these places provided in an otherwise completely agricultural society . . . [27·]

Two and one-half years later, during his second visit to Red China in 1962, Dr. Mendelssohn visited some of the first factories completed, and noted:

> Some of the new factories were (originally) equipped with Russian machinery, but by now this has been supplemented or even replaced by excellent Chinese made equipment.[27]

And on the occasion of his third visit to China, in the latter part of 1966, Dr. Mendelssohn noted great changes. Chinese manufacturing capability had made a great surge forward, having developed the capacity to produce, in limited quantities, most of the products available in the West, such as: ships, Diesel trains, electric generators, gas turbines, trucks and other automotive equipment; as well as such advanced items as electron microscopes, analogue computers, vacuum deposition units and synthetic diamonds for industrial use.

Also, Dr. Mendelssohn reported that frequent consulation was maintained between technical managers of factories and related university and research institutes. Following the Soviet pattern, these institutions for higher studies, in contrast to those of the West, are highly specialized (University of Peking for basic physics, Tsinghua for applied physics, etc.). In the classwork, more stress was placed on ability than memory; examinations were comprehensive, but open book. Despite the subservience to Mao in their technical papers, within their specialized areas scientists trained under this system are capable and are quite familiar with current research in the West, he found.*

The Japanese probably have the best insight into what is going on in Red China, outside that of the Free Chinese on Taipei (Formosa). The latter, of course, have a knowledge based partially on intelligence activity and so cannot disclose the extent of their information. The Japanese, then, generally provide first rate information on Red China, considering the restrictions applied to their contacts.

Genko Uchida, industrial secretary of economics in the Ministry of International Trade and Industry of Japan, has estimated that: Red Chinese technology, on the average, is some 10 to 15 years behind that of Japan; China's technology has passed the "takeoff" stage, and, if their economy expands at the same rate experienced in Japan since WW II, may expand sevenfold in the next 15 years; *from this rate of development, at the end of 15 years, the Red Chinese gross national product would approach the current level of the United States.*

He further comments that, at the present time, they tend to copy too much, without undertaking adequate specialized design. For example, some time ago they copied a poorly de-

---

*One must note that the matter of specialized schools is uniquely suitable for a Communist or Fascist state. A populace with an intellectual community which, in the main, has had only highly specialized technical training can be much more easily controlled by the party dictatorship. In other words, the functional structure of the State is best ordered by developing the students in accordance with state requirements.

signed Japanese tractor. Eventually, this Japanese firm went bankrupt. Although their production efficiency, in terms of labor, is low, being only one-fifth to one-tenth of that of Japan, they are now turning out a usable, 45-horsepower tractor at a unit price of $10,000 — only 30 to 40% higher than for a comparable machine in the West. Their steel production is expected to exceed that of Japan by 1973 (significantly augmented by the purchase of a rolling mill from Germany). As to the all-important machine tool production, he said:

> As I have mentioned, many of her factories are equipped with modern machine tools that were imported from various countries: East Germany, Czechoslovakia, Switzerland, West Germany, the United Kingdom, France and Japan. China herself is only beginning however, to produce machine tools of her own, and her progress so far is very uneven. Her output of tools of the grinding class, for example, is good, but her boring tools are far below standard. We can estimate the level of the Chinese machine-tool industry by noting that it does not produce transfer machines, grinders or jig borers and it cannot turn out really large machines . . .

> Her engineers are not inhibited by experience. They can boldly explore unorthodox approaches. For example, in a machine tool factory in Shanghai they have put all the operations, from machining of the various parts to final assembly, into one huge, temperature-controlled room — perhaps the largest room in the world for making machine tools.[28]

In some respects, the Red Chinese are advancing at a faster pace than the Soviet Union. The U.S.S.R. is not yet able to mass produce such simple items as cigarette lighters and ballpoint pens that work — let alone such products as flashlights with re-chargable cells or motor scooters. However, Red China manufactures these items for export, as shown by extensive, high-quality goods found in the shops of the Gaza Strip and Hashemite Jordan, following the Arab-Israel war. A survey of the Red Chinese products by the Israeli Bureau of Quality and Standards showed that the Chinese pens, which retailed for $.05, were comparable to the Israeli, Japanese and American pens selling for $1.50 to $2.50.[29]

No doubt the remaining elements of capitalism — estimated to be in the order of 300,000 families, who are allowed to live in comfortable circumstance and receive 5% return on their holdings — made a significant contribution to this progress.* Nevertheless, assuming continuation of a Communist regime in China, full utilization of industrial output for the benefit of the people is doubtful. This is clearly as true now as it was in 1960, when the following appraisal of the Red Chinese threat by the prominent defense strategist, Arthur T. Hadley was published:

> The picture of Red China in 1970 that appears in the best United States intelligence estimates is horrifying even for the kilo-megaton era. By 1970 the heavy industry of Red China will have developed to the point where it will be greater than that of India, Japan, and all her other non-Communist neighbors combined. By 1975 her output should be roughly comparable to that of Russia today. And this industrial complex will perch on top of a vast rural slum in which the peasants will still exist close to starvation.[30]

The first atomic explosion set off by the Red Chinese produced a special shock in scientific circles. The first blast was created with uranium-235, rather than from plutonium — which would have required a much smaller industrial development program. However, from a military viewpoint, development of the uranium-type device was sound; the uranium-235 could later be used to construct a hydrogen warhead for the intercontinental ballistic missile (ICBM) — required to threaten the United States. Because of the massive industrial facility required to produce uranium-235 by the process used by the United States and England, and the limited Red Chinese industrial capability, it was suggested that Red China had perfected a new, somewhat less expensive gas centrifuge process for producing uranium-235.[31] In addition to the direct economy realizable, this process would require much less electrical power to operate, and the processor-plant would be relatively unobtrusive — the low-level heat radiation from the centrifuge would reduce likelihood of detection by infra-red sensors on orbiting satellites.[32] (See Appendix B.)

Although various countries, including the United States, Britain, Netherlands, France, West Germany, Japan, and Sweden,[33,34,35] have been reported as interested in, or working on, the centrifuge process, Western efforts have been report-

---

*Such an arrangement would seem to constitute a Fascist-type license, which is not altogether illogical when one considers that fascism embraces socialism, although essentially nationalistic. And for that matter, the Red Chinese are highly xenophobic. Moreover, political ideology under a dictatorship, although necessarily limited by the intuition and reason of the elite, is generally employed as a rationalistic tool for the maintenance of control.

ed as unsuccessful.[36] News correspondent Hilaire du Berrier gives a colorful account of how Klaus Fuchs advised the Chinese on this simplified centrifuge process.[37]

Regardless of the process used for weapon construction, the Red Chinese set off their first atomic explosion on October 16, 1964 and their first hydrogen blast 32 months later, on June 17, 1967.* Japanese scientists said that the hydrogen bomb-test occurred at 100 to 150 thousand feet altitude – which would mean that the device was missile-borne.[38] Most American news reports, however, state that this test H-bomb was dropped from an airplane. Whether this first device was actually missile-borne or not, is apparently an academic question, as news reports state that a test firing of the first Chinese ICBM, with a hydrogen-type warhead, may be expected in the near future.

How the Red Chinese have been able to achieve their rapid progress with nuclear devices and rockets, is also more or less academic. It has been reported, however, that some 50 East German rocket technicians have been observed in Lanchow, where the missile development activity is centered.[39] Another report states that "most information indicates that the Chinese missiles are based on the best Russian blueprints."[40]

The deployment of Red Chinese missile systems from 1968 through 1975 is estimated by the *U.S. News and World Report:*

1968.   Modest production will start of reduced-weight H-bombs, able to be carried atop missiles. Early in 1968, at least four to eight missile launchers will be in place for rockets of 750 miles range. A new class of submarines with missiles for surface firing will appear.

1969.   H-bomb arsenal will grow. Tests of ICBM will continue and first intermediate-range missiles will be in production. The Red Chinese will introduce modern jet bombers with a range of 2,200 to 2,800 miles.

1970.   Red China will have perhaps 100 H-bombs, be ahead of Britain and France, but still far behind U.S. and Russia. Intermediate missiles will be operational, with a range exceeding 1,500 miles. Communists may have 80 to 100 launchers for these missiles.

1972-75.   China will be a first-class nuclear power with a full arsenal of H-bombs and warheads. ICBM's will be in production— about 75 actually deployed — with an intercontinental range of 6,000 miles.

*The French exploded their first atomic device in 1960 but were unable to conduct a successful test of a hydrogen device until 8 years later.

What China could hit in 1972-75 takes in most of the world—West Europe, Africa, all of Russia, Canada, Australia and western and northern stretches of the U.S. Particularly vulnerable to a Red Chinese ICBM would be the cities of Los Angeles, San Francisco, Seattle, Denver, Chicago, Detroit, Cleveland.[41]

Another estimate, issued in a report by the Joint Congressional Atomic Energy Committee on August 2, 1967, more or less confirmed the *U.S. News & World Report* data: for example, deployment of a few ICBMs capable of striking U.S. cities with H-warheads in the early 1970s was projected.[42]

One item in the *U.S. News & World Report* article needs elaboration. The Red Chinese already have submarines designed to launch missiles.[43][47] Their first submarines were obsolete types contributed by the Russians.[43] However, some of these were modified to carry two Soviet type T-10, surface-to-surface missiles vertically in the sail for a surface launch.[44] In 1966, tests of new Chinese submarines capable of launching missiles while submerged were reported.[46] Early in 1967, the number of Red Chinese submarines was reported[47] to be 50 and according to the British *Intelligence Digest* Red China will soon launch a *fleet* of nuclear powered subs.

Another possibility for a weapon system has been suggested by Dr. Ralph Lapp. He raises the possibility that a few mammoth H-bombs, with a yield in the order of 1,000 megatons each, might be placed off the West Coast of the United States with submarines for potential use by underwater detonation.[48] The resulting tidal wave would take out most of the low-level coastal areas, such as Los Angeles, and the high-intensity fallout would cover the country, perhaps as far east as the Mississippi, with lethal radiation (assuming no fallout shelters). However, from a weapons systems viewpoint, this sort of device is not logical. Of course, one can get into some rather complex discussions on logic — and it cannot be assumed that the Chinese would necessarily be entirely logical—but the basic purpose of nuclear weapons is for "bluff." This is especially true for the Chinese, for if they have a nuclear shield, they can then make excellent use of their unlimited manpower. Furthermore, the placing of such a weapon system offshore would involve some risk of detection and such an act of placement, would in itself, invite massive retaliation. Also, the effect which the Red Chinese would want to produce in an atomic war should be instant knock-out; this means maximum use of the blast effects, with reliance on fallout given second-order consideration.

Basically, the Red Chinese strategy is based on support of "people's wars" with massive ground forces — after they have deployed a number of missile systems with nuclear warheads, which provide a deterring counter-threat against U.S. nuclear forces by effecting a creditable threat against American bases in the Pacific area and against the continental United States (significant deployment and use of aircraft, except for defense against air attack, has been bypassed).[49] Whether Mao or a successor is ruling, this strategy seems fundamental and should be expected to continue.

In a boastful article published on September 2, 1965, the twentieth year after V-J day, the tenets of this strategy were set forth by Lin Piao, then Vice Chairman of the Chinese Communist Party Central Committee, Vice Premier of the Chinese Peoples Republic and Minister of National Defense, and more recently heir to Mao Tse-tung. Relating to the defeat of America he said, in part:

Today, the conditions are more favorable than ever before for the waging of people's wars by the revolutionary peoples of Asia, Africa, and Latin America against U.S. imperialism and its lackeys.

Everything is divisible, and so is this colossus of U.S. imperialism. It can be split up and defeated. The peoples of Asia, Africa, Latin America, and other regions can destroy it piece by piece, some striking at its head and others at its feet. That is why the greatest fear of U.S. imperialism is that people's wars will be launched in different parts of the world, and particularly in Asia, Africa, and Latin America, and why it regards people's war as a mortal danger.

U.S. imperialism relies solely on its nuclear weapons to intimidate people. But those weapons cannot save U.S. imperialism from its doom. Nuclear weapons cannot be used lightly.

However fully developed modern weapons and technical equipment may be and however complicated the methods of modern warfare, in the final analysis the outcome of a war will be decided by the sustained fighting of the ground forces, by the fighting at close quarters on battlefields, by the political consciousness of the men, by their courage and spirit of sacrifice. Here the weak points of U.S. imperialism will be completely laid bare, while the superiority of the revolutionary people will be brought into full play. The reactionary troops of U.S. imperialism cannot possibly be endowed with the courage and the spirit of sacrifice possessed by the revolutionary people. The spiritual atom bomb which the revolutionary people possess is a far more powerful and useful weapon than the physical atom bomb.

Vietnam is the most convincing current example of a victim of aggression defeating U.S. imperialism by a people's war. The United States has made South Vietnam a testing ground for the suppression of people's war. It has carried on this experiment for many years, and everybody can now see that the U.S. aggressors are unable to find a way of coping with people's war. On the other hand, the Vietnamese people have brought the power of people's war into full play in their struggle against the U.S. aggressors. The U.S. aggressors are in danger of being swamped in the people's war in Vietnam. They are deeply worried that their defeat in Vietnam will lead to a chain reaction. They are expanding the war in an attempt to save themselves from defeat. But the more they expand the war, the greater will be the chain reaction. The more they escalate the war, the heavier will be their fall and the more disastrous their defeat. The people in other parts of the world will see still more clearly that U.S. imperialism can be defeated, and that what the Vietnamese people can do, they can do too.

History has proved and will go on proving that people's war is the most effective weapon against U.S. imperialism and its lackeys. All revolutionary people will learn to wage people's war against U.S. imperialism and its lackeys. They will take up arms, learn to fight battles and become skilled in waging people's war, though they have not done so before. U.S. imperialism, like a mad bull dashing from place to place, will finally be burned to ashes in the blazing fires of the people's wars it has provoked by its own actions.[50]

One possibility which will have to be considered is that of distribution of limited quantities of nuclear weapons to "under-developed" countries by Red China. In a press conference on September 29, 1965, the Chinese Foreign Minister, Chen Yi stated:

As for the peaceful use of atomic energy and the building of atomic reactors, China has already been approached by several countries, and China is ready to render them assistance; as for the request for China's help in the manufacture of atom bombs, the question is not realistic . . .

Any country with a fair basis in industry and agriculture and in science and technology will be able to manufacture atom bombs, with or without China's assistance. China hopes that Afro-Asian countries will be able to make atom bombs themselves, and it would be better for a greater number of countries to come into possession of atom bombs.[51]

Dr. Chi-yuan Cheng, an authority on China and now with the University of Michigan, suggests that China might be willing to "lend-lease" a small stockpile of nuclear bombs to Egypt to gain a foothold in the Middle East.[52]

However, Red China's first goal should be support of the North Vietnamese. Documents captured in South Vietnam indicate that the Red Chinese urge engagement of the American forces by the Vietnamese, until China has developed their military units to allow an all-out Chinese offensive.[53] As discussed in Chapter 5, completion of new roads into North Vietnam – required for Chinese participation in Vietnam and for the launching of a strong drive into Thailand – would allow direct Chinese military support.

The fall of the Indochina peninsula would allow the Chinese to apply pressure on Japan by control of the Strait of Malacca. They could renew the revolutionary movement in Indonesia and gain control of much of the raw materials used by Japan – which might be expected to insure the success of a "people's movement" in that politically-troubled country.[54,55] The takeover in Japan, it would seem, would be gradual, with minimum use of force; on the other hand, the Free Chinese on Taiwan would be ruthlessly dealt with. India and Australia might then be integrated into the Chinese sphere of influence, as allowable under the circumstances prevailing.

The transition of leadership now being effected in Red China has heightened the Sino-Soviet rift, despite predictions by some State Department officials that the change would bring the two powers closer together.[56]

The indirect support to the Communist forces in Asia by the Vietniks, insurrectionists, obstructionists and other dissenting groups in the United States cannot be discussed here. Nor can any meaningful comment be made on divisive movements in West Europe, except to note that the neutralization of Europe, especially West Germany, and the breakup of NATO are well-known objectives of the U.S.S.R.

The presence of the Russian Army has been a threat to Europe since the end of World War II. With the advent of the ICBM, the security of the United States has been seriously threatened. Many groups in the United States and Europe have advocated that only disarmament – unilateral if necessary – and eventual world government can avert a world-wide holocaust. It cannot be denied that many of these ban-the-bomb movements, regardless of their motivation, have aided the Communist cause. In part, these groups have acted on the basis of incomplete knowledge of the nature of the threat and the countermeasures which may be taken.

One method for abating the extent of the nuclear threat has not been given adequate attention: this is the matter of shelters. In the United States, insufficient attention has been given to the role of fallout and blast shelters. Even the military has given the problem only limited attention. Upon becoming President, John F. Kennedy tried to promote private construction of family shelters, and later established the Project Harbor study for a national program to provide blast-type group shelters.* The Communists fully appreciate the role of passive defense: in their case, limitation of shelter systems is based on economic reasons. The shelter problem and its interrelation with the anti-missile missile (ABM)** is discussed in Chapters 7, 11 and 12.

The ICBM threat is creditable only if the threatened nation is without defensive capability to withstand the attack. Most defense analyses to counter the ICBM threat presented to the public have been based largely on the use of the ABM and have included only a modest expenditure for passive defense with fallout shelters. The following data, presented by the Department of Defense on potential U.S. and Soviet casualties assuming an all-out first strike by the U.S.S.R., is typical.

FATALITIES IN MILLIONS[57]

U.S. Programs	U.S. fat.	U.S.S.R. fat.
Current defense structure	120	120+
$11.4 billion for active† defense & .8 billion for passive†† defense	40	120+
20.9 billion for active defense & .8 billion for passive defense	30	120+

†Active measures include Nike-X deployment, improved defense against bombers and improved defenses against sea-based systems.
††Passive — minimal fallout shelter program.

---

*This study was under the auspices of the National Academy of Sciences and the National Research Council at Little Harbor Farm in Wood Hole, Massachusetts, during the summer of 1963. Perhaps significant interest in the results of their work passed with the President: in any case a comprehensive report on this study was not issued, as is common following such undertakings.

**The more descriptive term of anti-missile missile (AMM) is preferable over the more common term, anti-ballistic missile (ABM). The latter fails to identify the type of countermeasure, or "anti." And as missile technology advances intercontinental ballistic missiles are likely to be equipped with warheads which have special, maneuvering (i.e., non-ballistic) terminal flight paths.

There has been a plethora of studies on optimization of the active defense structure, with no corresponding consideration of variation in passive defense. Inasmuch as the public is responsible for participation in evaluation of the various alternatives, it would seem appropriate that they also be given the number of casualties which might be expected if a 10, 25 or 50 billion dollar passive defense program were implemented, in support of various levels for active defense. Also, the projected annual cost, over a period of say 20 to 30 years in the future, should be included for both types of systems, as passive defense measures generally do not become obsolete and require only low-cost maintenance. To support the breakdown on passive measures, data on activity in this area in Europe, and the cost involved could be nicely included.

According to reports on the Soviet ICBM threat, the replacement of Khruschev with Kosygin and Brezhnev has resulted in a sharp increase in deployment of offensive and defensive missile systems; their defense budget is now approaching that of the United States, despite the fact that their gross national product is lower by more than one-half. Moreover, since 1966 their budget in space and strategic weapons has been $25 billion, which is more than twice the comparable (declining) U.S. figure.[58]

The decisive leadership in the Kremlin in the past few years has brought about a situation which would have been considered impossible at the outset of the "decade of the Sixties." In November 1966, Secretary of Defense McNamara confirmed what news reports had said for three years, that the U.S.S.R. was deploying an anti-missile missile system. Since that time, according to separate studies published by *Fortune, U.S. News and World Report,* and the American Security Council, as American spending in Vietnam soars, and budget allocation for the U.S. strategic systems is limited to some $6-7 billion per year, the Russians have sharply stepped up their deployment of ICBMs and may achieve as much as 10:1 superiority in deliverable megatons over the U.S. in the early 1970s.[58,59,60] In 1967, the U.S.S.R. was reported to have spent roughly 70% of their defense budget on strategic offense systems and supporting weapon systems such as their

ABM, intended for possible use against the United States.[5]
The Red World, however, has one advantage not expres
sible in terms of budgets, army divisions, numbers of missile
in silos and submarine tubes. *The people in the Communis*
countries, perhaps unwillingly, have accepted a nuclear wa
as thinkable. Whereas, in the United States, serious consic
eration of the survivability problem has been almost com
pletely ignored, except by people connected with the civ
defense effort in some way. To what extent this has bee
brought about by ban-the-bomb, Vietnik and other types o
organizations − which generally include a number of dolsc
type individuals in their membership − is difficult even t
estimate. *However, the situation must be corrected, as th*
threat facing the United States and the rest of the Fre
World is not only immediate, but is increasing and will b
sustained.

Increasing the survivability of a country by deployin
an anti-ballistic missile system alone, is not an effective coun
termeasure; Mr. McNamara frequently pointed out that at th
same time an adequate civil, or passive, defense plan must b
implemented. Even the most rudimentary estimates of cas
ualties resulting from an all-out nuclear war, or exchange, be
tween Nation A and Nation B must include, as a part of th
supporting background information, the percent of shelte
capacity for the total population, the types of shelters avai
able, accessability, alarm systems, etc. Therefore, compre
hensive surveys estimating the relative deterrence existin
between the U.S. and the U.S.S.R., such as those given b
Fortune, U.S. News and World Report, and the America
Security Council, in References 58-60, should also includ
the percent shelter capacity available in each country an
other factors relating to the protection of the populace.

Another critical aspect of the Soviet threat develop
from the concept of a *nuclear detente.** Assuming that th

---

*Interestingly enough, former Assistant Secretary of Defense, Paul H
Nitze, once remarked that, "Only from a position of strength can w
hope for a detente (with the Russians)."[61] He did not say whethe
once a "detente" had been established, a position of strength would b
required to maintain it.

Russians are not able to exploit a detente with a technological breakthrough in weaponry,* *with the advent of the nuclear detente, they are in a unique position to support aggression under the guise of "wars of liberation," or People's wars.* In this way, under the pretense of co-existence, the cold-war may (continue to) be moved out into the underdeveloped areas, where the people are not well organized and do not have a clear grasp of the issues involved. The West European nations find it difficult to view this type of conflict objectively, inasmuch as the territories involved are generally former colonial states, which they were encouraged to give up by the U.S. State Department.[64]

Under the protective shield of co-existence, the U.S.S.R. has been protected from meaningful Western-based liberation movements aimed at freeing the Captive Nations. Co-existence also gives the Communists added respectability and improves trade relations with the non-Communist world.

The Red Chinese are preparing to expand their rule throughout Asia, by building military power and expanding highways to all borders — even to building military-type highways through Nepal to India under the guise of aid — and by seeking eventual control over the vital Strait of Malacca. At the same time, the U.S.S.R. is clearly continuing its drive for the neutralization of Europe and the take over of the Middle East. In addition to obtaining control of the Suez and the great sources of oil in the area, the Soviets would anticipate a secure land-link into Africa, which would be most useful in the subjection and control of that continent. Moreover, the nature and extent of the Soviet military program promises to allow a continued threat in the vital Middle East area, regardless of the course of events in Red China.

Naturally, the Soviets will try to support further military

-----

*For example, on February 21, 1963, in an address to the Senate, Senator Thomas H. Dodd reviewed the nature of the *neutron bomb* and the possible military advantages which could accrue to the nation which first developed it.[62] In this comprehensive discussion of the neutron bomb, Senator Dodd noted that the Russians had been working on this weapon since 1952, and that the advent of a practical weapon of this type would entirely change warfare. Although many applications for this type of weapon might we worked out, at once, the most unique potential would be for providing small, inexpensive nuclear weapons, with yields in the order of one kiloton.[63] Invading armies with a monopoly on the use of the neutron bomb could wipe out opposing forces without causing widespread property destruction, or delaying occupation because of radioactive contamination.

action in the Middle East with better "remote control" of the indigenous forces than was effected during the Arab-Israeli conflict. For example, in the latter part of 1967 over 1,000 Russian military "instructors" were sent to Algeria,[65] and in January 1968 the Israeli Minister of Defense, Maj. Moshe Dayan, estimated that the number of Soviet military support personnel in Egypt was increased from 600, before the Arab-Israeli War, to over 3,000.[66] Also, the Russians have taken over for Egypt in supplying republican revolutionaries in Yemen; Soviet-piloted MIG fighters and Ilyushin bombers were used to attack royalist villages.[67] Following the war, huge stocks of the latest types of military equipment were rushed to Egypt to replace the losses.[66] Considering the rapid increase in Soviet power in the Middle East, and the vital importance of the Suez Canal and oil resources there one might conclude that the U.S.S.R. was the major victor in the one-week war. The British *Intelligence Digest* concludes that, "If and when the Suez Canal is ever opened up again, the power of control behind the scene will be Russian."[68] Peking and Moscow have often declared advancing to the Cape of Good Hope as an objective.

Military build-ups such as that developing in the Middle East are difficult to control, and the possibility of an "inadvertent" nuclear war must be recognized. In June 1965, the perceptive global strategist, Herman Kahn, suggested that the United States would eventually become involved in a nuclear war, most likely from "backing into" a conflict between smaller powers such as Egypt and Israel.[69]

Of course, this projection was offered before the advent of the first Red Chinese H-bomb test, and the disclosure of the Russian ABM system — very lately followed by plans for a U.S. counter-deployment. Since then, too, the likelihood of development of atomic weapons by India and other nations has markedly increased. However, despite the suggestion by the former head of the Arms Control and Disarmament Agency, W.C. Foster, that continued spread of nuclear weapons might result in an attack on a country by an unknown power,[70] it can be reasoned that continued proliferation would augment the strength of the Free World. The advent of the low-cost gas centrifuge process for processing U-235 discussed above will add to the problems from the Nth country with nuclear power: Japan has undertaken research on this process and has refused to keep their results secret.[71]

Nevertheless, the possibility of inadvertent U.S. involvement in a "small" nuclear war seems to be generally accepted. In fact, as the era of the "Sixties" draws to a close, the expectations of interdependence, so hopefully mentioned at the beginning of the decade, appears to be being replaced with a dour, open-eyed re-appraisal of the elemental nature of the forces of the Communist world. Even former Vice President Hubert Humphrey was motivated to appeal for support for U.S. policies (in Vietnam and Moscow), saying that abandonment of Mr. Johnson's policy would be to deter "today's manageable troubles until they become unmanageable . . . a policy of Armageddon on the installment plan." [61]

Each year the military position of the United States *vis-a-vis* the Soviet Union becomes more critical, as shown by the following table on ICBM deployment. This data was taken from the book, *Containing the Arms Race,* [72] by Dr. Jeremy J. Stone, reports published by the British Institute for Strategic Studies and various releases by the Department of Defense, during both the Johnson and Nixon Administrations. A breakdown on multiple independent re-entry vehicles (MIRVs) is not included since the yields and number of warheads which could be used can be obtained from the total warhead yield – i.e., the SCARP carries one 20 or three 5 megaton warheads.

CAPABILITY OF US AND USSR ICBMs

CBM	Warhead Yield Mt.	Deployment			Megatons 1975
		1965	1970	1975 est.	
Atlas (L)	3	126	0		
Titan (SL)	5	108	54		
Minuteman (S)	1.7	600	1,000	1,000	1,700
		U.S. TOTAL			1,700
SS-6 Vostok (L)	10	100	100	0	
SS-9 Scarp (SL)	20	100	250	500	10,000
SS-11 Savage (SL)	5		1,000	1,000	5,000
SS-13 Savage (S)	5			1,000	5,000
		U.S.S.R. TOTAL			20,000

L – Liquid propellant, SL – Storable Liquid, S – Solid.

In considering the ICBM threat it is essential to also include the potential of the manned bomber. The following table was also compiled from data given in the ISS reports and the book by Stone.

BOMBLOAD DELIVERY CAPABILITY—US vs USSR

Bomber	Load lbs.	Deployment			Bombload in million lbs. 1975
		1965	1970	1975 est	
B-47	20,000	700	0	0	
B-52	75,000	630	600	250	18.7
B-58	12,000	90	10	0	
	U. S. TOTAL				18.7
Bear	40,000	70	100	100	4
Bison	20,000	120	110	110	2.2
Badger	20,000	1,000	900	900	18
Blinder	12,000	*	900	900	10.8
	U.S.S.R. TOTAL				35.0

*First deployment in 1962. Number in service this year not available.

Many of these bombers have been fitted with air-to-surface missiles, which would reduce their "bombload" capability. For example, two squadrons of the Badger-Bs were delivered to Indonesia in 1961.[73] This model carries two anti-shipping missiles and would have been most useful for control of Far East commerce, had the Red forces in Indonesia been able to take over control there. However, the total megaton yield from a bombload of the Soviet Bear may considerably exceed that from the U.S. B–52, for example, since the Russians apparently have a superiority in the megatonage yield-to-weight ratio over the U.S. by as much as five to one. [74,75]   In a nuclear war it should be expected that only one-way missions would be used—thus increasing bomb load.

Contributing to the sobering re-appraisal of the Soviet menace is the withdrawal of the British from the Far East and the rapid expansion of Soviet sea power. Following the withdrawal of the intermediate range ballistic missiles from Turkey by the U.S., the U.S.S.R. has built up its Mediterranean fleet. Also, it has delivered 40 of the Komar and Osa class boats, which carry anti-shipping missiles, to Mediterranean allies. Egypt used the Komar-class vessel and its surface-to-surface missiles to sink the Israeli destroyer Elath.[76] The U.S.S.R. is trying to line up a world wide system of ports-of-call: Singapore is to be available after 1971; access to Indian ports is being sought; Soviet takeover of Aden and Mers-el-Kebir is a definite possibility; and a base of some sort been

stablished at Port Said.[77,78]   The Russians are spending
ome $3 billion a year on their submarine program, which is
bout equal to the U.S. Navy's budget for the submarine and
nti-submarine programs − despite the fact that the gross
ational products of the U.S.S.R. is one-half that of the
.S.[79] The Soviet submarine program was markedly aided by
dept intelligence activity. Columnist Henry J. Taylor notes
hat:

> The convicted Konon Molody ("Gordon Lonsdale") spy
> ring in the British Admiralty damaged Anglo-American security
> terribly, and with lasting effect. It has been reported that these
> Red agents obtained the particulars about the Decca tracking
> system, and they also tapped our nuclear submarine secrets
> through our exchanges with the British.
> They scooped up the top secret data about Britain's "Dread-
> naught" nuclear submarine project, with which we've been coop-
> erating, and penetrated our own submarine base at Holy Loch,
> Scotland.[80]

Also, sales of British anti-submarine devices to India has
aused concern that the design of these equipments will be
ompromised to Soviet intelligence, since the Russians have
rranged for sale of three submarines to the India.[81]

According to the ISS report, *The Military Balance
968-69,* the U.S.S.R. had some 330 conventional and 50
uclear power subs in service. Only 13 of the nuclear and 30
f the conventional subs carry ballistic missiles, and only an
verage of three each. But according to *Aviation Week &
pace Technology,* the Russians are introducing a new sub
hich carries 16 missiles as does the U.S. POLARIS:

> Introduction of the Sawfly submarine-launched ballistic
> missile last year has given the Soviets an approximate equivalent
> to the Polaris A-3 missile, now deployed on 16-tube submarines.
> The Soviets are producing the submarines at the rate of seven per
> year. They have overall production capacity of one sub per
> month.
> Soviets appear to be experimenting with submarine detec-
> tion from satellites. . .a distinct threat to the Polaris.[82]

One of the key factors in supporting people's wars
hroughout the world is the capability of supplying the local-
ed forces with massive quantities of ordnance and supplies.
fter World War II, the U.S.S.R., recognizing this require-
ent, coordinated an expansion of their 400 ship merchant
arine with the expansion of their submarine fleet and sur-
ce navy.

According to *Jane's Fighting Ships,* in the period from
955 to 1965, the Soviet merchant fleet increased from

1,000 to 1,700. Current Russian orders and projections show that their merchant fleet will be twice that of the United States by the mid-1970s.[83] Moreover, the Soviet ships are of new design, whereas 80% of the U.S. merchant fleet is *now* 20 years of age or older (twenty years being the normal, economic retiring age for a ship).

The vital nature of shipping in a "limited" war such as Vietnam is shown by the devious approach used by the U.S.S.R. to obtain the use of ships owned by NATO allies to augment their own, fifth-largest merchant fleet. This is accomplished by chartering ships through the London-based Baltic Exchange, a blue-ribbon European shipowners "club." Thus, English, German, Greek, Italian, French and Scandinavian ships are used for "local," European traffic, while Russian ships are used for the Vietnam runs. Inasmuch as some of the Baltic Exchange ships are also utilized to service Red Chinese ports — from which smaller coastal vessels tranship to North Vietnam — the names of these shipping companies, and the number of the ships they have chartered to the U.S.S.R., is a closely guarded secret.[84]

In 1966, the Soviet Union spent over one billion dollars for new shipping, while the U.S. procurement dropped to $106 million. Many members of the Congress have expressed concern over this situation and the U.S. Navy has supported this view. In 1967, Adm. Thomas H. Moorer, Chief of Naval Operations, said, "This situation might not be of such concern if we could honestly say we were taking steps to correct it."[85] The Soviet program has produced more than a million tons of new shipping every year over the past five years.*

The Soviet merchant marine is a vital part of the "shield and sword" strategy. The nuclear "shield" is used to support the "sword" of conventional war. In the case Vietnam and the seizure of the U.S.S. Pueblo by North Korea the United States is restrained by a sort of a double shield. North Vietnam and North Korea are "shielded" by Red China, and the U.S.S.R. provides an overall shield for the Red Chinese and

---

*One way for the United States to bolster its relative position as a maritime nation would be by developing a nuclear-powered merchant fleet. However, the Johnson Administration would not make public a study said to favor more nuclear merchant ships[86] and the AEC the joint Congressional Atomic Energy Committee and Vice Adm. Hyman Rickover have prevented construction of another nuclear merchant ship.[87] The Chinese are completing their second nuclear merchant ship.

the smaller Communist powers.* But if the smaller powers were unable to obtain military supplies there would be no people's wars: Russia alone is spending $6 billion a year to aid North Vietnam.[88] Moreover, following the *Pueblo* crisis the U.S.S.R. was able to shoulder its way between the coast of North Korea and the U.S. Navy task force (sent into the area to bolster diplomatic talks) with a flotilla of 16 Soviet cruisers and missile frigates — thus checkmating the U.S. without recourse to a nuclear threat.[77]

There is a certain amount of gamesmanship employed in naming missile systems and making up acronyms. Take the examples of the U.S. missiles ATLAS, HERCULES, TITAN etc., denoting great strength. On the other hand, take the Soviet threat revealed by McNamara on November 3, 1967, which he identified as a Fractional Orbital Bombardment System, or FOBS. Since there is no possibility of following the Russian terminology for their classified weapons, this system could just as well have been described as the Semi-Orbital Bombardment System, or SOBS.

The role of this system, like most new missile systems, is most useful for bluff while development work is being completed and/or production is being pushed, prior to deployment. The unique objective of the Soviets in developing a FOBS (or SOBS) is that of providing a weapon with a lower altitude approach than realizable with an ICBM — hence, like an attack by aircraft, allowing less warning time to the U.S. defense command (in the order of 2-3 minutes to U.S. continental bases).

In announcing the Soviet FOBS, McNamara expressed the belief that this weapon system was designed to attack strategic bomber bases, rather than cities.[89] Perhaps so, but in this case it is difficult to hypothesize a likely scenario. Consider that the flight time for an ICBM warhead is 30 minutes from launch until explosion over target, and that likewise the time for FOBS is 20 minutes. If the U.S.S.R. launched their ICBMs and then, ten minutes later, launched the FOBS, as required for a simultaneous impact, the U.S. SAC forces would be alerted from the BMEWS detection

---

*In the early summer of 1968, three Soviet ships were captured by South American countries while spying in national waters or landing guerrillas for Castro: the *Idonobon Gromovoy* by Venezuela; the *Golfstrim* by Argentinia; and the *Kagestrov* by Brazil. The U.S. could have persuaded its Latin American friends to cooperate on a hostage deal for the Pueblo — instead we urged the release of the Red ships.

system (which gives a 15 minute warning of ICBM arrival) and much of the SAC force could get airborne and away in the remaining 15 minutes. However, if the Soviets elected to make an initial attack against only the SAC bases with FOBS, and not try to knock out a number of the MINUTEMAN and TITAN sites with an ICBM attack, then all of the U.S. ICBM sites could be activated for launch against the U.S.S.R. As evaluated immediately after the announcement of FOBS by McNamara, it is clearly designed as a terror weapon for a future confrontation. Lt. Gen. Ira C. Eaker said:

> There is something ominous about the haste with which the Soviet Union has tested FOBS – 11 shots in a month. This is further evidence that the Reds are determined to gain strategic superiority as soon as possible and lends credence to recent estimates that Russia will gain nuclear parity by 1969 and superiority in the early 1970s. It clearly is a terror weapon designed for nuclear blackmail.[90]

An effective, nationwide anti-ballistic missile could be used to neutralize a FOBS type attack, if it were commanded to destroy any approaching satellite for which a launch announcement had not been made and/or overflight permission granted.

The deployment of the "thin" ABM was announced by Mr. McNamara on September 18, 1967 – following months of bitter criticism on creating a missile gap – for protection against the possibility of a Red Chinese attack against the cities, and protection of some of the MINUTEMAN sites against a Russian attack. It was clear that Mr. Johnson had influenced the announcement, to avoid being charged with allowing a missile gap to develop. In reviewing the event, *Newsweek* lamented in its penetrating style:

> In the dread game of instant apocalypse wrought by the nuclear age – where cities stand only on sufferance and the score is kept in units of a million corpses – even brave men flinch and wise men fear to think . . .
>
> Last week, in a speech of rare clarity and candor, McNamara again spelled out U.S. nuclear strategy to explain his credo of restraint. But ironically, after fashioning an elaborate argument for keeping the arms race within bounds, McNamara proceeded to announce a new policy which, by his own reasoning, appeared to breach the restraining boundary.[91]

Actually, the McNamara statement[92] included a fairly basic survey on nuclear-age strategy. The one area not discussed, however, was that of the role of blast and fallout shelters. The *Newsweek* editorial writer, Edwin Diamond, apparently noted this omission. In an editorial, in which he lamented the decision for the deployment of the "thin" system, he said:

> Indeed, with the ABM escalation, the possibility of this supposedly "unthinkable" missile Armageddon is greater, not smaller. All of us have now been propelled by the logic of nuclear events that McNamara grasps so well toward the next era of the atomic age — the mole society where the cities and civilians of the 1980s may have to burrow underground to join the concrete MINUTEMAN silos sunk in the 1960s and the subterranean ABM control centers built in the 1970s.[93]

But it should be noted that more and more modern offices and factories are becoming suitable for moles — i.e., without windows to the outside.

The effectiveness of the Soviet ICBMs is assured, as long as the opponents delayed development of an American ABM system. On the other hand, if the Russian ABM system had only the capability to destroy a fraction of the incoming warheads, it would be cost-effective for them in terms of property damage limitation alone.

The U.S.S.R. as well as the Red Chinese may become concerned about a new approach to the missile defense problem being considered by the United States. This is the Sea-Based Anti-Ballistic Missile System (SABMIS),[94] Under this concept a number of picket ships would be placed in strategic locations off the coast of Asia and Europe. Interceptor missiles could destroy ICBMs while they were still over the Sino-Soviet territory. The State Department is especially interested in this approach, since it would also allow U.S. defense of allies without providing them with special equipment.[95] However, as only modest study efforts have been undertaken, the Communists need not become alarmed. Rather, the Reds can reflect that the Americans are unprepared in civil defense and have only a skeleton ABM underway — for defense of missile silos, not cities.

In comparing the 95% vulnerability of an ICBM over its launch site with difficulties of intercepting re-entering warheads one is reminded of the disparaging comment of the *New Yorker:*

> The important thing about missile defenses is that they will not stop all missiles. A certain number will get through. Perhaps twenty-five percent, perhaps fifty percent, perhaps seventy-five percent. No one really knows, and no one will ever know until the day of Armageddon.[96]

CHAPTER 7

THE HOLOCAUST

If there is to be a thermonuclear war, what would be it. nature? What course would it take? What would be the after effects and the conditions of the world in the post-Armaged don era? What advance measures could be taken to enhance probability of survival? These questions will be examined in a preliminary way, as permitted in the space allowable.

In 1962, the then Secretary of Defense, Rober McNamara exchanged thoughts on attack strategy with the Russians via public discourse.[1] McNamara advocated, "No cities except in reprisial," but the Russians quickly countered against all restraints on targeting.

The basic purpose of nuclear weapons is political — i. e. to win objectives desired without resorting to warfare. In a crisis confrontation the supposedly superior power has the obvious advantage. Defense strategists have made exhaustive analyses of various types of all-out nuclear wars, generally called an exchange. However, these efforts are almos simplistic, since the initiator of such an exchange cannot be considered as rational. If then, a nuclear exchange is started irrationally, there are too many ways of doing this to allow making meaningful analyses of all the various possibilities. For example, one possible result, not commonly considered by the U.S. but commonly studied by the U.S.S.R. is that of extended, "broken-back" warfare following the initial exchange.[2]

Prior to the advent of the ABM, the most common exchange scenario called for a quick, massive attack by Nation A on Nation B in which A would destroy most of B's military bases, major cities and all or nearly all of B's ICBM's. The ability to acheive such a knockout blow is called a *first strike* capability. Of course, if A miscalculates and B counterattacks, an extended broken-back war could result.

106

However, as both the United States and the Soviet Union deploy ABM systems, there are so many uncertainties introduced by the unknown performance of the two ABM systems that it is quite reasonable to assume that, if it should develop, a Soviet attack could be initiated by a few "warning" missiles aimed at missile bases. And should these missiles be effective in destroying the MINUTEMAN targets the Soviets could either demand surrender or launch a massive attack against cities, ICBM silos and airfields.

Further discussion on strategy will be included in subsequent chapters. It will be helpful to provide an outline of some basic weapons effects, to support the various strategies formerly limited to the U.S., England and the U.S.S.R., but now also open to Red China, France and Israel. And a steady increase of members into the nuclear club is to be expected.

As nuclear engineering knowledge increases, more insight is gained in the manufacturing techniques used in the production of nuclear weapons. Appendix B reviews some of the recently reported developments. Limitation of membership in the nuclear club seems to fade with each new technical development.

For an illustration of the order of destruction that can be caused, a 20 megaton thermonuclear warhead impacting on the ground for a surface burst will be assumed. A surface burst does not provide the greatest blast area damage, but it does produce the maximum size crater — in which shelters, of course, do not survive. Up to a point, as the altitude of the explosion is increased over the target site, the destruction radius increases: at the same time the amount of fallout decreases proportionally. However, the increase in blast range realizable by increasing altitude is not a gross one.

The damage radius for both blast and heat effects is estimated in Figure 1. The effects at the radii shown should be considered only as typical; variation in the range of the heat effects, as a function of the weather, would result. That is, on a hazy day the range of the lethal heat front would be reduced considerably. The "fireball" radius would be 2-3 miles; the thermal radiation produced would last several seconds. It is significant to note that 20 to 30% of the fatal casualties at Hiroshima and Nagasaki were produced from the initial flash burns, as distinct from flame burns.[3] Although these were only 20 kiloton weapons, the weather was clear and only light summer clothing was being worn at that time of the year.

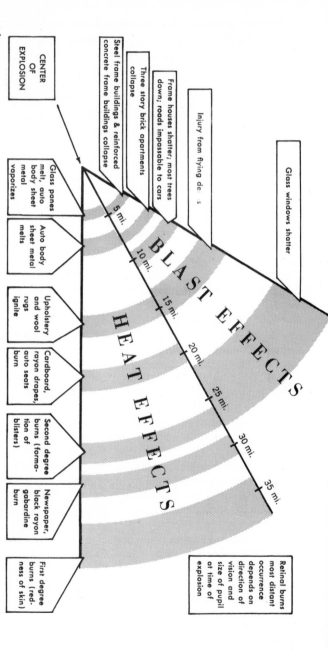

Figure 1.

BLASE AND HEAT EFFECTS OF A TWENTY MEGATON SURFACE EXPLOSION ON A CLEAR DAY.[4]
Reprinted by permission from "Target City" by Roger Signor, *Nuclear Information*, October-November, 1962.

CENTER
OF
EXPLOSION

Steel frame buildings & reinforced
concrete frame buildings collapse

Three story brick apartments
collapse

Frame houses shatter; most trees
down; roads impassable to cars

Injury from flying de   s

Glass windows shatter

Retinal burns
most distant
occurrence
depends on
direction of
vision and
size of pupil
at time of
explosion

Glass panes
melt, auto
body sheet
metal
vaporizes

Auto body
sheet metal
melts

Upholstery
and wool
rugs
ignite

Cardboard,
rayon drapes,
auto seats
burn

Second degree
burns (forma-
tion of
blisters)

Newspaper,
black rayon
gabardine
burn

First degree
burns (red-
ness of skin)

BLAST EFFECTS

HEAT EFFECTS

5 mi.
10 mi.
15 mi.
20 mi.
25 mi.
30 mi.
35 mi.

In addition to the heat effects, there is, produced simultaneously with the explosion, an intense radiation which is lethal to the same approximate range as for the heat and blast.(This is different from the fallout radiation which will be discussed subsequently.) This radiation consists of neutrons, X-rays and gamma rays; the latter having greater range and more capability for penetrating buildings, etc. The speed of propagation of the X-rays and gamma rays is the same as that of light, 186,000 miles per second.

The shock front, or blast, is propagated more slowly and will take a few seconds to reach the outermost limits shown in the figure. A few seconds after the passage of the blast front there will be, in some areas, a secondary "suction front" directed toward the center of the explosion. Generally, this will have a lower intensity than the initial blast, but will add to the destruction, especially causing damage to structures susceptible to the reversed force.

At the center of the explosion would be a crater some 600 feet deep. This crater would slope upward for a one-half mile radius to a 150 foot high wall of earth and debris which had been pushed up and out from the center of the crater. Thus in the one-mile diameter crater, shelter survival would not have been possible, unless the shelter had been 1,000 feet or more underground – which is generally not practical. However, 20 megatons is one of the larger yield weapons, and the surface burst taken creates the largest crater, so that this is a fairly realistic, near-worst example.

In addition to the blast, heat, radiation and cratering effects, there could also be what is called a fire storm. The intense heat ignited by a nuclear explosion might be expected to start countless small fires from buildings, stored fuel, trash, etc. If these numerous small fires tended to form a common flue-effect, sending a single large column of hot gases upward and consuming all available oxygen in the base fire, this would constitute a fire storm. As to whether such an effect would be produced, in many instances, can only be speculation, because of the obvious unavailability of data. The detractors from fallout shelters point to the occurrence of fire storms following the intense raids on Hamburg and Dresden during World War II, but the circumstances were entirely different and the results not directly applicable. However, these detractors are correct, fire storms should be considered – but the answer is better shelters, rather than none. Nevertheless, the problem has been exaggerated.

Thus the immediate effects of the explosion have been described. Although it would be relatively easy to provide shielding against the heat and radiation inside buildings, the blast would simply destroy these structures. Note that in Figure 1 building destruction is shown up to 10-11 miles. The blast effect is generally spoken of in terms of pounds per square inch, or psi. Frequently the blast is referred to as an overpressure of so many psi. This blast, or overpressure, in psi corresponds to wind velocity in miles per hour:

psi	wind velocity
2	70 miles per hour
5	160 miles per hour
10	290 miles per hour
20	470 miles per hour

The following table and discussion pertaining thereto provides an indication of the range in damage area which would be caused by lower yield weapons.

The lethal radii and lethal areas produced by nuclear weapons when used against cities and assuming air bursts at optimum burst height, may be tabulated as follows:

weapon yield in megatons	lethal radius (5 psi) in miles	lethal area; square miles inside 5 psi
½	3.45	37.5
1	4.32	58.6
2	5.41	93.
5	7.4	172.
10	9.3	272.
20	11.8	438.

Thus, as a first approximation, to select the proper weapon for use against a particular city, simply match the metropolitan area of the city as nearly as possible to the lethal area produced by a given explosion yield. For example, the metropolitan area of San Diego, California, is 275.7 square miles. The lethal area covered by a 10 megaton air burst is 272 square miles. So, 10 megatons would be a good first guess for civil defense planning for San Diego. But because cities are not usually circular, this estimate should be refined by local people who can figure the shape of the city, and the most effective blast pattern, together with more refined analyses of the relative target value of the city.[5]

There are several justifications for rating a given area as a potential target. Martin and Latham, in their exceptional work, *Strategy for Survival,*[5] have selected 303 likely targets in the U.S. Naturally, an area rated as a target for two or more reasons would receive a higher priority, generally speaking. The Martin and Latham table is given, in a condensed form, in the following pages. It should be borne in mind that this tabulation was published in 1963: there may have been a few changes since that time; for example, several of the smaller defense establishments have been closed and consolidated with larger bases. Also, the Atlas ICBM launching sites have been "salvaged." The following tabulation does not include reference to naval bases; however, Martin and Latham do provide a separate listing of naval target-areas, which may be obtained by referring to Appendix 10 in their book.

POTENTIAL TARGETS IN THE UNITED STATES*

City	Target Category	Possible Attack Level Megatons	City	Target Category	Possible Attack Level Megatons
ALABAMA			Santa Barbara	7	0.5
Birmingham	5	10	Stockton	7	1
Gadsden	7	1	Victorville	3	2
Huntsville	7	2	COLORADO		
Mobile	4,6	10	Colorado		
Montgomery	4,7	1	Springs	4,7	20-40
Tuscaloosa	7	0.5	Denver	1,2,5	95
ALASKA			Pueblo	7	0.5
Anchorage	4	2	CONNECTICUT		
Fairbanks	4	1-2	Bridgeport	6	10
ARIZONA			Hartford	6	5
Chandler	4	2	Meriden	7	0.5
Phoenix	4,5	10	New Britain	7	0.5
Tucson	1,2,3,6	185	New Haven	6	5
ARKANSAS			Norwalk	7	1
Blytheville	1	5	Stamford	7	5
Fort Smith	7	0.5	Waterbury	7	2
Little Rock	1,2,7	185	DELAWARE		
CALIFORNIA			Dover	3,4	2
Bakersfield	7	1	Wilmington	6	5
Fairfield-Suisan	1	5	DISTRICT OF		
Fresno	6	2	COLUMBIA		
Lompoc	1,2	5-25	Washington	3,4,5	8-15
Long Beach	5	1	FLORIDA		
Los Angeles	5	50-100	Fort Lauder-		
Marysville	1,2	50	dale-Hollywood	6	5
Merced	1,3	5	Homestead	1	5
Oakland	5	2	Jacksonville	6	5
Ontario-			Miami	5	10
Pomona	7	2	Orlando	1,6	5-7
Oxnard	3	2	Panama City	3	2
Pomona	7	2	Pensacola	4,7	1
Riverside-			St. Petersburg	6	4
San Bernardino	1,3,6	5-7	Tampa	1,4,5	5-10
Sacramento	1,3	7-12	Valparaiso	1,4	5
San Diego	5	10	West Palm		
San Francisco	5	30-40	Beach	7	5
San Jose	6	6	GEORGIA		
San Rafael	3	2-5	Albany	1,7	5

*By permission from *Strategy for Survival,* by Thomas L. Martin and Donald C. Latham,[6] the University of Arizona Press, Tucson, Copyright 1963.

City	Target Category	Possible Attack Level Megatons	City	Target Category	Possible Attack Level Megatons
Atlanta	4,5	20	Baton Rouge	7	2
Augusta	7	4	Lake Charles	1,4,7	5
Columbus	7	2	Monroe	7	1
Macon	1,4	5-6	New Orleans	5	10
Marietta	3	2	Shreveport	1,6	5-7
Savannah	1,7	5-7	**MAINE**		
HAWAII			Bangor	1,3	5
Honolulu	4,5	5	Lewiston-		
IDAHO			Auburn	7	5
Mountain Home	1,2	50	Limestone	1,3	5
ILLINOIS			Portland	7	2
Aurora	7	0.3 to 0.5	**MARYLAND**		
Belleville	4	1-2	Baltimore	5	20
Champaign-			Camp Springs	3,4	2
Urbana	7	0.1 to 0.15	**MASSACHUSETTS**		
Chicago	5	30-60	Boston	5	20-50
Davenport-			Brockton	7	1
Rock Island-			Chicopee	1,3	5
Moline	6	5	Fall River	7	1
Decatur	7	0.5	Falmouth	3,4	2
Joliet	7	1	Fitchburg-		
Moline	6	5	Leominster	7	2
Peoria	7	2	Holyoke	1,3	5-7
Rockford	7	1	Lawrence-		
Rock Island	6	5	Haverhill	7	2
Springfield	7	1	Leominster-		
Urbana-			Fitchburg	7	2
Champaign	7	0.1 to 0.15	Lowell	7	0.5
INDIANA			New Bedford	7	0.5
East Chicago	7	0.1	Pittsfield	7	1
Evansville	7	1	Springfield	1,3,6	5-7
Fort Wayne	7	1	Worcester	6	2
Gary	7	2	**MICHIGAN**		
Hammond	7	0.5	Ann Arbor	7	0.5
Indianapolis	6	5	Bay City	6	0.5
Muncie	7	0.3	Detroit	5	10
Peru	1,3	5	Flint	6	2
South Bend	6	2	Grand Rapids	6	5
Terre Haute	7	1	Jackson	7	0.5
IOWA			Kalamazoo	7	1
Cedar Rapids	7	1	Lansing	7	1
Des Moines	6	5	Kinross	1,3	5
Dubuque	7	0.2	Marquette	1,3	5
Sioux City	7	2	Mt. Clemens	3	2
Waterloo	7	1	Muskegon-		
KANSAS			Muskegon		
Salina	1,2	65	Heights	7	0.5
Topeka	1,2,7	10-14	Oscoda	1,3	5
Wichita	1,2,4,6	185	Saginaw	7	0.5
KENTUCKY			**MINNESOTA**		
Lexington	7	0.5	Duluth-Superior	3,7	5-7
Louisville	5	5	Minneapolis	5	40
LONG ISLAND			Moorehead-		
Westhampton			Fargo	7	0.5
Beach	3	2	Saint Paul	5	2
LOUISIANA			Superior-		
Alexandria	4	2	Duluth	3,7	5-7

City	Target Category	Possible Attack Level Megatons	City	Target Category	Possible Attack Level Megatons
MISSISSIPPI			Winston-Salem	7	1
Columbus.	1		**NORTH DAKOTA**		
Jackson	7		Fargo-		
MISSOURI			Moorhead	7	0.3
Kansas City	3,4,5		Grand Fork	1,3	5
Knob Knoster-			Minot	1,2,3	505-1505
Warrensburg	1		**OHIO**		
Saint Joseph	7		Akron	5	5
Saint Louis	5		Canton	6	2
Sedalia	1,2		Cincinnati	5	20
Springfield	7		Clevela	5	40
Warrensburg	1,2	505-1505	Columbus	1,5	5-15
MONTANA			Dayton	1,3,5	5-10
Billings	7	0.2	Elyria-Lorain	7	5
Glasgow	1,3	5	Hamilton	7	2
Great Falls	1,2,7	502-1502	Lima	7	0.25
NEBRASKA			Lorain-Elyria	7	5
Lincoln	1,2,7	65	Shelby	4	1
Omaha	1,2,4,5	50	Springfield	7	0.5
NEVADA			Steubenville-		
Las Vegas	4,7	2-3	Weirton	7	0.5
Reno	4,7	0.25	Toledo	5	5
NEW HAMPSHIRE			Warren-		
Manchester	7	1	Youngstown	6	5
Portsmouth	1	5	Weirton	7	0.5
NEW JERSEY			**OKLAHOMA**		
Atlantic City	7	2	Altus	1,2	65
Jersey City	6	0.25	Burns Flat	1	5
Newark	6	0.50	Elk City	1	5
Passaic	7	0.1	Lawton	7	0.25
Patterson	7	0.25	Oklahoma City	4,5	20
Trenton	6	2	Tulsa	6	2
Wrightstown	3,4	2	**OREGON**		
NEW MEXICO			Eugene	7	1
Albuquerque	4,6	2	Klamath Falls	3	2
Clovis	4	2	Portland	3,5	20-22
Roswell	1,2,3	65	**PENNSYLVANIA**		
NEW YORK			Allentown-		
Albany	6	1	Bethlemen	6	4
Binghamton	7	1	Altoona	7	0.2-0.25
Buffalo	5	10	Bethlehem-		
Newburgh	3,4	2	Allentown	6	4
New York	5	100	Erie	7	2
Niagra Falls	3,7	2-4	Harrisburg	6	1
Plattsburgh	1,2	65	Johnstown	7	0.5
Rochester	5	5	Lancaster	7	0.5
Rome-Utica	1,2	5-10	Middletown	4	2
Syracuse	3,4,6	2	Philadelphia	5	30
Troy	7	0.5	Pittsburgh	5	20
Utica-Rome	1,2,7	5-10	Reading	7	1
NORTH CAROLINA			Scranton	6	4
Ashville	7	1	Wilkes-Barre	6	2
Charlotte	6	2	York	7	0.25
Durham	7	0.5	Youngstown	6	5
Goldsboro	1,2	5	**RHODE ISLAND**		
Greensboro	7	2	Pawtucket-		
High Point	7	1	Providence	6	6-9
Raleigh	7	1	Providence	6	6-9

City	Target Category	Possible Attack Level Megatons	City	Target Category	Possible Attack Level Megatons
SOUTH CAROLINA			San Antonio	4,5	10
Charleston	3,4,7	3.5-4.5	San Benito	7	2
Columbia	7	2	Texerkana	7	0.5
Greenville	3, -	2	Tyler	7	0.3
Myrtle Beach	4	2	Waco	4,7	2
Sumter	4	2	Wichita Falls	1,7	5
SOUTH DAKOTA			**UTAH**		
Rapid City	1	50	Ogden	4,7	2
Sioux Falls	7	0.3	Provo	7	1
TENNESSEE			Salt Lake City	6	5
Chattanooga	6	5	**VIRGINIA**		
Knoxville	7	2	Hampton	3,6	10-12
Memphis	5	10	Lynchburg	7	0.5
Nashville	6	4	Newport News-		
Smyrna	4	2	Hampton	3,6	10-12
TEXAS			Norfolk	3,5	10-12
Abilene	1,2	65	Richmond	6	5
Amarillo	1,7	2	Roanoke	7	1
Austin	7	5	**WASHINGTON**		
Beaumont	7	2	Everett	3	2
Corpus Christi	7	2	Moses Lake	1,2,3	50
Dallas	5	40	Seattle	5	10
Del Rio	4	1-2	Spokane	1,2,3,6	12-17
El Paso	1,6	5-10	Tacoma	3,4,6	5-7
Fort Worth	1,5	20-25	**WEST VIRGINIA**		
Galveston-			Charleston	7	2
Texas City	7	10	Huntington-		
Harlingen-			Ashland	7	1
San Benito	7	2	Wheeling	7	0.5
Houston	5	20	**WISCONSIN**		
Killeen	4	1	Green Bay	7	1
Laredo	4,7	0.2	Kenosha	7	0.2
Lubbock	4,7	2	Madison	3,4,7	2
Midland	7	0.5	Milwaukee	5	20
Odessa	7	0.5	Racine	7	0.25
Port Arthur	7	2	**WYOMING**		
San Angelo	4,7	0.5	Cheyenne	1,2	19

KEY

1. SAC bomber base.   5. Population, 50 largest cities.
2. SAC missile base.   6. Population over 200,000
3. ADC base.   7. Population over 50,000
4. AF support base.

Before discussing the radioactive fallout from nuclear explosions, it will be helpful to briefly survey the effects of radiation, so that the nature of the fallout problem may be appreciated more fully as this problem is discussed.

The amount of radiation to which a person is exposed is called the *dose*. The most common unit of measure of the dose is the roentgen; although there are variant terms for precise scientific usage, this term is adequate for general usage. The dose may be effected in a flash, as would be the case in the vicinity of a nuclear explosion, or it may result from cumulative exposure over a period of days or weeks, as would be caused by radioactive fallout. Or the total dose received could be a combination of that from the exposure to the initial explosion and the subsequent fallout. The portion of the dose received from the fallout would accumulate over a period of days and would, therefore, accord the body defenses an opportunity for repair. However, the increase in total dosage allowable from the extended exposure of just a few days is not pronounced. Very roughly speaking the total dosage allowable is some 300 roentgens, whether received instantaneously, or over a period of days, or a combination thereof. (Over a period of years a higher dose can be tolerated.)

The clinical aspects of radiation exposure have been classified into six categories in accordance with the exposure levels experienced:[7]

Classifications	Roentgen Level
Asymptomatic	50 or less
Acute radiation sickness	
Group 1	50 to 200
Group 2	200 to 450
Group 3	450 to 600
Group 4	over 600
Group 5	over several thousand
Radiation injury to the skin	200 to 600
Internal radiation injury	not applicable in same sense
Late somatic effects	not applicable in same sense
Genetic effects	not applicable in same sense

Asymptomatic Exposure below 50 roentgens; no noticeable effects, blood count may be reduced slightly but normally no physical discomforture.

Acute Radiation Sickness Over 50 roentgens. General symptoms vary with exposure, but typically involve: weakness, nausea, low strength, abnormal urinary excretion, loss of hair and proneness to bleeding. Overall effect ranges from minor discomfort to early death, depending on dose and health of individual at time of exposure:

Group 1. 50 to 200 roentgens. Weakness, vomiting within 24 hours, restricted activity allowable.

Group 2. 200 to 450 roentgens. Vomiting soon after exposure and pronounced sickness for several days, followed by temporary recovery. Within 1-3 weeks the illness returns and the hair of the body is lost, but returns in a few months. Overall 50% chance of survival, but less as the 450 roentgen level is approached.

Group 3. 450 to 600 roentgens. Acute radiation sickness, similar to Group 2, only more severe; over 50% of these cases die.

Group 4. Over 600 roentgens. Effects more severe than Group 3, and additionally a bloody diarrhea. Life generally limited to about two weeks. (Succesful treatment of cases of this type have been made in a few cases of accidental exposure but mass treatments under the conditions envisioned would not be feasible.)

Group 5. Over several thousand roentgens. Produces severe damage to brain and nervous system; death comes in a few hours, or days at the most.

Radiation Injury to the Skin Itching commences almost at once and skin reddening occurs in two to three weeks. All of the hair is lost, if the dose is over 200 roentgens, but usually grows back in a few months if the exposure has been under 600 roentgens. (Amos 8:10. Isaiah 3:24 & 7:20?)

Internal Radiation Injury This effect would be produced in the days, weeks, months and years following a nuclear war by radioactive byproducts of the explosions inhaled or ingested with food and water. In addition to the foregoing general effects from the high level exposure to radiation, ingestion of low intensity radioactive materials can cause: glandular injury (iodine-131); anemia, bone necrosis, cancer or leukemia (strontium-90); and various materials deposited in the gastrointestinal tract can produce ulcers. Some of these effects will be discussed further in the subsequent section on long term fallout. It should be noted that even the most rudimentary shelters include dust filters to clean the shelter air of fallout particles.

Late Somatic Effects This category of radiation injury refers to effects produced a number of years following exposure. The possibilities include: leukemia, cancer, sterility, cataracts, developmental defects when unborn babies are exposed, and life shortening. However, these are injuries which all occur naturally. Apparently the exposure acts to increase the probability of occurence.

Genetic Effects What is involved here is the structure of the genes and reproductive cells. The effects are principally an increase in the number of female births (Isaiah 4:1?), an increase in still births, and natural abortions.

In the case of somatic and genetic effects only rough

estimates of the quantitative factors have been possible. However, recent limited observations in Guarapari, Brazil, which has 100 times the natural radioactivity common in the United States, have not shown a specifically identifiable effect.[8] Further tests are continuing under the sponsorship of the U.S. Atomic Energy Commission and the U.N. World Health Organization and should provide meaningful information in the next few years.

Now the nature of fallout may be discussed. This radioactive dust begins to settle down in the vicinity of the explosion in a few minutes and continues to be deposited downwind hours and days later. The heavier particles are of course deposited nearby. The radioactivity emitted by the fallout consists of: alpha particles, or helium nuclei; beta particles, or electrons; and gamma rays, which are similar to X-rays, but are more powerful. From the civil defense viewpoint the gamma rays provide the principal threat, as the alpha and beta particles cannot penetrate the simplest type of shelter. On the other hand, a few feet of earth, or other dense material is required to block the gamma rays.

The gamma radiation from the fallout is measured in roentgens; again the lethal danger point is in the order of 300 roentgens, with some added fraction for a continued rather than an instant exposure.* The intensity of the fallout radiation will continuously decrease every hour after the explosion. An approximate rule is that the intensity will decrease by a factor of 10 in seven hours. This decay is continuous, so that the following decrease in intensity occurs:

TIME (hr.)	DECAY	RADIATION INTENSITY
1	-	1,000 R/hr.
7	1/10	100 R/hr.
7x7=49 (2 days)	1/100	10 R/hr.
7x7x7=343 (2 wks)	1/1,000	1 R/hr.

The local or early fallout in the vicinity of the nuclear explosion is largely deposited within 24 hours. This fallout will be carried down wind at the prevailing wind rate. Figure 2 shows the fallout pattern from a surface burst of a one megaton weapon with typical wind conditions. (Ground zero refers to the point on the ground directly under the bomb at

---

*In professional Civil Defense work the radiation rate of roentgen/hour is convenient to use, but discussion relating to exact doses here will be limited to the total exposure over the entire time period involved.

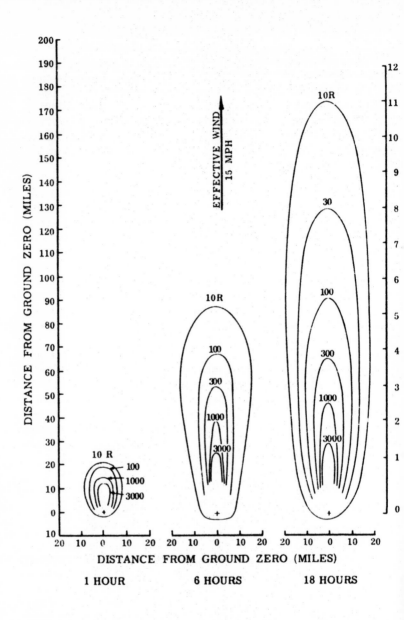

Figure 2.
TOTAL-DOSE CONTOURS FROM EARLY FALLOUT AT and 18 HOURS AFTER SURFACE BURST WITH 1-MEGAT FISSION YIELD (15 MILES PER HOUR EFFECTIVE WIN SPEED).[9]

the time of the explosion. The term is also used in the case of a surface burst.) Naturally, with higher yield weapons, the intensity and range of the "local" fallout will increase markedly.

To consider the effects of a country-wide attack, Figure 3 shows the fallout pattern resulting from an attack involving the release of approximately 1,500 megatons of fission energy under the prevailing weather conditions for the day chosen. This pattern was computed a few years ago, and with the passage of time weapon stockpiles have increased, so that a relatively heavier attack might very well be postulated for the future from the U.S.S.R. However, this level of attack is probably about the size which Red China or Red China and Cuba might be able to launch in the middle 1970's. It should be emphasized that this fallout distribution did not include massive underwater bursts off the West Coast mentioned in the preceeding chapter.

The radioactive particles, while still in the atmosphere, along with massive clouds of dust and other minute debris would tend to darken the sky, as during a storm. This darkening would be especially pronounced if the attack were launched in a time of the year when the forests were dry. Very likely, huge forest fires would be started, and no effort for control would be possible in areas where the fallout was intense enough to confine everyone to shelters. The smoke from the fires, combined with the blast debris, might very well provide a fulfillment of the Bible prophesies of destruction, shadowing of the sun, etc. (Isaiah 13:10; 24:6; 29:6; Joel 2:30; 31; 3:15).

In addition to the local fallout, about 25% of the finer particles are carried up into the troposphere (25,000 to 50,000 ft. altitude) and deposited in a belt around the world, taking up to a year to return to the earth. However, with the passage of time most of the radioactivity decays.

Having managed to live through the initial high intensity radiation from fallout, the survivors, in addition to the massive physical restoration and relocation problems, would have to cope with the long threat created by residual, low intensity, long-life radioactive products, principally strontium-90 and cesium-137. These elements are deposited in the soil, taken up by the plants, and so carried into the body. It is the unusual characteristics and effects produced by these elements that constitute the problem; the amounts produced are not large. However, a study of the strontium-90 problem

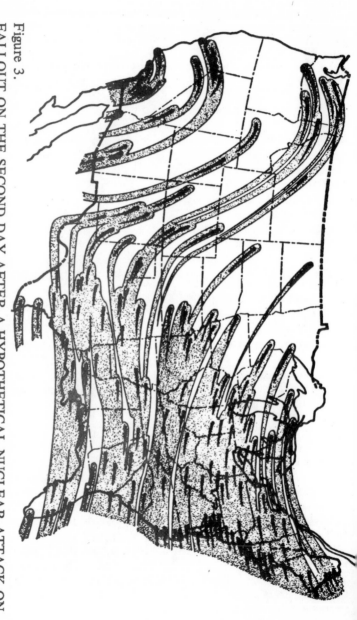

Figure 3.

FALLOUT ON THE SECOND DAY AFTER A HYPOTHETICAL NUCLEAR ATTACK ON OCTOBER 17, 1958.[10] By permission from *Fallout*, edited by John M. Fowler, Basic Books, Inc., 1960.

by the authors has shown that this need not present a serious post-attack problem.[11]

As to the cesium-137, this isotope is formed in a quantity only some 50% greater than that of the strontium-90. However, the maximum permissible concentration in the body is approximately ten times that for strontium-90, because of the dispersion of the cesium throughout the muscles and because of its rapid passage from the body. As noted above, the addition of potassium alone to the soil effected a reduction to 1/10 of the original concentration. No doubt, other control measures could also be used, if required, but as the up-take in the plants from the soil is only 1/10th to 1/100th that of strontium-90, it may be that the potassium additive alone would provide an adequate countermeasure.[12] Since the effect of cesium-137 is genetic, it would be desirable to support such world-wide usage of the soil-additives countermeasure as could be provided under the prevailing circumstances.

Carbon-14 is also a long-life by-product of nuclear explosions; it has a half-life of 5,760 years. Its radiation could possibly contribute to genetic changes, but Herman Kahn has pointed out that the global distribution of this isotope is such that it need not be considered as a major problem, much of it being deposited into the ocean.[13]

It has been shown that long-term fallout is more in the nature of a serious minor problem, but not on a par with that of the immediate local fallout, directly following the attack. To survive this period, considering current and possible future threats, the entire nation should have ready access to adequate, well equipped shelters — whether at home or at work. In non-target areas the simpler fallout shelters would be adequate. In larger cities, blast shelters, equipped with some type of air supply and cooling, are needed. Underground steel and concrete structures are needed for protection against blast; air supply and cooling are needed for protection against the possibility of fire storms.

Protection from fallout is obtained by shielding from the gamma rays. The extent of shielding provided is proportional to the mass of the material; for example, two readily available shielding materials, earth and concrete, provide the following protection values:

	Protection Factor	
Barrier, Feet	Earth	Concrete
1	10	30
2	100	300
3	1,000	3,000
4	10,000	30,000

The effect of the barrier, or shield, is to absorb gamma radiation. For example, assume that outside the shelter the total dose from fallout over a period of two weeks was 10,000 roentgens. Then, in an underground shelter, with three feet of earth on top, the total dose from the fallout would be under 10 roentgens — which would not be sufficient to cause any noticeable ill-effects. (In a small shelter the protection would be increased considerably because of shielding from the sides.)

Some protection can be obtained from distance also. In the center of, or especially in the basement of large buildings, relatively high protection factors are present.

In addition to protection from fallout, civil defense shelters should be fully equipped with air filters for protection against chemical and/or biological attacks. These filters are quite effective, would only add a small cost to a fallout shelter system, and would actually minimize the likelihood of a chemical-biological (CB) attack, as an auxiliary phase of a nuclear attack. It should be noted that the CB threat is given much consideration in the extensive civil defense courses and training exercises in the U.S.S.R.

In a properly equipped fallout shelter, the survivors should expect to spend approximately two weeks, or perhaps considerably more time, depending on the intensity of the local radiation. However, in many cases it would be possible to spend short periods out of the shelter, surveying local conditions, obtaining additional food, or in decontaminating the immediate area. It should be explained that the fallout, or radioactive dust, generally having the appearance of a white powder, can be swept up, washed away with a hose, or otherwise disposed of. Such methods can be expected to reduce the residual radiation intensity of the decontaminated area by as much as a factor of one-hundred.

One of the most effective ways of warding off the threat of a nuclear war, from a military viewpoint, is simply to provide adequate blast and fallout shelters for the populace. Clearly, the anti-ballistic missile system is needed, but the role of the ABM is to provide some protection for people not getting into shelters quickly enough, and for property damage limitation. Even with the anti-ballistic missile system, shelters are essential – otherwise the enemy can spot ground bursts, which produce the most local fallout, 100-200 miles up-wind, out of range of the anti-missile defense for the area involved, and depend on the usual wind patterns to wipe out the population down-wind with fallout.

Thus, it can be stated that the primary concern of the United States should be survivability – to use a term the Soviets like to use. And survivability means first and foremost: well designed *blast and fallout* shelters, well stocked and adequately equipped with emergency facilities. *In short – shelters for survival: the anti-ballistic missile for added protection and for property damage limitiation to facilitate post-attack recovery.*

The Johnson Administration considered the possibility of asking the Congress for an "inexpensive," relatively speaking, fallout-only shelter system for major cities. The Nixon Administration should give the American people a full breakdown on costs for alternative shelter systems which provide blast, fire storm, and fallout protection.

The Russians have managed to quietly build a nationwide shelter system while keeping all news of this from their leading newspapers and frequently denying the existence of their shelter system to Westerners. For example, in 1963 an American authority on civil defense in the U.S.S.R. and a member of the Rand Corporation, Leon Gouré, testified before a Congressional committee that 40 to 60 percent of the people in Moscow could be sheltered – mostly in blast shelters.[14] Since then, shelter construction has been intensified.[15] The Soviet program will be discussed more fully in Chapter 11, it is enough here to include the summary of Mr. Gouré's presentation to the Congressional Committee:

> Soviet authorities have stressed the need for shelters as the most effective means of defense against nuclear, chemical, and bacteriological weapons. The Soviet shelter construction program is primarily a mass shelter program which appears to have gone into effect in 1949 or 1950, with special attention to industrial plants and new housing construction. All permanent urban shelters provide varying degrees of protection against blast and a high degree of protection against collapsing buildings, radiation, fire, and chemical and bacteriological agents. They must be equipped for relatively long-term occupancy.
>
> Soviet publications have shown the design of a variety of types of shelters. These include:

1. Very deep or heavy shelters for a large number of persons, designed to withstand in excess of 300 pounds per square inch; these shelters are intended for use by members of the elite and the administration;

2. Large detached shelters for 100 to several thousand persons, and designed to withstand 100 to 150 pounds per square inch; these shelters are intended for use by industrial workers as well as the public;

3. Subways in Moscow, Leningrad, and Kiev;

4. Basement shelters in public buildings and apartment houses designed for 10 to 100 pounds per square inch;

5. Various types of simple fallout shelters which can be built very quickly by the population in the event of an emergency and which will provide the principal form of protection in rural areas;

6. Suburban and rural family shelters, utilizing existing deep root cellars and other underground structures, to be constructed by the population.

7. Soviet literature has also described shelters for cattle.

The permanent shelters are equipped with double steel doors and filter ventilation units for removing radioactive dust as well as chemical and bacteriological agents. Also included are water, light, heat, toilets, bunks, and in some cases bottle oxygen. Food is apparently stored in most public shelters but not in apartment house shelters. In the latter case the population is instructed to bring its own supplies when taking cover. Civil defense teams control the shelters and operate the equipment.[16]

What would be the potential benefit from a complete shelter system to the U.S.S.R.? Before the advent of the Russian anti-ballistic missile system, one estimate was that:

With a massive civil defense program, Russia could reduce casualties from a U.S. retaliatory attack from around 130 million of the population killed to between 5 and 10 million dead.[17]

This was considered as a maximum estimate; many authorities did not consider such low losses possible — however, now the added protection of the anti-ballistic missile system would be included!

Many prominent Americans have tried to spur the development of a nationwide system of shelters. Dr. Edward Teller, Congressman Chet Hollifield, Military Strategist Herman Kahn, Governor Nelson Rockefeller, and many other prominent leaders have vigorously worked for a more extensive shelter program. Dr. Eugene P. Wigner of Princeton, a Nobel Laureate in physics, says that:

Effective civil defense would make a war less likely by decreasing the preponderance of offensive weapons over defensive ones. This preponderance creates an unstable situation by giving a great advantage to the aggressor. Strengthening the defense will

contribute to stability by decreasing the aggressor's advantage
and by making it less possible for him to exact repeated concessions by threats of attack. . . .We should trust the common man;
his destiny is at stake; he should make the decision and no information should be withheld from him.[18]

And in the following comment General Nathan F. Twining also notes that, without shelters, the United States clearly
will be subject to nuclear "blackmail":

There is no question that a nuclear war can be "won," as
wars of the past have been won — by the side which is best prepared to fight it. This preparation of which I speak includes as
top-priority items civil defense measures as well as military offensive and defensive power. The tenacious attitude, incidentally,
of Americans in refusing to recognize and heed civil defense
measures is just about as idiotic as would be the action of an in-
fantryman facing certain rifle fire and refusing to get into a fox-
hole.

Nevertheless, the defeatists believe that no one can win a
nuclear war, that civilization will be destroyed; hence, the human
urge to fight must somehow be channeled into limited, non-nuclear wars. This approach is a different way of arriving at the
same weak answer. If ever the belief that "no one can win a nuclear war" becomes completely dominant and controlling in U.S.
national policy, the enemy will know it. The enemy will know that
America will go to any lengths to avoid nuclear war, and then by
virtue of his geographic and demographic advantages, he will be
in position to destroy us.[19]

Can America afford to have a better shelter program?
Can America afford *not* to have a complete blast and fallout
shelter system? The fire insurance rate on real estate is something like 0.3% of the building value per year. Assume an
average house, or apartment, of a value of say $15,000; and
that this is the home of four people. The cost per annum, per
person for fire insurance is 0.3% of $15,000, divided by four—
or $11.25 per year. Blast and fallout shelters do not become
obsolete, like military hardware. Therefore the cost can be
amortized over a period of 25 to 50 years. The average person
is now spending $281.25 for fire insurance for a 25 year per-
iod — and he never really expects to have a fire. As shown in
Chapter 11, this order of cost could provide some fairly decent single-use shelters.

The Department of Defense has estimated that 150 million casualties in the U.S. would result from an attack by the
U.S.S.R. in the early 1970's.[20] Moreover, from a military
viewpoint, other factors aside, the survivors might very well
be required to set up a Communist State, in light of superior

Russian survivability. This was based on current shelters! Considering the effects of an attack and the benefits realizable from blast and fallout shelters, the British *Intelligence Digest* reported:

Present Defences

As American defences now stand, a full-scale Soviet nuclear attack on the leading 150 industrial and population centres, 132 strategic military bases, and 21 Atomic Energy Commission installations, with resultant fall-out from surface bursts, would inflict 130,000,000 deaths. Over two-thirds would be from immediate blast, thermal radiation, and initial nuclear radiation. The remaining deaths would occur up to a six month period from radioactive fall-out. A national community fall-out shelter programme costing $10 billion could save those lives.

Blast Shelters

A system of blast shelters in America's 150 largest cities could reduce casualties to 25,000,000, according to a Rand Corporation study. The Nike-X ABM system would further reduce the casualties.

An effective national blast shelter programme could cost as much as $100 billion. Due to this high cost, such a programme has not yet been recommended by the Defence Department.

An engineering study has been made of the problem of protecting the population of New York City by blast shelters. By excavating 800 to 1,000 feet into the solid rock underlying Manhattan Island, a system of deep rock shelters for 4,000,000 people could be built at a cost of $500 to $700 per person. [21]

In Chapter 11 an alternative approach to the shelter problem is proposed—based on multiple use construction, planned and financed by local government units. It is shown that there are unique advantages in this approach. *What is needed is for a few cities to establish a thorough-going shelter system, to start the trend.*

It is possible that future historians will be able to note the effect of the American decision to support an *adequate* anti-ballistic missile system with an effective complement of blast and fallout shelters on the survival of the Free World — at least in the form in which it now exists.

PART III

CAN ARMAGEDDON BE AVERTED?
BUILD THE RESOLUTE SOCIETY

Red strategy and effective U.S. countermeasures

CHAPTER 8

THE ULTIMATE WEAPON

In consonance with the modern management principle of proposing solutions for each problem as presented, it seems essential to conclude this volume with suggested measures applicable to the entire nation. And, although no effort will be made to discuss the philosophic problem posed in endeavoring to ward off an Armageddon, as opposed to spiritually preparing for such an event, a common course of action can be pragmatically outlined which applies, in the main, to either view. That is to say, whether the Communist-thermonuclear-Armageddon threat has developed as a result of divisive social forces and actions (including recent wars) or whether it is an essentially inevitable event, preceeding a forthcoming millenium, cannot be considered here. But a single positive program to mold and augment our defense position, and in most respects, at the same time, insure spiritual development, can be provided. Further, it should be realized that in many respects, every age, every generation, and perhaps every individual, has its or his own Armageddon — and following the critical tribulation period, may expect to enter into a phase of living more secure, serene and rewarding, assuming that the problems have been met forthrightly.

The key to the problem of strengthening the defensive shield and increasing spiritual preparedness lies in the source of strength. At the present time there seems to be a morbid preoccupation with thermonuclear weapons which are viewed as ultimate or doomsday devices. But, is there such a thing as an ultimate weapon? No doubt, the bow and arrow, the military use of gunpowder (in several phases), etc. were each, at one time, considered ultimate weapons. But these devices alone were ineffective and useless. It took a unified command — a monolithic national will — to effect a purposeful use of these weapons. And this is invariably based on the subjective, social attributes of the people, their integrated effort, their responsive and responsible action, their mutual

129

consideration – in short, *their character.* Now it does seem that this quality of character has been the primary factor affecting the development of the American nation, of past decades, the America of today, and the country-to-be. For example, the following observation by General Ira C. Eaker (USAF, Ret.) may be considered:

> The fundamental basic elements in national security in their order of importance are: the intelligence and determination of the people, the wisdom of their leaders, and the adequacy of their military forces.[1]

In short, one may say that *the ultimate weapon is character.*

But we are now faced with the erosion of this national character by subversive and divisive forces operating openly within our country, which are difficult to control by procedures established for our open society in the past. It must be our objective to clarify our national thinking, to strengthen the national sense of purpose and to control and eradicate subversive and divisive influences which tend to undermine that purpose. Problems of this nature are not new. True, they may be magnified in our time, but the historic answers, such as the following written by the ancient Chinese philosopher, Lao Tsu, still apply:

> Truly, once the way is lost,
> There comes then virtue;
> Virtue lost, comes then compassion;
> After that morality;
> And when that's lost, there's etiquette,
> The husk of all good faith,
> The rising point of anarchy.[2]

Note especially line five. Isn't it interesting that a Chinese philosopher, some 2,500 years ago, could identify a trend which is widespread today – that of substituting "intellectual morality" for the classical standards upon which our society was founded?

The necessary procedure for controlling the divisive, iconoclastic forces is also outlined by Lao Tzu:

> That which lies still is easy to hold:
> That which is not yet manifest is easy to forestall;
> That which is brittle (like ice) is easy to melt;
> That which is minute is easy to scatter.
> Deal with a thing before it is there;
> Check disorder before it is rife.
> A tree with a full span's girth begins from a tiny sprout;
> A nine-storied terrace begins with a clod of earth.
> A journey of a thousand li begins at one's feet . . . [3]

All of which indicates that the problem of survivability is basically a subjective one, resting on a coherent, unified and purposeful national outlook. But a nation's outlook can only be derived from the cooperate sum of each and all of the individual citizens. In a dictatorship, such as found in the late Fascist states of Italy and Germany, or in the perhaps even more dictatorial Communist states today, the national outlook is forcefully aligned and unified by a politically omnipotent government. This control of thought, alignment of individual outlook, and resulting conformity in personal action is in fact essential to the existence of such a power structure and is therefore effected by rigid control of all mass communication media, school activity, employment, etc.

On the other hand, in a free society such as ours, serious dilution of this national outlook, by organization of subversive movements, is all too easily produced. For example, we have the group demonstrations for such specious causes as anti-Vietnam, ban-the-bomb, free-filth speech, legalize-drug-addiction, etc. The effect of all these essentially diverse movements, each of which alone is not too significant, is to integrate into one single drive the deterioration of individual character and the confusion of the sense of national purpose.

CHAPTER 9

FROM MARX TO MARCUSE

The revolution in America is underway! Whether it was quietly signaled following McNamara's tutorial efforts at The Bay of Pigs, or began with the 1968 campaign in New Hampshire by Senator Eugene McCarthy on an anti-Vietnam platform, or the conflagration at Watts, or whether it was the assassination of President Kennedy — no matter. *What is important: the revolution is.* It is not cast in the crude physical mode of a classical revolution — although the razing of whole areas of cities is rather physical — but it is, in general, a sophisticated, controlled action, carefully metered by the intellectual elite whose cause it serves.

Although the identification of motivation is generally a hazardous undertaking, it is fairly obvious that the Red Revolutionary, to use an inclusive categorization, has some warped understanding of the relationship of strength based on moral character and therefore directs his efforts to debase as an essential adjunct to subversion. As to the question of a Mephistophelian link, it should at least be noted that Goethe's *Faust* was a bible for Karl Marx, and that he frequently would sign his name "Old Nick" when writing to friends.[1] And, although the scourge of communism cannot be entirely placed on Marx, it is important to note that in his first serious writing, the poetic drama *Oulanem*, the major theme was an admixture of homosexuality, seduction, Satanic power, and the ruin of the world. Yet this affectation with the illusion of demonic power — for it will here be held that the *power* is illusionary, although the effect produced within the deluded one may be all too real — is unfortunately a not too uncommon attitude. Dostoevski's *Underground Man*, for example, was prompted to say, "Unless I can have my cup of tea, let the whole world perish." Or again, another nihilistic cry, from *Faust, "Alles, was besteht, ist wert, dass es zugrunde geht."* ("Everything that exists deserves to perish.")

According to Gustav Techow, a contemporary of Marx —

132

who has perhaps left us the best picture of the man — Marx's motivation was not unlike that of these fictional characters:

First we drank port, then claret which is red bordeaux, then champagne. After the red wine Marx was completely drunk. That was exactly what I wanted. I found out the truth about certain things which would otherwise have remained suppositions.

The impression he made on me was that of someone possessing a rare intellectual superiority, and he was evidently a man of outstanding personality. If his heart had matched his intellect, and if he had possessed as much love as hate, I would have gone through fire for him, even though at the end he expressed his complete contempt for me, and had previously indicated his contempt in passing. He was the first and only one among us all to whom I would entrust leadership, for he was a man who never lost himself in small matters when dealing with great events.

Yet it is a matter for regret in view of our aims that this man with his fine intellect is lacking in nobility of soul. *I am convinced that a most dangerous personal ambition has eaten away all the good in him . . .* The only people he respects are the aristocrats . . . In spite of all his assurances to the contrary, and perhaps because of them, I took away with me the impression that the acquisition of personal power was the aim of all his endeavors.[2]

The purpose of those obsessed with power is well described in three lines in Milton's *Paradise Lost:*

Here we may reign secure, and, in my choice
To reign is worth ambition, though in Hell,
Better to reign in Hell than serve in Heaven.

And in these lines lie the key to a fullness of understanding of the Communists and their movement which, even they, do not have.

They cannot hope to gain a free world, imbued with the charitable traditions of (classical) Christianity: first, that world must be destroyed. Whether this is accomplished through propaganda, demoralization, mass slaughter, destructive wars, Machiavellian political coups, sensitivity discussions, or a combination of these is simply a matter of tactics.

Perhaps the most dangerous aspect of the Communist movement is the obsession to subvert all traditional standards of decency, to the benefit of the Communist world revolution. In fact, it appears that the Communist leaders will progressively "evolve" in callowness as to become entirely insensitive to world wide destruction.

But the shifting craftiness of the Communists was apparent at the outset. *Why an organization which professed atheism should be founded to promote an end to crime, oppression, and inhumanity of man to man, Marx never got around to making clear!* After Lenin and Trotsky organized the Red revolution to seize power in Russia from the provisional government led by the socialist Kerensky, it was quickly apparent to the world that this was no benevolent dictatorship. On February 8, 1920, Sir Winston Churchill summarized the situation in Russia the *Sunday Illustrated Herald:*

> From the days of Spartacus-Weishaupt, to those of Karl Marx, to those of Trotsky, Bella Kuhn (Hungary) Rosa Luxembourg (Germany), and Emma Goldman (United States), this worldwide conspiracy for the overthrow of civilization and the *reconstruction of society on the basis of arrested development and envious malevolence,* and the impossible equality has been steadily growing. It has been the mainspring of every subversive movement during the nineteenth century. And now at last this band of extraordinary personalities from the underworld of the great cities of Europe and America have gripped the Russian people and have become the undisputed masters of that enormous empire.

As to Churchill's reference to American support for the Red revolution in Russia, although the American financial aid was significant, American aid to European revolutionaries did not start in 1917. For example, during their first years in England the Marx family subsisted largely on income provided by articles Marx wrote for the American, Horace Greely—publisher of the *New York Herald Tribune.* Greely planned to abolish: slavery, consumption of alcohol, and capitalism, and to establish a utopian socialism.

According to philosopher-historian Will Durant, the most significant event in Western civilization during the past few hundred years is the decline of the Christian religion in Europe. The relationship between this decline in Europe and the upsurge of communism there is easily apparent. What is relevant to the average American is the extension of this trend in the United States. Symbolic is the appearance of the inverted "peace" cross, or Aldermaston throughout the country (in the Dark Ages, called the "Witches' Foot"), the interest in mediums, black masses, and other mummery. But notably, there is heard no great outcry by the National Council of Churches: perhaps they are too occupied with the collection of funds to support militant activists, opposing the war in Vietnam, and working for the admission of Red China to the U.N.

Even the Catholic Church, once considered the greatest single bulwark against the onrush of communism, is rapidly shifting its position to prepare for the possibility of co-existence in a Red Europe and South America. In a sweeping review of the changed position of the Vatican *vis-a-vis* communism, *Look* reported:

> The ecumenical movement has such large boundaries that Roman Catholicism is warming to an accommodation with a more pliable communism . . . Communism had drawn its first clear concession from Catholicism a few days before Pope John's Council opened in 1962. And though it has not since adapted any known Catholic teaching to Marxist doctrine, and is not about to, the Church has quite plainly retreated from its holy war against communism and settled down with it quite serenely . . . Any Socialist or Communist state where citizens are free to worship is now quite acceptable to the papacy.[3]

In the loosely organized revolutionary movement the Communists have established in the United States — now in about the same stage as that in Russia in 1905 — there is need for diversity in leadership in their varied programs, such as: teaching youth to look to government for economic support rather than the family, promotion of the use of narcotics, sexual promiscuo''sness, acceptance of perversion, promotion of hatred between ethnic groups or the campaign to vitiate all religion. But if it were necessary to designate a "Director of Strategy" of these diverse activities, it would be difficult to select a more capable candidate than Professor Herbert Marcuse of the University of California at San Diego (UCSD). Realizing, as Sigmund Freud did before him, the essential nature of monogamy and respectable family life as a foundation of civilization, Marcuse — who advocates destruction of civilization — reverses Freud with the simple formula of social destruction through "sexual freedom." Marcuse also proposes that freedom of speech not be allowed to conservative groups, but be a privilege reserved for the New Left and the like.

Certainly the work of one college professor, even though a Marcuse, could not hope to precipitate a revolutionary movement in the Nation's youth — by such activity as being the principal lecturer to a UCSD student seminar on revolution — but, as discussed in Chapter 13, the Supreme Court has swept away every loyalty oath and other restriction against the employment of Communists and fellow travelers in schools and colleges. It is that Marcuse is an example of a society tolerating a force organized to destroy it. According to Governor Reagan, the student guerrillas would not have got anywhere had it not been for the fellow traveling anarchists on the faculties.* Reacting to this situation, Harvey H. Hukari, a Stanford University Graduate student remarked:

> I'm sick of being taught by those refugees from reality, whose only saving grace is that they have tenure, and then being told that I'm receiving a liberal education. I'm sick of seeing political work for liberal candidates being done by university employees on university time and with university facilities. . . I'm tired of professors who speak strongly about academic freedom and then assign a reading list which does not contain one author whose political philosophy is to the right of *Ramparts* magazine. The Black Student Union wants to know how many black people are in teaching positions at Stanford. I want to know how many Republicans there are on the faculty of the political science department.[4]

As to Mr. Hukari's question about the political affiliation of his professors, he would perhaps be interested to note that 95% of the faculty at UCSD are registered Democrats and 5% are registered Republicans.[5] The results of the substitution of political propaganda for scholarship — to call a spade a spade — is reviewed in an article in the special January 1969 issue of *Fortune* devoted to student unrest entitled, "The Faculty is the Heart of the Trouble:"

> They hold in high esteem a "gut commitment" to a cause, despising any careful analysis of the facts and background bearing on whatever situation engages them emotionally. Many activists describe, in an offhand way, their political position as Marxist. This does not lead them, as it led radical students in the Thirties, into an avid reading of Marx, much less into an intellectual controversy over differing interpretations that could be found in Kantsky, Lenin, or Trotsky. Today's student Marxists tend to take their Marx from quotations from Mao Tse-tung, most of which are about as intellectual as a toothpaste ad.

---

*According to the prominent educator, Dr. Sidney Hook *(U.S. News & World Report,* May 16, 1969) the worst excesses of student violence have occurred at the most liberal universities, large or small. One of the most objectionable issues for the "liberal" politician is the Communist root of the student revolts. But Senator John McClellan's investigations have uncovered shocking evidence of Communist infiltration among militant students and blacks. Typically, James Forman of SNCC advocates armed revolution to establish socialist government in the United States.

As the revolution in the United States develops — unless it is stopped by effective counteraction — it will be pulled together with more central control. On June 1, 1969, FBI Director J. Edgar Hoover reported that the *Old Left* was more and more gaining control of the students' groups such as the Students For Democratic Society (SDS). The one major division which was resisting direction from the Moscow-dominated Old Left was the pro-Peking Progressive Labor Party (PLP). However, this schism is of little consequence since both factions support continuous revolution with gradually increasing tempo to establish a Communist government in the United States. Special guerrilla training centers have been set up in Cuba and Sweden to train revolutionaries on urban warfare and riot tactics in America. More and more activity of this sort should be expected, as long as it is tolerated.

According to Director Hoover, much of the financing for student revolutionaries and other New Left activities is derived from gifts from wealthy individuals, foundations, and from honoriums paid to speakers. For example, some of the prominent contributors are a Cleveland industrialist who has long been a Soviet sympathizer, a New York industrial leader who was formerly editor of *Soviet Business Today* and past chairman of the Congress of American-Soviet Friendship, and an heiress in the New England area who is married to a prominent educator. What has not been discussed in the news of late is the $3 billion that are supplied directly by agents from Moscow and Peking — 95% for the Red activity in Free World schools and colleges.[6]

As to the Russian-Chinese split, this situation is working so well for the Red World that if it were not real there would be good reason to invent it. Regardless of the Hollywood-quality news film released by the U.S.S.R. on the border clashes with the Chinese, the common policy of destruction of capitalism is fundamental. And there are far more areas of cooperation than there are differences. It will be remembered that the break only started from disagreement with Khrushchev over nuclear policy.*

---

*One interesting indication of basic union of the two powers was shown by the Red Chinese diplomatic discussions with the U.S. These were held in Poland, where Russian monitoring microphones could be conveniently installed *(Los Angeles Times* Feb. 17, 1969).

These differences are basically jurisdictional and philosophical. With independent control of the two blocs, continued competition for a single power structure may be assumed as a matter of course. *However, this should be expected to be a controlled competition, centered largely in the drive for new Red colonies in Asia, Africa, and South America. This at once averts direct conflict, provides competitive expansion of communism, and allows a certain amount of limited warfare between the two groups — which may be conducted largely by indigent colonial forces.*

As to the philosophical differences between the U.S.S.R. and Red China, this difference may be gradually eliminated in the near future. Since the original difference arose under Khrushchev, the U.S.S.R. has returned to Stalinism and has shown it will not allow significant deviation by the East-European satellites — witness Czechoslovakia. From the Czech invasion has come the so-called Brezhnev doctrine which supports the policy of armed invasion of "socialist" countries. Now this is quite similar to the basic Red Chinese program for expansion. The Red Chinese expect to expand through support of guerrilla activity — now in Vietnam, and later through Peking trained "liberation fronts" already established in Assam, Burma, Thailand, and India. Whereas, the Russians, under the Brezhnev doctrine, would like to feel free to occupy bordering nations who had been forced into socialism via a political coup or subversion directed from Moscow.

As noted by Winston Churchill, communism essentially involves "reconstruction of society on the basis of arrested development." The achievement of this "norm" is the objective of the Chinese Communists, and as discussed in Chapter 14, tolerance of meaningful individual freedom in a Communist state is not feasible. In the course of time, the Russian and Chinese internal policies should, pragmatically, evolve toward a common norm., leaving only the external, expansionist differences.

The denial of absolute references or standards of morality in the Communist world can only lead to cunning malevolence, which crushes individual creativity. This adds to the difficulties arising from inefficient Communist methods of production and limits the amount of consumer goods and food products which can be produced. That is, not only does the Communist control of agriculture provide the major reason for an impending world food shortage, *but it influences Communist expansionist policy to gain control of more land to produce more food (inefficiently).*

Cooperatively, or competitively, the common objective of the Soviet Union and Red China is the completion of the takeover of Asia and Africa. In 1953, Mao Tse-tung sent Stalin a comprehensive memorandum outlining a new program for World Revolution *(Congressional Record,* 1954, p 5708) which included the following observation:

> With Asia and Africa isolated (under Communist control) in the Capitalistic countries in Europe there will be a total economic collapse in Western Europe. Their capitulation will be a matter of course.

However, it may not be necessary for the Communists to await complete takeover of Africa and Asia to establish a communised Europe. Throughout the 1950s, as Russia's nuclear capability rapidly developed, greatly aided by their intelligence efforts in the U.S. and England, the Soviet "power shadow" over Europe was in many respects countered by the amazing economic recovery in West Germany under the leadership of Konrad Adenauer. The Adenauer government was strongly anti-communist and the Communist Party was outlawed. After Adenauer's retirement, his Minister of Finance, Ludwig Erhard became Chancellor and continued the same enlightened economic and strong anti-communist policies. But despite strong warning of the consequences, in 1966 former Secretary of Defense McNamara and President Johnson forced Erhard to continue support of the U.S. outflow of dollars (and gold) by purchasing some $700 million worth of U.S. weapons — which Germany could no longer use (since its army was then already fully equipped for the scheduled 12 division standing). When Erhard yielded to the Johnson-McNamara demands, despite a recession then affecting the German economy, this produced such a violent reaction in Germany that he was forced out of office and subsequently replaced by Kurt Georg Kiesinger. This government was characterized by the number of socialists and (former?) Communists it contained — notably the Foreign Minister, Willy Brandt, socialist, and one of his Deputies, Herbert Wehner, who after fifteen years as a Communist *declared* himself to be a socialist. Also there was the new Minister of Justice, Gustav Heineman, who sometime after he was installed in office, consulted with the *outlawed* Communist Party and advised them how they could circumvent the outlaw provisions of the constitution. The Communists made a few minor changes in their party organization and the party name and quickly started building up as a quasi-respectable political party. Justice Heineman was bitterly assailed for engaging in secret talks with members of the East German Communist party. Also Heineman legalized adultery and homosexuality between consenting adults and removed legal barriers to journalists in the publication of classified government information. For these achievements Heineman was subsequently maneuvered into the semi-honorary office of President.

Symbolic of the situation, during the 1969 political campaign, Willy Brandt maintained that by adopting a stronger pro-Russian policy, Bonn's bargaining power with the Western allies would be augmented! The strong man of Brandt's Social Democratic Party is Herbert Wehner. The Brandt-Wehner policy toward East Germany is *Entspannung* or "detente" – which should be more properly translated as union with East Germany to form a socialist state. Also there are an estimated 5,000 Communist agents in West Germany and frequently tips of the espionage iceberg are uncovered, as occurred with the rash of "suicides" of German officials in October 1968.*

On September 28, 1969, the point beyond which a return can be expected was passed in Germany. The Brandt (read Wehner) led Social Democratic Party (SPD) – aided by Red-led mobs which thoroughly disrupted the gatherings of opposing parties – managed to pick up enough votes to gain control of the government. Short of a historical event as rare as the advent of a Joan of Arc, Germany, and Europe, have passed the political point of no return and may be expected to be moving steadily eastward to closer agreements with Moscow. It should be expected that Brandt will slyly work for the withdrawal of the U.S. Army from Germany, as a necessary step for reunion with East Germany to form a "neutral" country.

This withdrawal of the American forces from Germany would signal the break-up of NATO, put Europe under Soviet domination, and leave the United States to contemplate its self-ordained fall from world leadership and its chances of survival in Fortress America.

Already the Reds have seized impressive blocs of power in the unions throughout Europe and are constantly gaining

---

*Added to this is the Soviet penetration of NATO. On March 23, 1967, the discovery of a Communist spy network in NATO with over 300 members was reported.

by the simple plan of unifying behind one candidate while the opposition is divided. The 1968 student-led "revolution" in France barely failed to topple the Government — but only because the formal Communist organization held back from full participation. Apparently the time was not right. Although the passing of De Gaulle from the political scene in France will strengthen the position of the West, France will continue to be handicapped by the extensive infiltration of Communist agents in their government — which condition De Gaulle simply would not recognize. As reported by *Life,* April 26, 1968, a former French intelligence officer in the service of the Russians defected to the West and testified that the Soviets, through French spies in NATO, had a whole library of secret NATO documents. When they wanted an additional report they would simply order it by the NATO numbering system, and get a microfilm copy in two or three days. But De Gaulle would not recognize the situation.

By 1966 it had become apparent that the Communists could paralyze the British industry any time they wanted to do so.[7] Even if the (Fabian Socialist) British labor government were replaced by an (only moderately) conservative government at the next general election, the Communist union strength can hardly be affected by this change.

In Italy the control of government is held by the socialists, and they are split into five factions — which division is largely responsible for the success of the Red technicians there. The Communist popularity at the polls is just over 30 percent: the foreign minister is a "Marxist-Leninist." As a result of this situation, a popular front government including the Communists appears to be a grim possibility in the near future.

The Russians will realize however, in the coming power struggle for Europe that time is of the essence since, as discussed in Appendix B, nuclear capability is rapidly developing in Europe. Therefore, the European nations and/or NATO must be taken over from within. Above all, the Russians fear a rightist Germany armed with a large stockpile of assorted nuclear weapons, which they fully control.* The

---

*The Russians are not concerned about a fascist movement, although this is a convenient smear term to use to discredit any group they choose to oppose. Under prevailing circumstances the Communists could easily penetrate any fascist group from within to limit its effectiveness since, as discussed in Chapter 14, fascism is politically close to communism.

Communists will be counting on their extensive infiltration of various European governments and NATO to facilitate take-over. Coupled with this, will be economic pressures generated by control of the Suez Canal — if it is reopened — and they will expect to control shipping around the Cape of Good Hope after gaining control of South Africa — although the Red Chinese also aspire to gain suzerainty there.

In countering this Communist drive to take over Asia, Africa and eventually the rest of the world, there are many things which could be done which are not receiving attention, but the most potent weapon is information. True, full military capability is needed to provide a protective shield, but the Achilles heel of the Red World is truth. Internally the Communist rulers must brainwash the people to maintain control, and therein lies their weakness. Externally, the Reds find massive propaganda a most effective technique for softening up a country for takeover. The use of propaganda warfare against the Reds has frequently been considered, but little has been done because of the bad connotation of the term. However, what we would want to (aggressively) impart to the Red World is really not propaganda, but information. Therefore it would seem important to use the name of *information warfare* in lieu of propaganda warfare.

Some of the religious organizations are getting sizeable amounts of Bible excerpts into Russia by the simple method of having a network of supporters mail their tracts in assorted styles of envelopes to individuals in the U.S.S.R. A similar approach could be used to mail salient news summaries into Russia — thus countering the propaganda they are mailing to individuals here and the presence of *Soviet Life* in our libraries.

Since the current volume of mail into the U.S.S.R. makes censorship impractical, there is little the Russians could do as a countermeasure. As discussed in Chapter 15, some good effects are produced by radio transmissions but, in general, when these stations carry unfavorable news they are jammed. In Eastern Europe especially, the satellite nations still hope for freedom — though the diplomatic courtesy of a Presidential visit to Roumania must have dimmed hopes for changes there.

There is so much that could be done on the national scene, given the motivation. As discussed in Chapter 6, both the Russian and Chinese military production is awesome, but their economy is still small when compared to that of the Free

World. The gross national product for ten of the leading industrial nations is shown in Figure 4. Also the Reds are dependent on Free World engineering for many products, which they buy and copy to eliminate costly design work.

If this country would undertake a campaign of *economic warfare* against the Communist bloc — instead of trying to mellow them with expanded trade — their economy could be sharply curtailed. In really using the strength of the American GNP, the trade between other Free World nations and the Red bloc could also be largely stopped. England periodically comes to the United States for financial assistance but is one of the

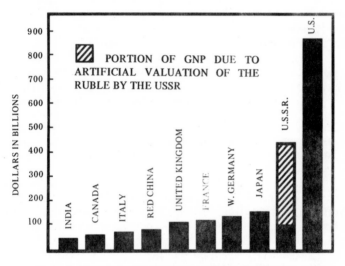

Figure 4. TEN HIGHEST GROSS NATIONAL PRODUCTS, 1968

biggest exporters to the Red World — even providing credit in many instances. Japan, who ships two to three percent of its export trade to Red China, ships some 30 percent of its exports to the U.S. Only a little economic "arm twisting" would be required to stop Japanese exports to China. Seventy percent of Red China's trade is with our allies. The lamentable state of affairs is illustrated by the following. In March 1969, following the "hostilities" between the U.S.S.R. and the Red Chinese, Soviet "civil" aircraft started making refueling stops in India while enroute to North Vietnam with heavy cargos of "merchandise" and "civilian tourists." India receives over one

billion dollars of foreign aid per year from the United States.*
By using hard realism and forcing the Communists to rely on
their own resources by establishing more efficient production
they will have to give more authority to their factory and
farm managers, thereby eroding the power structure of
the central government. But what is being done could hardly
be more helpful to the development of world communism.
In the first four months of 1969, Department of Commerce
export licenses showed $18 million of vital machine and
chemical products being shipped directly to Russia. And
normally several times the amount of the direct shipments
is filtered in through the satellite nations and European
countries. And the $37 million supplied by the U.S. to finance
the Russian Fiat plant[8] represents the sort of action that
motivated the writers to coin the term *dolsc.*

Although the trade the Reds have with the Free World
is relatively small in terms of dollars, the items they purchase
are vital to their endeavor. Columnist Henry J. Taylor remarks:

The Red bloc buys from the West only − only − what it
cannot otherwise obtain. During my 1965 trip in Iron Curtain
Europe not a single commissar denied that to me. They admit,
of course, that they are helped − often critically − when they
buy. Are we to fight communism in the world by helping it to
succeed?[9]

The only way of curbing Red trade is, through accelera-
tion of the grass roots movements for sanity, to establish
reality in Washington: but the indications are of an opposite
policy. On September 15, 1969, fourteen NATO nations and
Japan held a trade conference and announced that they were
lifting most of the remaining trade restrictions with Eastern
Europe and the U.S.S.R. To assume that the U.S. State Department had not agreed with the foregone conclusion in advance would be to question the efficiency of that organiza-

---

*Although this situation was widely reported in Europe and Asia
and Radio-Budapest announced that military equipment would be
included in the cargos, the American "free press" and radio-TV news
service cooperated with the Nixon Administration in withholding
news coverage. Further, American Officials informed various governments, notably Pakistan and Thailand, whose territory was being
violated by the over-flights, that the U.S. did not want an outcry
over the matter, as this might be domestically embarrassing.

tion. And a few months hence the State Department can justify increased Red trade because of the Russian trade carried on by the NATO allies.

Since World War II the Reds have been steadily increasing their lobby-power in Washington (except during the short-lived McCarthy period). For example, in *Washington Confidential,* a seamy expose of the Red use of dope and sex in Washington circa 1961, the veteran reporter Lee Mortimer said:

> Some members of staffs of Congressional committees (who are not investigated by the FBI) are suspected of being card holders, and some administrative assistants of left-wing liberal Senators (who actually run their bosses) are more than friendly to the evil Soviet apparatus.[11]

And in 1969, Eric F. Goldman, in reviewing his period on the White House Staff, related in his book, *The Tragedy of Lyndon Johnson* that President Johnson once remarked to a small group that it was the Russians who were behind the Vietnam War, and as Goldman reported the conversation, the President said:

> It was the Russians who stirred up the whole agitation for a suspension of the bombing of North Vietnam. He knew better, but he suspended the bombing to show the nation how foolish such a move was. The Russians were in constant touch with anti-war senators — and he named names. These senators ate lunch and went to parties at the Soviet embassy; children of their staff people dated Russians. "The Russians think up things for the senators to say. I often know before they do what their speeches are going to say." (From CIA and FBI reports.)[12]

Among those present only Mr. Goldman registered surprise — apparently the others were calloused to the situation.

As conceived by Marx, the revolutionary movement to establish communism would be a mass uprising of workers. In the intervening century, what has now developed is the use of "peoples wars" in the under-developed areas and in Europe and the United States the gradualized takeover based on demoralization of the people after the manner of Marcuse provides a slow "strangling" revolution. According to the Marcusians, the essential formula now is deception and destruction. Following Soviet guidance through some estimated 350,000 secret agents in the Free World, sympathetic college students are financed, counselled, encouraged not to reveal their real views — and instructed as to the organizations they should join.[10]

It would seem that the nine day seizure of Stanford University's Applied Electronics Laboratory — which contained classified files — by militants in April 1969, signifies the end of real security in defense laboratories, which are dependent on recruiting from the nations colleges and universities each year.

Another aspect of the influence of subtle Red propaganda in America has been the drastic limitation of civil defense appropriations by the Congress and promotion of the idea of the hopelessness of civil defense against a nuclear attack. At the same time the entire Red World is dispersing their industry and population at a maximum rate. Even North Korea is putting new industry underground and has established several underground air bases, with only runways above ground. Hangars, administrative centers, hospitals, depot facilities, and barracks are all permanently established in a distributed underground net, connected together with tunnels. A jet airplane may land on a runway and taxi into a hangar secured in the side of a mountain. Many shore defenses and costal-defense guns are also secured underground.[13]

CHAPTER 10

PRE-EMPTIVE URBAN EVACUATION

Under the prevailing international circumstances, the idea of extensive renovation of the large cities, of further concentrating the population and industries, simply denies reality.

Yet, each year brings forth more and more appropriations for costly federal bulldozer operations to rebuild urban areas which are already overly concentrated. But the cost to date, and that admitted to for future refurbishment of urban areas, might ordinarily be considered as representing a somewhat excessive but acceptable rate of expenditure — were it not for the city-hostage problem. However, the current rate of expenditure is only a modest start on that required to accomplish the complete urban transformation now being envisioned in the long range planning stages. For example, in a special feature television program entitled "America the Beautiful"[1] the figure of one trillion (one thousand billion) dollars was cited as a "ball-park" estimate for the countrywide urban transformation. A subsequent article in the *U.S. News and World Report* discussed an estimate by the National Planning Association that two trillion dollars would be required for this purpose.[2]

Well, that sort of money would pay for quite a lot of urban re-distribution, shelters and missile defenses — as required to immunize, to a large extent, the population from the threat of thermonuclear attack.

The existing major cities have grown and developed largely in an unregulated way from an essentially economic stimulus. That is, the location had certain natural advantages for trade, manufacturing, etc; and people gravitated there for employment. Moreover, this concentration was intensified on the east coast because of the prior settlement, and because of the tendency of immigrants from Europe to settle in eastern port cities. The immigrants found it advantageous to set-

147

tle in the ports at which they arrived, because often they did not have adequate funds for travel inland. Also, they could generally find a colony of old-country nationals in the port cities and settling there eased the transition problems.

These factors were all-important two-hundred, one-hundred and perhaps even fifty years ago. But consider the rapid development which this technological age is bringing about:

- Instant communication countrywide
- fast transportation everywhere
- automated factories, requiring smaller labor forces
- additional leisure time — suggesting the desirability of convenient access to the "big outdoors"
- nation-wide, and forthcoming world-wide TV, and excellent availability of consumer goods everywhere.

Under these circumstances, it is only logical to examine the need for and the desirability of continuing urban concentration.

An examination of the desirability of big cities seems to be developing from a more or less philosophical viewpoint. For example, the New York Times writer, James Reston, remarks:

> New York is giving us these days a glimpse of just how brutish and helpless life may be in the great clattering American cities in the future . . . The place is a political jungle and the general reaction of most of its citizens seems to be that nothing can be done about it. . .
>
> Here are many of the most creative and individualistic minds in the nation . . . But in the life of the city as a whole the individual seems lost . . . The cynical shrug of the shoulder has become the automatic New York reaction to most complaints about the filth of the streets, the paralysis of the traffic, or the bankruptcy of the railroads . . .
>
> Is this what Thomas Jefferson with his dread of cities was warning about? There would come a day he feared, when men and women would live in such numbers that they would become indifferent to one another's needs or cares, and the whole democratic process would then be in jeopardy . . .
>
> New York is not yet in this position but sometimes it seems to be well on its way.[3]

Jefferson's concern for the maintaining of the democratic process is perhaps the most critical factor, outside of the thermonuclear danger. For example, consider the following UPI news item, of July 17, 1965:

> NBC television commentator David Brinkley told Ohio University students Saturday that the "decline and fall of the 50

state governments will be completed within our lifetime." The movement of political power from state capitals to Washington D.C., is inevitable and unstoppable whether we like it or not, the Capitol correspondent said bluntly.

Brinkley said the power shift from local to Federal Government is caused by the problems of "large cities which are becoming unmanageable and uninhabitable. . . "

The newsman predicted however that the Federal Government would "legislate wisely."[4]

And now consider the following quotation from William L. Shirer's, *The Rise and the Fall of the Third Reich*, describing one of Hitler's first steps:

Thus within a fortnight of receiving full power . . . he had abolished the separate powers of the historic states and made them subject to the central authority of the Reich . . . The state governments are from now on merely administrative bodies of the Reich.[5]

And another news commentator, George Bordman, is concerned about the danger to the democratic process accruing from continued "federalization" and urbanization. He quotes from the book, *The Urban Complex* by Robert C. Weaver, former Secretary of the Department of Housing and Urban Development, and then comments on Mr. Weaver's proposed program:

"Originally this Nation was developed largely by offering people absolute control over wide areas to facilitate the rapid improvement of the land. Now we are trying to recover control over the way land is used so as to achieve a proper type of development of our urban areas and of the whole country. Our current objectives are to secure the open space needed for urban and rural recreation, to protect wildlife, to promote conservation, to eliminate scatterization, and, of course, to provide sites for the shelter required by our population. Thus we seek to recapture control of the use of the land, most of which the government has already given to the people. . . "

His reference to land, "most of which the government has already given to the people," is typical of the socialist-fascist point of view . . . of course bureaucrats hate scatterization. Massed populations are much easier to control . . . [6]

It is interesting to note that Weaver said he felt that the Federal land recovery program could be augmented by restricting the use of privately owned automobiles. In an address to the 60th annual convention of the National Association of Real Estate Boards, he stated:

Limiting the freedom to use automobiles and to use up land will be as important to the future of urban America as extending the freedoms to choose housing and to live in entirely new communities . . . Our children and grandchildren will have

150   BUILD THE RESOLUTE SOCIETY

to decide whether each American has an irrevocable right to drive his automobile to wherever he wants to go.[7]

Some consideration should be given to the basic philosophy in building civilization. To this end, the following excerpts from two articles by eminent writers probing the structure of civilization as related to cities are appropriate:

TO CLEAR THE DROSS*
Louis Bromfield

It is a long-established belief of historians that vast concentrations of population in cities are one of the principal factors in the weakening and eventual decline of great nations. It is not for nothing that the great preponderance of the leaders of every modern nation have come from small communities or agricultural areas.

I think it can be said with justice that the only element of the population which has made any real and permanent gain through the concentration of industries into vast cities like Detroit or Pittsburgh is that minute segment of the population which owned the earth upon which cities such as these were built. And in any decentralization of cities that is the only element of our population which would not gain in every possible sense. Followers of Henry George would hold that most of these owners of real estate are not entitled to the vast fortunes which they have acquired, not through their own initiative, brains or enterprise, but simply through the fact that they happened to own the land or purchased it, speculating or profiting upon the results of the brains, initiative, and honest hard work of more worthy citizens. Consequently the single taxers would assert they have no right to special consideration or protection. In any process of decentralization this tiny element of our nation will be the only one to protest and their outcry is scarcely worth consideration in face of the immense gains to be achieved by a more reasonable distribution of population . . .

The development of the Tennessee Valley Authority has shown the way toward one important kind of decentralization, by taking over an area larger than the British Isles and developing it simultaneously along *both* agricultural and industrial lines, under a plan by which enterprises in both fields exist side by side without the disadvantages that exist in our crowded industrial areas.

MORAL AND CULTURAL ASPECTS OF
DECENTRALIZATION**
Roy Smith

. . There is something overpowering about a great mass of humanity. The very crowds upon a city's streets suggest to the indi-

*From *Cities Are Abnormal,* by Elmer T. Peterson. Copyright 1946 by the University of Oklahoma Press.

**Ibid.

vidual his utter incompetency. His protests are so inadequate; his opinions are given such scant attention; his sufferings provoke little sympathy; his loneliness attracts little notice. If he is a work-er he feels miles removed from his employer. The likelihood of bitter class conflict increases in direct ratio to the mass of work-ers, because of the disappearance of the close personal touch be-tween employer and employe. If the metropolitan dweller is a voter, he is separated by an almost impassable distance from "the administration," particularly if the governing body is a large bureaucracy in a centralized scheme. If he is a consumer, he is separated by a great gulf from the producer, and in the logistics of a supposedly peaceful working world, his supply line is length-ened to the point where he becomes almost frantic with anxiety for government-conferred security. All this has the effect of destroying in him all sense of his importance as an individual. The only way he can hope to count is by becoming a member of some organization. This means pressure groups. It means that tenants are arrayed against landlords; employers and employes do not live in "one world."

Dr. Carl Jung, the psychologist, declares that the majority of those who suffer from mental derangements have previously lost their religious faith. There seems to be a definite connection between a vigorous religious faith and mental health, according to the testimony of other authorities equally competent. As the pressure of the city destroys faith it undermines the forces of religion. . .

With a welcome turning from a destructive to a construc-tive thesis, we may contemplate the possibilities of creating a cli-mate in the smaller cities and towns for faith, science, and cul-ture, which, in ages past, have sprouted miraculously from relig-ious backgrounds and inspirations. To say this is not to set up a special pleading for religion — it is merely to say what happens to be a fact. We all know how learning and the arts were nourished through the Dark Ages in the monasteries, and how our greatest universities were founded.

In education and the arts, some of the very best accom-plishments have come from the smaller places or rural areas in America . . .

On the whole, it would seem that the encouragement of regional cultures, in decentralized environments, would provide vast new outlets to creative arts that now seem to be "cribbed, cabined, and confined" by steel and concrete urbanism. Consid-erable emancipation may be anticipated when culture finds its way naturally among human beings who live close to the soil, and there should be a great and significant freshening of current.

All of which indicates that there are many valid argu-ments for gradually dispersing the large cities in addition to the central one advocated here: minimizing the susceptibility to an atomic attack. And, of course, other factors associated with life in the larger cities could be considered, such as: excessive commuting time, crime and violence, air pollution, slums, etc. But these are so well recognized that discussion is hardly required.

As to the process of dispersing the cities, this should be started on a limited scale at once by migration from the major urban concentrations. Especially young people and those who are retiring should consider establishing their home away from the dense urban areas. Methodical steps should be undertaken by families and industries — new positions or factory sites sought for, and moves made, with a minimum of financial inconvenience. Industries as well as families will find many advantages outside the larger cities. Housing costs are generally lower, commuting problems reduced, water supplies more adequate and less poluted, community life superior, and taxes generally less.

Industrial relocation is already underway, as shown by a recent study conducted by the *U.S. News and World Report.* U. S. factories, except for the heavy industries — steel, autos, machinery, etc. — are moving from the traditional Maine-to -Illinois "cradle of industry" to the south and west. For example, in the last ten years: New York has lost 186,000 factory jobs; Michigan, 95,000; Ohio, 58,000; and Massachusetts 43,900 jobs. On the other hand, Arizona leads in job increases — from 32,700 to 62,300, or a 91% increase in the ten year period. Florida, Mississippi, Tennessee, Arkansas, New Mexico and Utah each have had over a 25% increase in industrial jobs over the last ten years, with lesser increases in all of the western and southern states except Kansas.[8]

It is difficult to judge the influence of the nuclear threat on industrial dispersion, but it is significant to note that, according to the Office of Civil Defense most of the top 500 corporations have established some sort of alternate headquarters, including microfilm duplicates of key records. The larger banks are also establishing alternate headquarters. Industries such as U.S. Steel, American Telephone & Telegraph, Standard Oil of New Jersey, Western Electric, and Hughes Aircraft have elaborate provisions for use of alternate emergency headquarters. Probably the most elaborate of these emergency facilities is one buried deep in a mountain near Hudson, N.Y. Russell Watson, staff writer for the *Wall Street Journal,* reports on this underground facility used by a number of major U.S. corporations:

Quietly, and sometimes secretly, many of the nation's biggest companies are building alternate headquarters safe from nuclear attack. Buried underground or dispersed away from big target cities, they would be vital in keeping the economy functioning if ever   H-bombs fall.

Near here, for example, a mammoth corporate bunker lies hidden in the hollowed-out core of Iron Mountain protected from blast, heat and radiation by countless tons of rock, soil and iron ore. A 28-ton steel door in the mountainside swings open, and a visitor wanders through offices, kitchens, dormitories, communications facilities. New York, 115 miles to the south, could be incinerated but Iron Mountain offers protection against all but a near-direct hit by a multi-megaton weapon . . .

Once inside, it is hard to tell that the headquarters are underground. Walls are painted in a variety of bright colors, and vivid prints adorn them. Offices look much like those in modern skyscrapers. There is also a lounge area, a medical section complete with examining room and hospital beds, and a "music" room where easy chairs and _ red-and-gold couch invite comfortable listening to piped-in concerts.[9]

A new era in urban development is in the making. Complete cities are being planned with integrated location of residential, industrial and commercial areas. Parks, schools, transportation routes and shopping centers are all conveniently worked into the composite master plan. [10,11,12]

In the early 1960s, architects, real estate developers and city planners, in considering the multiple problems incurred in new construction, realized that the "new towns" of Europe, especially those of Finland and England, offered many unusual advantages. Among the benefits to be derived from a "completely designed" city are: reduction in (equivalent) housing cost; industrial parks dispersed throughout the city; commuting and parking problems minimized; lower taxes; streets laid out for efficient highways and bus routes; overall planning for schools, hospitals, civic buildings, libraries, golf courses, lakes and parks; special lanes for foot and bicycle traffic; and increased safety from atomic attack with opportunity for efficiently integrating community shelters into schools and other public buildings at a minimum cost. (The latter advantage not being widely appreciated as yet.)

Two of these new towns, Columbia, Md. and Reston,

Va.*, have received considerable national publicity, but actually some 70 large communities which resemble the new city concept were at least as far as the planning stage early in 1967. The following table lists thirteen of the largest of these ambitious development projects.

MAJOR 'NEW CITIES' BEING DEVELOPED IN THE U.S.

Name	Locale or Vicinity	Projected Population
Clear Lake City	Houston, Tex.	150,000
Columbia	Howard County, Md.	110,000
El Dorado Hills	Sacramento, Calif.	75,000
Irvine Ranch	Orange County, Calif.	80,000
Janss/Conejo	Ventura County, Calif.	87,000
Laguna Niguel	Orange County, Calif.	40,000
Lake Havasu	Lake Havasu, Calif.	60,000
Litchfield Park	Phoenix, Ariz.	75,000
Mission Viejo	Newport Beach, Calif.	80,000
New Orleans East	New Orleans, La.	175,000
Rancho California	between Los Angeles and San Diego	250,000
Reston	Fairfax County, Va.	75,000
Valencia	Los Angeles County, Calif.	200,000

Quite significant is the fact that these new cities are being financed from private sources rather than by federal assistance. The total cost of a typical new city, including the new industries, is estimated to be $1 billion for a city of 100,000 population. [11,14]

It is interesting to compare the cost per person for a new city resident with that for the projected nation-wide complex of refurbished major cities — costing some two tril-

---

*The change in tact which developed in the management of the Reston project resulted in part from above-the-market architectural design, which resulted in a low sales rate. The financial backers, the Gulf Oil Co., assumed control and effected a major reorganization of the project city. It is important to note, however, that the sales record for Columbia exceeded that expected, so that it was necessary to accelerate the construction program there. [13] The architecture of both towns has been criticized because of a "world's fair appearance." Especially noteworthy is the lack of harmony at Reston between buildings and the existing topography — which factor was considered so important by Frank Lloyd Wright. [11]

lion dollars. Assume that the total population of the rebuilt major cities would be some 50 million*; this would represent a cost of some $40,000 per resident. On the other hand, the cost per person in a new city would be $10,000 per person, including the cost of the associated industry. Thus, from these preliminary data, it appears that the new city approach is economically far more attractive. Naturally, extensive trade-off analyses are needed to provide exacting comparisons.

In an address to the 1967 meeting of the American Association for the Advancement of Science, Athelstan Spilhaus, president of the Franklin Institute in Philadelphia, flatly said that the old cities must go. "Without exception," he stated, "our cities are hopelessly bound by tradition, outmoded building codes, restrictive legislation, and the abortions of their historical development." He called for the construction of equally spaced smaller cities, with a maximum population of 250,000. Spilhaus, Buckminster Fuller, Gen. Bernard Schriever (U.S.A.F., Ret.), and others have formed an Experimental City Steering Committee to plan and create a pilot community incorporating their unique ideas.[16]

Aside from the economic and civil defense problems involved—where do the people want to live? A 1966 Gallup Poll found that: only 22% of the people wanted to live in the cities, 59% preferred the suburban areas and small towns, 18% the farms, and only 1% undecided.[17]

Industrial migration from the eastern seaboard and dispersion throughout the south and west, although apparently resulting from economies in labor costs, tax reduction and a lessening of transportation problems, benefits also the military-defense position. The individual can help to accelerate this dispersal by checking with his broker on the location of the physical assets of the firms in which he has ownership; acquisition of new stocks should be limited to firms with a major part of the assets in or near cities under 250,000 population. Widespread adoption of this policy for new stock acquisitions will provide a powerful leverage to the cause for dispersal. Further, for those individuals located out of the larger urban centers, each portfolio might very well include a certain percentage of holdings in local firms.

---

*At the present time, approximately 20 million people live in cities with a population over 1 million.[15] Although the major cities are generally surrounded by suburbs, these, it would seem, would not be involved in the renewal projects.

As to financing industrial dispersal, government financing would not only be undesirable from a bureaucratic-boondoggle angle, but such an undertaking might be considered as an "overt act" by the U.S.S.R. and/or Red-China — despite the fact they are both spreading out as fast as they can with their limited means. Actually, the cost involved in a gradual relocation of industry should not present a prohibitive barrier to private financing, as industry is spending on the order of $50 billion per year on plant renewal and expansion.[18]

Much study and discussion by business, financial, industrial, and local and state governmental groups are needed. Hopefully, plans can be worked out which will allow an orderly migration over the next two decades. It will be paramount to avoid upsetting the economy or causing personal and corporate hardship. The crux of the problem was recognized by the Secretary of Agriculture, Orville L. Freeman, in an address to the Symposium on Communities of Tomorrow, in December 1967. He said, in part:

> It is time to take issue with the urbanist school that believes the megalopolis is the wave of the future, with the countryside being preserved as a kind of a huge national park where urbanites rest their nerves before plunging once again into the maelstrom of the city.[19]

Additional guidelines can be taken from the civil defense and urban dispersal plans being followed in the U.S.S.R., discussed in the next chapter.

CHAPTER 11

DESIGN FOR CIVIL DEFENSE

The establishment of an adequately sheltered society involves some added financial obligations and some variations in living patterns. The costs involved, special training required, and adjustment to an occasional drill-alert represent relatively minor hardships when evaluated in terms of the benefit derived. These inconveniences may be accepted by citizens of resolute character, as Americans generally are. For certainly, this country can tolerate shelter expenses and training activity on a par with that of the U.S.S.R. Perhaps the best way to highlight the burden involved is to review the status of civil defense in the Soviet Union, having already mentioned the policy of dispersal by Red China in Chapter 6.

But, before reviewing the Russian civil defense activity, it should be stated that discretion should be used in comparing the Soviet accomplishments with those realized in the United States, under the direction of the Office of Civil Defense (OCD). This agency has organized units of the Federal, State and Local governments, and key elements of industry for various degrees of emergency. The contrast between civil defense in this country and in the U.S.S.R. results largely from the difference in the funding levels applied, and from the natural advantage accruing to the monolithic state. From 1950 *through* 1961 the United States spent $532 million of federal funds on Civil Defense.[1] To this should be added an equal amount of local funding, as an estimate. In the same period the U.S.S.R. spent some 500 million to 1.5 billion dollars *per year* for this purpose.[2] This is to say that the Soviet government spent roughly ten times more for civil defense during this period. Moreover, the control of building codes and location of new facilities realizable in a dictatorship provided supplemental advantage not suggested by the financial disparity.

The U.S.S.R. has accumulated a major advantage over

the U.S. in population dispersal, which must be considered as a civil defense measure. For example, in 1959 the ten largest Soviet cities had a combined population of 17 million people, while the ten largest U.S. cities had over 40 million. The Russians established a policy of decentralization during the 1930's in which development and relocation east of the Ural mountains was encouraged. Following World War II and the advent of the atom bomb, this policy of population dispersal was intensified. The size of cities was limited to 250,000 people and special control measures were imposed: buildings were limited to five stories, wide streets were required with sizeable greenbelts (i.e. parks, etc.) provided, and utilities were buried deeply underground. New factories and colleges were located in smaller towns, but established facilities were not relocated. Figure 5c shows a preferred city layout; an ideal city size is 100,000 to 300,000.[3]

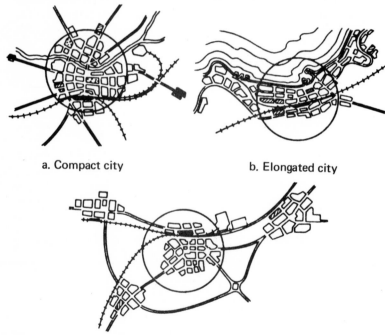

a. Compact city   b. Elongated city

c. Dispersed city with satellite towns

Figure 5.

EFFECT OF CITY DESIGN ON DAMAGE WITHIN
ENCIRCLED AREA OF DESTRUCTION.

As for shelters, the Russians had a big advantage at the outset with their elaborate subway system in Moscow. Most of these tunnels and station platforms are very deep, some being 120 feet below street level. Subway access is by means of escalators. Much of this ornately constructed system was completed prior to WW II (under the direction of German engineers). During the war hundreds of thousands of Moscovites used the tunnels for shelters from air raids. Since this time, the subway system has been extended and enlarged and an auxiliary shelter section added. About this addition, New York Times correspondent Harrison Salisbury reported in 1954, upon returning from a five year stay in the U.S.S.R.:

> . . . It (the Soviet Government) has recently completed what undoubtedly is the world's largest and safest air-raid shelter under the guise of building an addition to the Moscow subway system. The shelter is called a new "radius" of the subway. Actually it has no transport purpose, merely paralleling existing lines. But it extends under the whole of the central part of the city at a very great depth.
>
> It is possible that, along with use of existing subway links, a large percentage of Moscow's 6,000,000 population could find space underground in case of an attack.
>
> But not one word of the civil defense side of this construction has appeared in the Soviet Press.[4]

Although the Moscow press has given no indication that the subway system has been adapted as a huge shelter system, there are visible in the subways what appear to be covers to huge bulkhead-doors, which would be required for adequate shelter operation. If properly equipped, these subways could provide some 1,000,000 blast type shelter spaces—enough for 20% of the population of Moscow. Similar deep subway systems have been built in Kiev and Leningrad which would shelter like percentages of the population there.[5]

Also the basements of public buildings and apartments provide for mass sheltering; apparently specially constructed deep shelters are provided for key personnel. The following article on basement shelters in the U.S.S.R. by Leon Gouré, a prominent authority on Soviet civil defense, shows the utility of a well designed basement shelter:

BASEMENT SHELTERS*

It is said in the Soviet Union that one of the more widely available collective means of protection are the shelters, built into

---

*From *Civil Defense in the Soviet Union* by Leon Gouré, University of California Press, Berkeley, 1962. (Figure numbers changed.)

the basements of multistory apartment houses, and industrial, school, and public buildings.[28] According to a civil defense handbook, they are

"... simple and at the same time reliable means of defense. They protect [the population] from the effects of an atomic bomb explosion (at some distance from the center of the explosion), from the effect of the blast wave and of splinters resulting from the explosion of high-explosive and fragmentation bombs near the shelter, from toxic and radioactive matter, and other known means of destruction.

These shelters are located in the basement part of buildings, which is very convenient for those who seek shelter. People

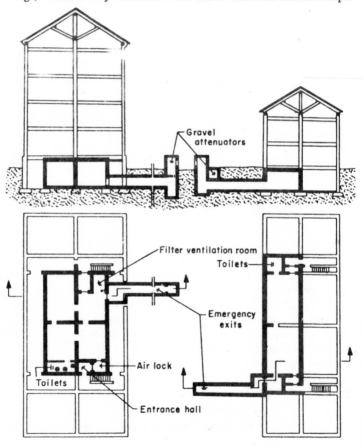

Figure 6. BASEMENT SHELTER.

---

[28] *Voennye znaniia,* 1957, No. 1, p. 24

can rapidly descend into such shelters at any time of the day when the air alert is sounded."[29]

The typical Soviet basement shelter is thus more than merely a cover against fallout. It is customarily designed to provide space for 100 to 300 persons, 150 being the recommended capacity.[30] Usually, it will occupy only a part of the basement. Ideally, the shelter will be in the center, so as to take advantage of the double shield provided by the external walls the basement (see fig. 6).[31] If this is not possible, the shelter to use one or more of the building walls. Entirely below ground, the basement shelter must have a roof of reinforced concrete long enough to withstand the blast wave of an atomic bomb "some distance" from the explosion or a direct hit on the building a high-explosive bomb, and if the building collapses, it be able to bear the weight of the debris.[32] Furthermore, the roof has to be fireproof and sufficiently insulated to shield the shelter occupants from the heat of large fires. The walls of the shelter may be made either of reinforced concrete or of several thicknesses of brick. For added strength and safety, the shelter is compartmented by a number of bearing walls of concrete or brick, and the roof is further supported by steel or ferroconcrete beams or plates.[33] Depending on the construction material used and the thickness of the roofs and walls, the basement shelter is designed to withstand a blast pressure of 10-100 psi.[34] Most of them are likely to be built to survive in the lower range of blast pressure.

To render them proof against radioactive, chemical, and bacteriological agents, the entrances to the basement shelter are each protected by double steel doors of the bulkhead type, which are edged with rubber to make them fully airtight.[35] The filter ventilation unit is located in a separate room inside the shelter to avoid endangering the occupants if it becomes contaminated by radioactive or toxic agents.[36] Some shelters have an exhaust

---

[29]Miroshnikov and Zapolskii, *op cit.*, pp. 134-135.

[30]*Ibid.*, p. 139; Baratov, *op cit.*, p. 134; Gvozdev and Iakovkin, *op. cit.*, p. 173.

[31]*Voennye znaniia*, 1957, No. 1, p. 24; Miroshnikov and Zapolskii *op. cit.*, p. 135; Supron and Sverev, *op cit.*, p. 306.

[32]Miroshnikov and Zapolskii, *op. cit.*, p. 136.

[33]Gouré, *Symposium*, p. 108.

[34]*Ibid.*, Doyle, *op. cit.*, p. A-1079

[35]*Voennye znaniia*, 1957, No. 1, pp. 24-25; Supron and Zverev, *op. cit.*, p. 303; Lebedeva, *op. cit.*, p. 18; I. A. Koniushenko and A. M. Miasnenko (eds.), *Bakteriologicheskoe oruzhie i mery zaschity ot nego* (Bacteriological Weapons and Means of Defense Against Them), DOSAAF, Moscow, 1959, p. 7

[36]Supron and Zverev, *op. cit.*, p. 304; Miroshnikov and Zapolskii, *op. cit.*, p. 140; Miroshnikov, *op cit.*, p. 24.

system as well. The required emergency exit (see fig. 7) consists of a tunnel, about half as long as the building is high, which usually terminates in a concrete block above ground, with one or more openings covered by louvered doors or plates; occasionally, the tunnel merely leads into a manhole.[37] According to the manuals, all exits are equipped with gravel blast attenuators. Basement shelters in adjoining buildings may be connected by underground passages, which also serve as emergency exits. The exits are usually in the backyards of the buildings or in adjoining gardens.[38]

For long-term occupancy the shelters are equipped with water, toilets, special containers for drinking water, heat, electric light and power, storage batteries, double-decker bunks, telephones, radio receivers, medical supplies, and fire-fighting and digging apparatus, and they may also be provided with bottled oxygen.[39]

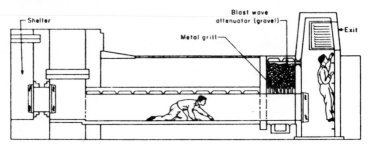

Figure 7. SHELTER EMERGENCY EXIT.

The type of basement shelter described here is usually mentioned in connection with new construction, rather than with respect to buildings erected before World War II. Little is said about adapting these older basements, or World War II shelters, to modern requirements. The Soviets admit that the older facilities, which were adequate protection against conventional weapons, would not be effective against nuclear weapons.

Civil defense publications do state that some older basements with particularly strong cover — especially vaulted roofs — lend themselves to being turned into shelters.[40] It is said also

[38]Miroshnikov and Zapolskii, *op. cit.,* p. 137; *Voennye znaniia,* 1957, No. 1, p. 24.
[39]Gvozdev and Iakovkin, *op. cit.,* pp. 170-171; Miroshnikov and Zapolskii, *op. cit.,* p. 143; *Umppt,* p. 33; Miroshnikov, *op. cit.,* p. 26.
[40]*Voennye znaniia,* 1958, No. 9, p. 29.

that basements with strong roofs can be reinforced and made fire-proof, and that window wells may be filled and sealed. One recommendation is to strengthen the roof with reinforced concrete slabs resting on steel beams and supported by concrete, brick, or wooden supports (see fig. 8).[41] To improve the shelter's fire and heat resistance, and as an additional shield against radiation, the roof may be covered with a foot-deep layer of sand.[42] An emergency escape tunnel and exit would have to be added, and blast and sealing doors, filter ventilation facilities, and other essential equipment would need to be installed.

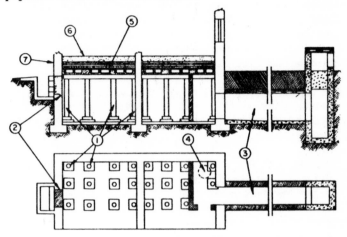

1. Posts (dia = 20 cm)
2. Covered windows
3. Emergency tunnel
4. Filter-ventilation unit
5. Wooden boards to guard against splinters
6. Layer of earth (30 cm) to reduce instant radiation
7. Concrete slab

Figure 8. ADAPTATION OF A CELLAR TO SERVE AS A SHELTER.

There seem to be no individual family shelters in the cities, although in the rural areas it is quite possible that many of the deep farmhouse basement-cellars have been adapted for shelter use.[5]

Although the Soviets try to create the impression abroad that they are without shelters and are not about to start a shelter program, travelers in the U.S.S.R. have observed shelters from the Baltic Sea to Central Asia, and from the Gulf of

---

[41] Supron and Zverev, *op. cit.*, p. 313; Miroshnikov and Zapolskii, *op. cit.*, p. 136; Moskalev *et al.*, *op. cit.*, p. 65.
[42] Supron and Zverev, *op cit.*, p. 313.

Finland to the Black Sea.[6] And starting in the early 1950's all new building plans for housing and factory construction were reviewed by civil defense to insure inclusion of adequate shelters. Since 1954 four separate courses in civil defense have been organized, ranging from 10 to 20 hours each. Every adult was requested to take these courses and it is estimated that 50 to 100 million people did. Since 1958, elaborate city-evacuation plans have been organized for the larger cities — to allow evacuation within a few hours notice. Evacuees are to bring extra clothing and their own food — enough for several days— although there are apparently food stockpiles established at the staging areas some fifty miles outside of the cities. Perhaps it is anticipated that an attack might develop from a slowly developing crisis, or that there is a good likelihood that they otherwise might have some advance warning. Although gas masks (to provide protection against chemical and bacteriological attack) have not been issued, the use of these devices was covered in the training courses. Since the cost of these devices is only a few dollars, it is quite possible that they have been stockpiled for mass distribution. Elaborate decontamination procedures have been established and some consideration has been given to the sheltering of animals.[7]

The following news item in the May 16, 1961, *New York Times* effectively summarizes the above discussion on Soviet shelters.

> Washington, May 16 (UPI) — The Nation's Civil Defense Chief said today a secret report indicated that the Soviet Union was building enough shelters to protect the great majority of its population from fallout in the event of a nuclear war.
>
> Frank B. Ellis, director of the Office of Civil and Defense Mobilization, told a House appropriations sub-committee in testimony published today the study showed Russia was spending from $500,000,000 to 1.5 billion a year on shelters.
>
> Mr. Ellis asked for $2,000,000 to provide shelters in twenty-nine Federal buildings and $6,200,000 to include shelters in planned buildings. He said he hoped the project would encourage Americans to build their own.
>
> Congress rejected a similar request last year and Mr. Ellis ran into hostile questioning in renewing the appeal.[8]

These preparations have put the U.S.S.R. considerably ahead of the United States in the area of civil defense, since they have been equipping new construction with both blast and fallout shelters — whereas we have largely limited our efforts to identifying existing buildings which are suitable for or may be adapted to use as fallout shelters. However, the Soviet shelters unquestionably would not be comparable to

hat this country could provide, if it undertook an all-out
1elter program — as will now be proposed.

The Eighty-First Congress, recognizing the importance
nd urgency of a national shelter program, promptly "dis-
osed" of the problem by establishing the first civil defense
lan, on December 1, 1950. Under this plan the various
tates were "authorized" to provide the appropriate shelters
or their communities. Since that time, the Congress has,
owever, supported Federal financial assistance to the states,
aving supplied much of the funding requested by various
dministrations to support local Civil Defense activity.

The provision of blast and fallout shelters for the entire
opulation of the country at minimum cost will certainly re-
uire multiple use of the shelter space. Facilities that are to
e used in everyday life should be designed, located and there-
ore paid for at the local level. There have been several in-
tances of this type of dual-use construction already provided.
'or example, the Robert H. Goddard High School recently
ompleted in Roswell, New Mexico, is normally occupied by
50 students, but it can also be used as a fallout shelter for
,500 people. Although most of the classrooms are 15 ft.
nderground, there has been no difficulty from absence of
vindows. (After all, where are the windows in supermarkets,
owling alleys and the like? Also many modern office build-
ngs and factories are windowless.) One advantage noted in
his type of construction is the wonderfully low noise level
n the classrooms — so often penetrated by the shrill grind
f traffic noises. This school is completely equipped with
mergency power, water, oxygen, food and other facilities
equired for shelter operation. It was built entirely from local
unds and cost approximately $10.50 per square foot, which
s rather a minimal value for school construction. The
dditional cost of the shelter facilities and construction was
130,000. For a shelter capacity of 6,500 people this repre-
ents a cost of $20.00 per shelteree. The radiation protection
actor is over 600, which is rather good protection.[9,10]

Thus, it does seem within the reach of local communities
o finance shelter construction for multiple use facilities. The
'ederal Government in providing multiple use shelters can
nly function as sort of a financial middleman. The local gov-
rnmental units can exercise enough responsibility, initiative
nd foresight to fully provide for local needs. *Local financing
neans local control. Federal financing means Federal control
f choice of building sites, design of multiple use facilities,*

condemnation of existing structures for shelter construction, establishment of some low-universal protection factor*, control of the number of shelter spaces allowable to each community, establishing distances between sites, providing some minimal food stock, etc.

Performance of the Federal Government in the area of urban renewal may be taken as indicative of Federal capability. Many cities have found the "Federal bulldozer" coming to their town to be a torturous blessing. For example, in Washington, D.C., thousands of low and middle income Negroes were forced to leave their homes to make way for plush high rise apartments and town houses which, when completed, rented upward from $130 a month per room; or in California, in the period from 1950-60, 126,000 houses were torn down under the Federal program (of which 25,000 were in good condition) and only 30,000 replacement units provided — and they were so posh that only a few of those displaced could afford them.[11] This is but one sample of the Federal record on a routine, non-emergency and small program (in comparison to a massive shelter system). Moreover, during eight years of this period, the urban renewal program was under the direction of a Republican administration. The problem is simply not one of Federal *mismanagement*, but one of Federal *management.* Characteristically, so many fixed rules and procedures have to be followed that local problems can never be adequately recognized.

The recognition of the nature of Federal management was shown by voters in: Salt Lake City, Utah, Waukegan, Ill., St. Petersburg, Fla., Spokane, Wash., and other cities who have rejected Federal funds for urban renewal and civic construction because of the controls and entanglements involved.[12]

It is proposed, therefore, that a nationwide system of shelters be built from state and local funds and that the shelters be designed for multiple usage, in accordance with local needs, desires and wisdom. This would allow local groups to discuss, debate, review plans for models of their own facilities, and finally make choices — by voting, if desired. As for financing, shelter construction would cost more with Federal financing; actually, funds collected from the taxpayers by the local governments may be deducted on Federal income-tax

---

*Standards for local Emergency Defense Centers were gradually lowered from 1,000 to 40.

returns. In other words, given equal construction cost (which is not the case since Federal construction would undoubtably provide different shelters than local), it would cost the taxpayer less in total taxes for shelter construction by local government units than from the Federal Government. Moreover, if it is desired to keep as much of the local autonomy as is now left, then local governments should not become obligated more by further dependence on Federal funds — the expenditure of which generally involves certain "standards."

Now this is not at all an unworkable approach. The Orange County Civil Defense organization at Santa Ana, California, operates almost entirely from local funds. The only assistance they receive from Federal funds is a few hundred dollars a year for one-half of the cost of the stand-by-for-alert telephone lines. Operating under this basis, their shelter identification program compares favorably with the national overage, as generally operated on the cost-shared basis with the Office of Civil Defense.

But cost is not an overwhelming problem in providing shelters, especially if the shelter system is designed for efficient dual use — even permitting two shelter spaces for those who work at a distance from their home area. First, unlike most military weapon systems, shelters do not quickly become obsolete. Well built shelters should have a life of 40 to 50 years. This would allow financing from long term bonds, thus spreading the cost over the useful life of the facilities.*

Cities under 50,000 in population normally should need only fallout shelters, unless located near a military target area of some type. The additional protection of a blast shelter in cities from 50,000 to 250,000 is desirable, although such a city may not be a high priority target. Cities with a population over 250,000 definitely need blast shelters. A list of 303 potential city-military targets is given in Chapter 7.

The degree of protection obtainable in a blast shelter

---

*A very useful book on shelters has been written by Dr. Thomas Martin, Dean of the College of Engineering of the University of Arizona, and Research Specialist Donald C. Latham of the Martin Co. This book, entitled *Strategy for Survival*,[1] is an excellent source of practical and theoretical information. It also has an extensive bibliography list.

A free booklet, PL-84 "Atomic Energy and Civil Defense," is available from the Government Printing Office.

The International Civil Defense Society, P.O. Box 124, Geneva, Switzerland publishes a monthly bulletin (in English, French, and German) which is an excellent source of information.

in terms of ground range (from the point directly under the burst) is a function of the depth of the shelter and the strength of construction. For protection immediately under a 10 megaton ground burst the shelter would have to be over 1,000 ft. deep. That certainly would not be suitable for a multiple-use facility, as we would think of it. Moreover, the access time required from the surface would be excessive. Therefore, a compromise depth of 100 feet or so should be accepted. This is in the order of depth that would be reasonable for a deep subway system. It is interesting to note that during his visit to the U.S. in 1959, the First Soviet Deputy Premier F. Kozlov, recommended to Governor Rockefeller that deep subways be provided for shelter protection of New York City.[13]

Of course, a similar degree of protection could be obtained from shelter construction other than subways, placed at the same depth and designed with equal strength. Also, by not using a subway shelter, the complexity of the button-up doors to segment the subway into separate "cubicles" could be avoided. But there is an outstanding strategic advantage in the subway type of system. Also there are several practical advantages.

It is quite possible that if an exchange should occur it would develop from some crisis, such as the Cuban missile crisis in October 1962. In such an event, the President would merely have to push the shelter-alert button. Everyone would then take shelter, *and those entering the subway — now protected from anything except an overhead hit — would now start walking through the shelter-subway to the perimeter of the city.* Each "cubicle" should be joined with a blast-proof revolving door of some type. And extra shelter space should be provided in the suburbs of the city to provide for workers during non-working hours. Further, if the attack were without any type of indication or warning, there is a fair possibility that many of the cities would be left for bomber attack (a few hours later) and that the first attack, by missiles, would be directed on the missile and SAC bases. In this case also, those people in the center of the cities would have an opportunity to evacuate in advance of the attack.

The subway would seem to provide the best multiple use facility for a large city. It probably will have a struggling bus transportation system and a growing auto traffic problem. A new subway with well laid out lines would relieve traffic congestion and provide rapid transportation to the uburbs. Secondly, the subway has the advantage of being continually in public use, so that there is never any confusion as to *where* the nearest entrance is. Thirdly, the subway shelter may be advantageously used to cope with the fire storm problem.* Shelters designed to withstand a fire storm are cut off from overhead sources of air, which creates a humidity and temperature control problem.

With the tunnel shelter, after the blast, the damaged sections are identified by intercommunication links and doors between the intact cells are re-opened. This will allow the pulling in of air from outside the fire storm area with huge fans

---

*Recent analysis by civil defense authorities of the fire storms in Germany and Japan during WW II has shown that only the older, eastern cities in the United States with a "building density" (percentage of ground area that is covered by buildings) would support a fire storm following a nuclear attack.[14] In most of the larger cities provision for the possibility of a fire storm might very well be included, however. To obtain this protection, overhead air intakes in the center sections of the cities must be disallowed.

Clorate candles and lithium hydroxide can be used to supply oxygen and absorb carbon dioxide, respectively, but provision must be included for disposing of the cumulative body heat and humidity. Although air conditioning would do this effectively, it is expensive and an adequate source of emergency power must be provided.

On the subject of fire storms it should be mentioned that although the fire storm is a terribly real threat — and certainly one of *the* justifying reasons for a system of self-sustaining blast, as opposed to fallout shelters, there has been considerable hysteria on the subject of fire storms issuing from "pacifist" scientific groups, in which the WW II firestorm at Dresden is cited as the prime example. The figure of 250,000 deaths there, frequently cited by the ban-the-shelters-too scientist, was that issued by Dr. Goebbles. See the "Apocalypse at Dresden," *Esquire,* November, 1963.

No scientist denies the reality of the fire storm danger. What has not been brought into public consciousness, is the opposition of the many dolsc-scientists to shelters. As the blast shelter question comes into public discussion — as seemingly it must — they will most likely condemn it even more heartily than they have the various proposed fallout shelter programs. For example, by a speech in the Tivoli Concert Hall in Copenhagen, on January 3, 1964, Linus Pauling was able to contribute to the influence against a vote on some Civil Defense funds for Denmark, and these credits were not pr ided.[15] This, despite the fact that a country the size and geographical location of Denmark would not expect a nuclear attack. Further, its relative distance from potential target cities in Germany, France and England would allow ample time for the people to enter the fallout shelters before windborne fallout would arrive. Blast shelters would not be required.

to supply fresh air, cooling and humidity control. These fans would also be equipped with chemical and bacteriological filters. They would be operated from emergency power, but less power would be required than in the case of air conditioning equipment. The shelterees could gradually walk to the perimeter of the damage area, where surface areas could be decontaminated more quickly.

And lastly, one aspect of the subway-tunnel system which should be considered is the possibility of the return of the electric auto.[16,17] Current research on fuel cells and new light weight batteries may again make the electric car competitive with the gasoline-guzzler. The advent of a practical electric auto would allow adjacent channels of the subway-shelter tunnels to be used for auto traffic.

It has been found in a few test cases in the U.S. that the public prefers commuting via a modern electric-railway with close-spaced, fast schedules to driving in a personal auto.[18] No doubt, the improved service provided in these cases could be considerably increased — given a widespread development program, which seems to be coming along anyhow because of the auto traffic problems.

In Montreal, Canada, a much more significant test of the potential for subways has been made. Calling on the many modern architectural and engineering techniques available, Montreal Mayor Jean Drapeau guided a design team toward the creation of a new subway system using small sleek cars with airline styling. High-level lighting and tasteful styling was used to produce bright and pleasant stations. In reviewing the opening, *Fortune* reported:

> Montreal opened its Metro, which cost $213,700,000, last October. The system was an immediate hit. Passenger traffic is about 50 percent higher than expected. Instead of two rush hours a day, the system has four. Service is so swift that many businessmen are relaxing back to a fine old European custom: going home for lunch. U.S. politicians might note than Drapeau ran for re-election last fall. He pulled a record 94 percent of the vote.[19]

In summary, the advantages of the subway type of dual-use shelter are:

- Rapid city evacuation during a crisis period while being sheltered.
- Entrances are conveniently located.
- Location of entrances are well known.
- Uniquely adaptable to cope with the fire storm problem.

The essential factors favoring the use of rapid mass transportation, such as subways, are:[20]

- With the advent of local bus/auto transportation to the rapid transit stations, suburban station spacing may be increased from one mile (formerly considered a maximum) to five miles, which increases speed of service.
- During rush-hour peaks, one rapid transit track can carry 2,200 passengers per hour; eighteen freeway auto lanes are required to carry a comparable number of commuters.
- Typical speed of rapid transit is 57 miles per hour, as compared to some 30 miles per hour for the auto traveling on the freeways during the rush period.
- Schedules for rapid transit are regular and not affected by traffic accidents or tie-ups.
- Considering the construction cost of the freeway vs. rapid transit, the latter does five times the work (passengers carried) at one-fourth the cost.
- Lower construction costs mean lower taxes.
- Limitation of commuting by auto is perhaps the best way of controlling smog.
- Time spent on high speed transit may be used for light reading, etc.

As to the smaller cities in the 50,000 to 250,000 population range, a number of alternatives are feasible — perhaps even including subways, bearing in mind that either blast or fallout shelters may be selected in these areas. Types of primary use structures, other than subways, might include: city auditoriums, fire stations, libraries, convention centers, hospitals, schools, warehouses, grocery stores, bowling alleys, theaters, parking lots, light industries, etc. These facilities can be built by the municipalities and leased to various business and industrial firms. Or, privately constructed shelters, normally used for business purposes, can be given a reduced tax rate. On the other hand, "penalty" taxes could be placed (on larger firms) which did not provide shelter spaces for employees during working hours — thus forcing the municipality (or state) to provide for the working-hours shelter requirement.

There is a rapidly increasing trend for the financing of construction of industrial plants by means of tax-free bonds. The local governments issuing these industrial-aid bonds are in a unique position to arrange for provision of shelters in new plants. In 1967, some $700 million of these tax-free bonds were issued, as compared to approximately $10 million in 1957.[21]

For the towns and cities under 50,000 population the fallout shelter alone should suffice in most cases. Large community type fallout shelters should be placed in the center of town and numerous smaller shelters provided in the suburbs. Full use should be made of basements of stores, factories, apartment buildings, schools, etc.

In the country family style shelters should be provided in the home for those homesites located more than a few minutes drive from the nearest community shelter. Family shelters can be just as effective as the larger community shelter, even if built into the corner of a basement, but the planning must be carefully done and the shelter properly equipped. Adequate guidance should be obtained from local Civil Defense officials.

Certainly, some farmers will want to shelter and care for their animals. Some information has been published on the care and protection of animals from fallout.[22] Adjoining family-type shelters are needed for those caring for the animals.

One of the major problems with an extensive shelter system maintained over many years is the maintenance of the necessary food supply. Specially packed and staple food can be stored for a two to five year period, but thereafter must be replaced. One estimate shows that this replacement would cost, on the average, $10 to $20 per person per year.[23] For the home shelter food storage is not a serious problem as the shelter area can be used for storage of normally used staple foods and constant replacement be provided. It would seem that for the community shelters the problem could be solved in a large-scale application of the home-shelter plan.

In the smaller towns and cities the community shelters could be combined with, or located under, grocery stores. This would provide a constant turnover of a potential emergency food supply. In the larger cities the same approach could be used and extended by tying in grocery warehouses with the subway shelters.

In the main, *the essential factor would be resolute community action. Forthright action, as judged appropriate in each community, is urgently needed — to provide shelters for every American, whether at home, at work, at school, or wherever.*

Having outlined very briefly a proposed shelter program a cost estimate should now, normally, be presented. But unfortunately, the multiple use shelter has not received sufficient examination to date to allow doing so. Hopefully, this subject may receive more extensive treatment as a part of the established Civil Defense operations. However, fairly good information is available on the cost of special purpose shelters. These data will be presented to illustrate the magnitude of the problem, and to point up the need for expanded analysis of the various possibilities for multiple use shelters — which, though functionally superior (in the case of the subway), should cost considerably less.

COST OF SINGLE USE SHELTERS PER SPACE[24,25]

Shelter Capacity	Class I (100 psi 10,000 pf)	Class II (50 psi 200 pf)	Class III (10 psi 100 pf)	Class IV (Present CD shelter, pf 40, min.)
100 space	$300	$250	$200	$10, average
1,000 space	$175	$140	$110	

It is interesting to note that the Goddard High School provided fallout protection with a protection factor of 600 at a cost of $20 per space (blast data not available, but protection probably good).

For a comparative view it may be added that in the following countries the inclusion of fallout shelters in new construction of multiple family units is obligatory: Denmark, Finland, the Netherlands, Norway, Switzerland and Sweden.[26] Sweden also has a program for deep blast shelters for portions of the population and industry. Recently, West Germany has also established a similar program calling for shelters in basements of new constructions.

To facilitate the use of a nationwide shelter system, a complementary alarm system is required. Such a system is under development. It will operate by making use of all (electrically operated) radio and TV receivers. A "black box" is to be installed on each set which will automatically turn on the radio or TV; warnings would be broadcast on all channels.

Although it is possible that missiles could be launched from submarines to attack coastal cities without allowing a few minutes warning, as with ICBMs, this is unlikely — except in the special case of the small, limited attack. The optimum way to launch an all-out attack is to fire the ICBMs and the sub-launched missiles so that they would all impact at the same time on the target country. This would require that the offense get its long range ICBMs out of the silos first. The submarine-based missiles would be fired minutes later.* Thus it seems that at least a fifteen minute warning could be expected. This should be adequate to shelter a well trained society. The American people can respond to defense organization if the issues are put squarely to them. By way of illustration, the Milwaukee Director of Civil Defense, Brig. Gen. D. C. Carleton (USA, Ret.), reported that Milwaukee had a special public-participation exercise. In this exercise the public had been asked to get off the street and take cover when the sirens blew. In the question and answer period following an address discussing this operation, Gen. Carleton remarked:

> I watched the exercise from a helicopter over the city and it was quite an amazing sight. This was the first time we tried it and everybody thought we would fall on our faces. But that is exactly what prompted me to say in my talk that the reaction of the public is in great proportion to the effort you make to tell them what to do. When the signal went off, the streets were cleared as by magic. Within 30 or 40 seconds you could have shot a cannon up Wisconsin Ave. and you wouldn't have hit a thing. Everything pulled off the streets. The people evacuated the cars and busses and what not, and got indoors.[27]

By making proper long-range plans we can greatly simplify the Civil Defense problems. But those plans require action by resolute citizens — the display of real character — in working for changes in building codes, planning new community facilities, developing new cities and towns, providing tax incentives, etc.

In some cases it may be desirable for areas in which rapid population growth has been experienced to limit or control growth by not providing new freeways, encouraging new industries, and developing additional water resources. For example, limitation of growth has been advocated for California by the Population Reference Bureau because of increasing difficulty with smog, water, and the problems associated with a projected population of 1.5 billion for the state in 2066.[28]

Does the concept of transforming the United States into a sheltered, distributed society seem to be outside the limits of feasibility? In considering this same problem, following World War II, Sweden elected a policy of *survival without surrender* and established a vigorous shelter program. And,

---

*Simultaneous launch of all missiles would give an additional warning time of about five minutes to U.S. ICBM & SAC bases.

despite some reduction in productivity by fractional social-ization, Sweden has provided fallout and blast shelters for over 30% of the population. Civil Defense activity is placed on a par with military duty by also conscripting men for CD billets. Over one-half of Sweden's electrical power stations, both hydro-electric and atomic, are in blast-hardened shelters. There are many factories located in deep-rock shelters, blasted out of the mountains. The development of these factories was started during WW II, and since then many new factories have been "dug" — it having been found that the cost is only about 10% above conventional above-ground construction.[29],[30] The following from Reference (29) explains briefly how this plan was financed:

> Most of the larger rock constructions have been made immediately available for peacetime uses such as garages, warehouses, schools, public assembly halls, or recreational centers. Income from rent thus helps amortize the capital expended.

Although only limited information on military facilities is available, by 1953 two caves opening into North Sea inlets had been blasted out of solid rock to house destroyers of 2,600 tons, as well as submarines and other navy units. At that time it was said that the entire navy would be provided with similar shelters. Numerous shelter-hangers for aircraft have also been established; in many instances, these are designed so that the jet fighters can complete three quarters of their take-off runs on runways inside the caves.[31]

It should be mentioned that, depending on the time of year of an attack, it is possible that an entire crop of the U.S. could be lost (or the crops of the entire Northern Hemisphere, for that matter). Also, regardless of the time of the attack, most of the domestic and wild animals would be lost. This points up the need for adequate food storage and additional research on a vegetarian diet suitable for a post-attack recovery period.

As for the strontium-90 problem, there are many things that would be helpful as advance measures. And many of the corrective measures could be provided for after the nuclear exchange, providing that there was sufficient industry intact to supply the needed equipment, since the adverse effect from strontium-90 is of a slow, cumulative nature. For example, standby ion-exchangers could be installed in city water supplies[31] and dairies,[32] but as pointed out in Chapter 7, the strontium-90 problem should be considered only as a potential cause for adding fractionally to the problem.

There has been considerable public discussion about the anti-ballistic missile (ABM) for the defense of the U.S. This weapon defense system has been sponsored by the Army, favored by the Congress, and has been considered nervously by the Department of Defense for many years – in what have may very well have been considered by the outsider as a period of indefinite procrastination. The influence on the deployment of the ABM by the Soviet Union, effected by the Department of Defense, is discussed in the next chapter.

Since the ABM system cannot be expected to be more than 70-80% successful, it is essential to have shelters to supplement the protection provided by the interceptor missiles. *Further, shelters are absolutely essential to prevent the negation of the ABM system by an up-wind ground burst (out of range of the ABM interceptors), which would inundate the area being protected by the missile system with intense fallout.* Basically, blast and fallout shelters are for the protection of the populace; the ABM supports this function, and also minimizes property damage.

The objective has been to consider the techniques for survival – and thereby minimize likelihood of attack, on a society so sheltered and equipped as to make such an attack grimly unattractive from a hard military viewpoint. *That is to say, the most effective way of minimizing danger – or damage – to America from an armageddon is by making adequate preparations for that possibility.*

Passive defense alone, including fallout and blast shelters, city evacuation plans, etc. could virtually shift the international power balance in favor of the U.S. And were it not for the widespread restrictions imposed on strategic planning by *dolsc* politicans in Washington, the entire Red military scare could be eliminated. For example, as discussed in the next chapter, satellite weapon systems could provide the U.S. with orbital weapons which are secure from surprise attack. It would take weeks to neutralize defense or offense weapon systems in space, constantly ready for target assignment. The Communist psychological warfare club over the U.S. would then be eliminated, as ICBMs became obsolete with the advent of space weapons. The armageddon scenario would be shifted – IF INDEED THE RED WORLD WERE TO CONTINUE ITS EXISTENCE, THROUGH FREE-WORLD ECONOMIC SUPPORT – FROM A 30 MINUTE EXCHANGE AGAINST POPULATION CENTERS TO A PROTRACTED CONTEST TO ELIMINATE OPPOSING WEAPONS IN SPACE.

CHAPTER 12

THE DEFENSE DILEMMA – A MUTED TRUMPET

On November 28, 1967, the news broke that McNamara was being "promoted" to a relatively obscure position as head of the World Bank. In reporting this event, *Newsweek* asked the question of why, and then proceeded to answer it:

.... Had the Defense Secretary been discarded as a political liability in the '68 Presidential campaign? Was the switch the first augury of a major Cabinet re-shuffle to give a beleaguered Administration a new look? What kind of successor would Mr. Johnson tap to run the Pentagon?

In the end, it was Vietnam – "McNamara's War," as some dissenters once dubbed it – that proved Super Mac fallible after all. *The cold logic and obdurate rationalism that made him a superb crisis manager were insufficient to give him mastery of that ultimate irrationality, war itself.* Time and again, his carefully analyzed intelligence reports proved faulty, his carefully calculated predictions embarrassingly wide of the mark.[1]

In other words McNamara was fired because he made a mess of the war in Vietnam and even *Newsweek,* though a leading liberal publication, could not gloss over the issue. Since American survival in the 1970's is problematical – because of McNamara's role as Secretary of Defense – it is important to review his policies.

Although various new policies may now be introduced into DOD, the *seven year rule* will still apply, in the main. This "rule" states that seven years are required to provide a major new weapon system, when the time from initial concept to field deployment is considered. During McNamara's seven years in office, there were relatively few new weapon systems initiated and many of those started under the Eisenhower Administration were cancelled in a summary manner.

Among the major arms and weapon systems cutbacks, cancellations, demobilization of essential military bases, premature retirement of important weapon systems and slashing of essential developments initiated by the Eisenhower Administration by McNamara were:

- B-70 Bomber – Cancellation of production of this long range aircraft left the U.S. without a successor to the B-52 bomber. One of the justifications for the cancellation was the existence of the SKYBOLT missile being developed for the B-52's.
- SKYBOLT – Cancellation of this 1,000-mile range nuclear tipped missile for the B-52's and the British Airforce produced an international crisis because, in effect, Britian was reduced to a second class power as a result.
- SAINT – An advanced loiter type ABM. The U.S.S.R. is now reported to be testing this type of ABM as a preliminary step to deployment *of what would be their third generation ABM.*
- DYNA-SOAR – This cancellation was calculated to keep the U.S. Military out of space – regardless of consequences.
- LASV (PLUTO) – Completion of this low-altitude, nuclear-powered missile would have provided insurance against the U.S. becoming a second-rate power *vis-a-vis* the U.S.S.R. in the 1970's.
- MOBILE MINUTEMAN and MRBM – In a typical McNamara stratagem the mobile MINUTEMAN was cancelled and the mobile medium range ballistic missile was set up as a paper study – then later cancelled.
- European SAC Bases – The United States had a ring of B-47 bases around the borders of the U.S.S.R. The B-47 was retired and most of the bases closed.
- DAVEY CROCKETT – Removal of these low-yield field weapons from the U.S. Army in Germany took away the only real deterrent they had against the Red Army.
- ABM – Early versions of the ABM system were deftly kept in the development stage and out of production by periodically increasing performance requirements.
- Nuclear Fleet – Construction of vitally needed nuclear-powered submarines and aircraft carriers was stopped and the anti-submarine warfare program was drastically curtailed.
- Bases – Closing of many important shipyards and military bases caused months of delays in supplies for Vietnam, when the action started.

It is hardly necessary to include a detailed discussion of the F-111 (TFX) boondoggle, in which McNamara tried to build a "universal" airplane and wound up with a flying Edsel. Also, the Bay of Pigs, the Berlin Wall, the loss of Laos, etc. should be left, primarily, to the State Department and the President.

As a result of the McNamara cutbacks in defense, the growing influence of the dolsc-dominated peace-at-any-price-in-Vietnam movement, the deterioration of NATO, continued cutbacks in defense under the Nixon Administration, and the rapid growth of Soviet military power, on the other hand, the United States is started on the way to becoming a second rate power.

McNamara and his top aides were very adept at misleading the public without exactly lying. McNamara also suppressed much intelligence data which, if generally known, would have discredited his cutbacks and defense restrictions. For example, he suppressed intelligence data on the Soviet deployment of the SS-9 ICBM's and when the succeeding Secretary of Defense, Melvin Laird, had to expose the looming threat in testimony to the Senate in support of the ABM, Laird's statements were given skeptical reception.[2]

One of the surprising defense policy innovations introduced by the incoming Kennedy Administration, which had campaigned on an (imaginary) missile gap, was the introduction of the detente concept. Although the detente principle has a certain appeal from a basis of logic, those advocating this policy have not supported the validity of logic in this application. Classical philosophers held that, in relation to each other, *sovereigns were in a state of nature*. And who can support the existence of an improvement over this situation in the present era? The noted French political scientist, Raymond Arrow, has commented at some length on the American policies in his book, *The Great Debate*. Some of the key points he makes are:

> American analysts have barely touched upon the conditions under which a nation might avail itself of its "conventional sword" in order to advance under the protection of the "thermonuclear shield" . . .

> The American analysts, while regarding thermonuclear war as possible, have given little thought to conditions under which such a war would *intentionally* be unleashed. They have examined various sets of circumstances that might lead to war without its being deliberately wanted by either of the principals, but they have always assumed a common interest on the part of both Russia and the United States to avert fighting a war unto death . . .

The entire American theory is based on rationality; it attempts to reconstruct the manner in which a strategist would behave if, like his hypothetical counterpart in economic theory, he were both intelligent and well-informed. But how many real-life chiefs of state resemble this idealized portrait? How many of them are always able to abide by the dictates of reason, at least reason defined by the theoreticians?

. . . Countries in possession of nuclear weapons may be at the mercy of military juntas, revolutionaries, or adventurers, and once a truly irresponsible head of government joins in the game, the worst may come to pass. [3]

A policy of detente requires a controlled exposure of military technology. This tends to deny the value of secrecy in military capabilities and allows the possibility of either under-exposure or "magnification" of military resources by a ruthless nation. Moreover, preoccupation with a detente detracts from development of survivability. The Red Chinese strategy is based on survival of nuclear war with sufficient resources and unified will to win any broken-back war which could follow the initial exchange.

During the Eisenhower Administration the doctrine of *massive retaliation* was essentially a fixed policy. As a result, much defense planning was based on the massive threat concept, although strong conventional forces were maintained as a matter of course. In 1959, General Maxwell Taylor, who had always been a strong advocate for large conventional forces, retired from the Army as Chief of Staff. Soon thereafter he published a book entitled, *The Uncertain Trumpet.* * In this book General Taylor held for a "balanced" force to minimize the "brush-war" threat. The Kennedy Administration, being interested in a detente, quickly adopted the concept of the balanced force.

The Eisenhower-Dulles policy of massive retaliation was replaced with that of a controlled response — variously known as the *doctrine of the pause,* or *flexible response.* Most regrettably this change precipitated the exit of France from NATO. [4]

As a result of the American participation in the 1956 Suez crisis, and subsequent refusal by the Eisenhower administration to supply the French with technical information on the manufacture of nuclear weapons — knowledge which the

---

*For if the trumpet give an uncertain sound, who shall prepare himself for battle? I Corinthians 14:8.

Russians already had and which would have saved the French some $2 billion [5] — French-American relations had undergone serious erosion. But when the French learned of the application of the doctrine of the pause to NATO defense, during a NATO exercise in September 1964, they were incensed. [6] The subsequent response of the French Premier, Georges Pompidou, in defending their withdrawal from NATO in an address to the French National Assembly, is historically significant. In part, he said:

> The strategy approved by the NATO council was that of massive and immediate atomic retaliation. Officially it remains the NATO doctrine and the council has never been in a position to adopt a new strategic concept. In actual fact, this concept, still theoretically in effect, has been abandoned by the Supreme Command in favor of the concept of the flexible response. It sufficed for McNamara to renounce Dulles' concepts for a strategy that the NATO council had never approved to become, in fact, that of the command.
>
> Certainly we protested. We refused to take part in the exercises that were too obviously based on the new theory. We discussed — that is, we upheld throughout conferences of military leaders and diplomatic representatives — our thesis conforming to the official NATO doctrine. The entire apparatus, nontheless, obeyed the directives of the American government.
>
> And I affirm, without violating any secrets, that a large part, perhaps even the majority, of the Allied military leaders share our point of view. But as soon as the discussion becomes public, not one of our allies contradicts the sovereign thesis of the United States. This is what integration is? [7]

The doctrine of flexible response was a major contribution to the deterioration of NATO and the Socialist tide in Europe, discussed in Chapter 9. And, as pointed out in the above quotation by Arrow, many of the analyses supporting the limited response and detente concepts did not consider the effect these policies had in encouraging "limited" wars such as the Arab-Israel and Vietnam wars, and the blatent Communist aggression elsewhere in Asia and Africa, and the developing insurrection in South America.

Another area of simplistic analysis, which hopefully will soon be corrected, was that a nuclear war would necessarily be both instant and decisive. The various possibilities of a slowly developing crisis, followed by a gradually developing exchange and a prolonged period of "broken-back" warfare could not be adapted to the simplistic logic and formulas used and perhaps would have otherwise been deliberately disallowed.

The advent of the ABM, and the more objective management of defense policies under Secretary Laird should influence the exploration of the possibilities of a slowly developing nuclear crisis. For, if Nation A and Nation B both have ABM systems, each will also have an elaborate system of penetration aids (electronic devices to defeat the opposing ABM). If Nation A elects to attack Nation B it may precipitate a preliminary limited exchange by threatening to destroy three major cities unless B retreats from some position supporting a minor power or takes some such restrictive action. If B holds firm, then A would probably fire a few ICBM's at the three cities. If A's penetration aids were effective, then B would be at the mercy of A's missiles. However, A will not know how effective B's penetration aids will be in allowing B's missiles to defeat A's ABM — unless Nation A has had good intelligence data on B's penetration aids from spies working in B's defense department.

Many more possibilities could be discussed for a slowly developing exchange. *But the most important factor to the average person is the vital role of the fallout and blast shelters — given hours of time for access.* If this factor became generally appreciated a public demand for a massive group shelter would develop. It is certain, however, that the communists and dolscs will oppose effective shelters even more than they did the ABM in the summer of 1969.

McNamara's decisions based on cost effectiveness rather than military effectiveness was but another of his simplistic policies. In a mathematical sense, cost effectiveness is basically an inappropriate procedure for use in guiding weapons systems development. But, if it is used, the associated confidence limits should be included. However, this is seldom done, as the result is a variable answer which may even be meaningless.

The optimum procedure to be employed in solving a military-weapon problem is that of "synthesis." This, considerably more imaginative and sophisticated process, requires that a statement of the military problem in question be given as an input to the technical working staff. This group then develops the characteristics and specifications for the best weaponry design for the problem. Cost may be given only secondary consideration, with primary emphasis on performance. The function of a synthesis-orientated technical team is to augment, to help, to support the work of the military — rather than to manage, direct or supersede it.

Occasionally, the process of synthesis can penetrate right to the heart of a complex issue, as it were, to provide a simply-derived solution. For example, the author was able to show that, with the advent of the anti-missile missile, the aircraft had suddenly become a much more attractive weapon system, in terms of penetrability.[8] Moreover, the perspective provided by synthesis supports initiative and tends to circumvent the need for spasm reactions to May-day parades in Moscow — to develop a counter-capability to a newly-displayed Soviet weapon.

For strategic superiority, either the bomber or the ICBM could be advanced sufficiently by American technology to effectively penetrate the Soviet defenses — given the drive to do so.

What is developing now is the art and science of electromagnetic warfare—the battle of electronics countermeasures (ECM)—vs—electronics counter-countermeasures (ECCM) on the defending radars. For missiles which attack aircraft or missiles which destroy ICBM warheads must be guided by large complex radars located on the ground. These radars can be jammed by ECM devices carried by the aircraft, or accompanying the ICBM warheads. On the other hand, the radars generally have special ECCM circuits to assist in countering the operation of the ECM devices. The ECM devices are small and relatively inexpensive; the advantage tends to accrue to the ECM equipment, given sufficient flexibility in design. And it is possible to design and deploy many types of anti-radar homing devices which use the radar as a beacon for guiding the radar-killer device to it.

Both with ECM and with radar ECCM techniques, the technological state-of-the-art is constantly advancing. For example, the U.S.S.R. is spending large sums of money on ECM techniques,[9] and even the Cubans are expanding instruction at the Havana University School of Technology to include electronic and electric-power sabotage techniques — largely financed by a U. N. grant.[10]

In the field of electronic countermeasures McNamara was also able to drastically curtail the American capability. The British, having lower performance aircraft than the United States, had concentrated on highly sophisticated counter-measures techniques and had developed special, high-power jammers for their aircraft. According to the *Washington Observer,* when adaption of the British jammers for American planes was proposed:

Briefly, the story of this weapon, which is still very much hush-hush insofar as the high echelons in the Government are concerned, because it can upset the Soviet-American power balance, is as follows:

Back on October 14, 1961, a joint exercise was held by the U.S. Air Force and the Royal Air Force to test North American defenses. It was the second such exercise and was called "Skyshield II." In it eight Vulcan bombers of the R.A.F., coming over the North Pole and Canada, equipped with a new type of gear producing electro-magnetic waves that simulate magnetic storms, flew over New York, Chicago, Washington, D.C., Detroit, etc., photographing their "targets" with clocked film, without being detected by the ground defenses.

The latter reported "no overflight," but when confronted with the clocked film and checking it against the film taken by the ground radar, found that "atmospherics, due to magetic storms" had occurred at the very moments when the Vulcans' film showed the passage of those nuclear bombers over the cities in question.

The operation was a great success from the viewpoint of the R.A.F. commanders, who had been urging their American colleagues to install the same gear on the B-52 bombers. It showed conclusively that the Soviet nuclear bases could be knocked out with the greatest ease in one single raid, before the Soviet authorities even learned that the magnetic storms over the U.S.S.R. had been artifically induced.

But for the Kennedy-Yarmolinsky-Rostow Administration the whole thing was a bad jolt. They had just adopted a global policy for the U.S. based on a Soviet-American partnership and news management directives had already been issued to promote the idea of "The Two Nuclear Superpowers — USA and USSR," and all efforts were to be directed towards the elimination of England as a nuclear power. But this invention, which put Soviet Russia at the mercy of the R.A.F. Bomber Command, risked undermining the whole set of premises on which a Soviet-American partnership and eventual alliance could be sold to the American public. [11]

The objection the defense planners have had to the airplane has been its susceptability to being shot down by surface-to-air missiles. But the electromagnetic war has just been started. Radars can be jammed, and "jam-proof" radars *can* be developed. A variety of anti-radar missiles can be provided to knock out radar sites. The innovation of entirely new concepts and techniques is not related exactly to "cost-effective" management, but more to creativeness or invention.

On the other hand, a parity-detente policy discourages invention and development. Moreover, as will be discussed in

Chapter 14, the parity-detente school of thinking provides the Communists with motivation to try to achieve a knock-out superiority. For example, had DOD continued with the development of the Low Altitude Supersonic Vehicle (LASV), which was nuclear-powered and could have flown around the world at supersonic speeds to penetrate the surface-to-surface missile defenses by "tree-top" flight, the U.S.S.R. would have had much more difficulty in justifying the deployment of their anti-ballistic missile system.* *For if the U.S. had had the additional capability for massive retaliation with a low-altitude nuclear-powered missile, and perhaps also had had new bombers on the way for early production, the deployment of an anti-ballistic missile system would have made little sense on their part.* In other words, "cost-effectiveness" (i.e., cancellation of the LASV by DOD) made their ABM system *cost-effective.*

It is fundamental that the existence of a marked military superiority or capability for "unlimited retaliation," discourages "brush-fire" wars, such as Vietnam – which will surely cost the United States at least $100 billion. And Vietnam is only a problem because of the massive cutback in new weapons under McNamara. An operational LASV system in the U.S. arsenal alone would have provided a major deterrent to the Soviet sword and shield strategy in Vietnam.

Although the Kennedy-Johnson-McNamara policies have had tragic effects in the 1960's and left America facing a peril in the 1970's, this danger is being magnified and increased, instead of corrected, by subtle influences seeking to ruthlessly slash defense budgets. It is apparent that each phase of the ABM system will be fought with irrational criticism, for example as in July 1969, and a Chappaquiddick incident cannot be expected at the time of each Senate review of appropriations to detract the opponets.

The critics of the ABM have three main points: that the American system would not work; that it would cost a lot of money; and that it would scare the Russians into a spasm reaction. Perhaps it is just the trend of the   es that there is no necessity for these critics to also explain why the

---

*Dr. Edward Teller has said that the cancellation of the LASV was the biggest blunder since the failure to go ahead with the development of the ICBM following WW II, thus allowing the Russians a near-superiority in this vital technological area in the late 1950's.[12]

Communists would have become alarmed over the U.S. construction of an expensive defense missile system which didn't work!

Or, if one is quite gracious with the ABM critics, one could consider the possibility of their objections being based on lack of information, more than cynicism, even though this would imply that the critics were remiss in following developments reported in the news media, such as the items discussed in References 13 through 28, and are still considering the now obsolete NIKE-X technology. The following excerpts from these references, and related comment, will provide the reader with some background on this subject:

It is now clear that Russia has made a breakthrough in missile defenses that has U.S. scientists and military men openly and seriously concerned.

What the Russians have done is to perfect an antimissile weapon that produces the so-called "X-ray effect" in intense proportions. That fact is now evident to officials in this country.

X rays are one of the most hazardous forms of radiation spewed out by a nuclear blast, and it has been discovered that above the atmosphere these X rays travel for thousands of miles. They carry enormous pulses of energy — enough to paralyze or disintegrate attacking U.S. missiles before they re-enter the atmosphere and while they are hundreds of miles from their targets.

U.S. scientists stumbled unto the X-ray effect inadvertently, long after the Soviets had witnessed its effects in actual tests in 1963. [13]

All of which supports a 1966 report by Vice Admiral Ruthven E. Libby (USN Ret.):

They (The Russians) have exclusive knowledge concerning the atmospheric and space effects of very high yield fusion warheads (knowlege they gained during their unilateral violation of the test moratorium and which we do not possess). [14]

Thus a conscientious ABM critic would want to discuss at some length this X-ray kill and the change on the requirements for ABM guidance from that for the Nike-X system by this new technique. In reviewing the published information he would also find in a 1967 issue of *Technology Week:*

At altitudes above 90 miles there is no longer enough atmosphere to absorb the X rays. They spread their energy over thousands of miles. Consequently, the range at which they can produce destructive effects within a missile is greatly increased, reducing the severity of the anti-missile guidance problem. Exact range at which the X-ray effect is damaging depends on the yield of the device and how energy is partitioned.[15]

And in news reports of May 10, 1967 the Department of Defense revealed that the U.S. was also adopting the X-ray kill for the American ABM system:

> Because the destructive range of the X-rays extends for several miles, a defensive missile has only to be fired in the general vicinity of incoming warheads ... A change in the concept of the nuclear warhead had permitted an "advance" in ballistic missile defenses which made the area defense feasible ... The change was to a high-yield (over one-megaton) thermonuclear warhead ... which would depend on X rays for its destructive effect.[16]

The strategy of the U.S.S.R. in sneaking an advance on the U.S. was reviewed by the *U.S. News and World Report:*

> The mystery of the X-ray effect, described as a "thriller" by U.S. scientists, started during Soviet and U.S. atomic tests in 1958. At that time the Soviets, but not the Americans, apparently first recognized the full potential of the X-ray effect. These were quite apart from the other effects of a nuclear explosion known to the Americans — blast, heat and radioactive fallout.
>
> Shortly after the discovery, the Russians called off their atomic tests and started stirring up worldwide propaganda for a moratorium on all testing.
>
> It was during the moratorium, officials now report, that the Soviets devised a series of new tests to thoroughly check out the X-ray effect. The Soviets suddenly broke the moratorium in 1961, taking the U.S. by surprise. During subsequent tests, the Russians on one occasion destroyed two incoming missiles with a single antimissile warhead more than a hundred miles over the arctic.
>
> American scientists, unaware at the time, did not work on the X-ray effect in their own high-altitude tests of 1963 and have never actually destroyed one missile with the explosion of another. Over the protests of top military men and many scientists, the Administration in 1963 signed the test treaty that now bans all above ground tests.[17]

And if an objective anti-ABM critic continued to search for background information as to when the U.S. started to parallel the Soviets efforts, he would discover, in a November 17, 1967, news article:

> In censored testimony last May before a Senate disarmament subcommittee, Dr. John S. Foster Jr., director of defense research and engineering for DOD, confirmed that the United States was developing a missile defense system using the principles of the

spectrum bomb (i.e. the X-ray bomb) ... What the Administration kept secret was that the new defense system required the design of an entirely new type of atomic weapon and that development of the spectrum (X-ray) bomb began in 1964 and has been pursued in intensive underground testing at the Nevada test site.

With its explosive yield of about one megaton, the spectrum bomb will be carried by the three-stage Spartan missile, capable of intercepting incoming missile warheads above the earth's atmosphere. [18]

Thus the now more informed critic of the ABM might be inclined to reflect on the capability of an already deployed Soviet ABM system using a high-altitude X-ray kill interceptor missile. He would find reports such as Reference 13 which tell of projects to develop protective shields for the MINUTEMAN and POLARIS warheads, to make them resist the penetration of the X-rays. And he would perhaps run across the following Pearson-Anderson report of how the U.S. underground tests are conducted:

The Nevada tests consist of exploding large doses of nuclear energy in vacuum compartments underground. The vacuum compartments are supposed to simulate the lack of air density in outer space since the ABM counter-missiles would be exploded at a very high altitude.

So far the tests have indicated, according to some scientists close to the scene, that the ABM would be able to knock out any Chinese missiles, but not the Russian missiles which are highly sophisticated. [19]

As to paragraph two, this is interesting if true. But the important thing about these underground tests was that the Russians made a tremendous breakthrough after breaking the Test Ban Moratorium then tricking the United States into signing the Test Ban Treaty. This prevented the U.S. from duplicating the Soviet high-altitude X-ray tests after the nature of the Russian breakthrough was discovered. *And this clever use of the Test Ban Treaty by the Russians was not mentioned in the Kennedy-sponsored book, ABM, thus suggesting that the authors were cynical in their "analysis" of the ABM problem.*

Another interesting aspect of the ABM issue developed right in the White House: many observers commented on the lack of any sustained drive by the President for his ABM program. And the Capital observer, Stanley M. Andrews, noted:

The hidden Machiavelli who wore down Nixon's support for the ABM is the powerful Dr. Henry A. Kissinger, Nixon's unofficial Secretary of State . . . It is known that while he gave lip service to the Safeguard ABM program he was secretly against it. It was his assistant who prepared and leaked to foes of ABM, reports giving the strongest possible case against the ABM programs.[29]

After luring the Kennedy Administration into the Test-Ban Treaty, thus fixing their superiority in ABM technology and limiting any U.S. tests of ABM warheads to rudimentary underground simulated tests, the next Soviet objective was a ban on space weapons. By the time this treaty came around for approval, Pavlov conditioning had been established so that only limited opposition was voiced. *The Communists had pulled another coup: had the Americans grasped what could be accomplished by space weapons the entire Red strategy for world conquest through nuclear blackmail could have been countered by deployment of the first American space weapons.*

Moreover, the Kennedy Administration imposed an "off-limits" philosophy in DOD on thinking about space warfare and there has been no indication that this fetishism will be abandoned.

Although space is an inefficient place to store weapons, because of low reliability, extra booster power for launch and other factors, deployment of space weapons at once gets the first battle areas off the earth's surface. If the U.S. had a first strike capability deployed in space the first overt act on the part of the U.S.S.R. would be an attack against the satellite weapons. Since this attack would involve hours to days to destroy all the satellites, there would be ample time for city evacuation and occupation of shelters.

For example, the U.S. could launch, over a period of several months, a number of orbital bombs. These could be placed in a whole pattern of orbits so complex that no computer could determine if a military purpose was involved. Each satellite would probably carry several bombs, similar to the multiple independent re-entry vehicles (MIRV's). For a first strike the U.S. could, potentially, de-orbit the satellites at a certain date on which a synod (confluence) would be formed. Although the U.S.S.R. would have some apprehension as to the nature of the orbiting bombs, they could never be sure without sending out a manned inspector. This would keep them occupied for years. But the way things actually are, there is speculation that the Russians may be preparing to deploy such a system against the United States. [30]

On the other side of the Iron Curtain a Soviet Ministry of Defense text, entitled *War and Politics,* considers the subject of new weapons and tactics and includes this summary remark:

> The Soviet Government is not limiting itself to those military means which the adversary has. Undoubtably, this would be insufficient. The creation of new methods of combat which the imperial aggressors still do not possess is a task of Soviet science and technology.[31]

In following a similar philosophy, the United States would be producing a nuclear fleet, deploying a new manned bomber, providing both area and point defense ABM protection for the major cities and reviving some of the weapon systems cancelled by the former Secretary of Defense. Also, a major emphasis would be placed on research and development related to new and advanced types of weapons systems. The public would be advised and trained for proper appreciation of civil defense, and communities would be vigorously encouraged to provide adequate blast and fallout shelters— fully equipped with air filters, emergency power and medical facilities. Industry would be encouraged to disperse.

Meanwhile, in the U.S.S.R. the philosophy of maximum capability has not been noticably abated by treaties to limit nuclear proliferation and deployment of space weapons. As the U.S. has concentrated on Vietnam, the Soviets have applied their resources to the development of new strategic weapon systems—including space weapons. General Bernard A. Schriever, USAF (Ret.) notes:

> The most significant element in that new strategic force, however, has been a space development—the orbital missile.
>
> The orbital missile was first displayed in the November 1965 anniversary parade and it was proudly identified by Soviet spokesmen as an orbital missile. The Soviets, by the way, never called the weapon anything less than an orbital missile. They declared in 1965 that its warhead could be brought down to earth on command "on the first or any other orbit."
>
> In addition to an expanding force of ICBM's and an orbital-bombardment system, the Soviet strategic threat is supported by an antiballistic-missile system. ...I feel compelled to add that no Soviet spokesmen have ever expressed the thought that those Russian lives their system may someday save were not worth the cost. Nor have they indicated that the purpose of the system is to defend the country against a secondary threat, while the primary threat is ignored. Nor have any Soviet spokesmen expressed even the slightest concern about the possibility that some nation might interpret their ABM system as provocative or destabilizing.[32]

CHAPTER 13

THE SUPREME COURT VS. NATIONAL SECURITY

Since Earl Warren took the oath of office to become the Chief Justice of the Supreme Court in October 1953*, the Court has been more or less continuously in the public eye, as a result of widespread criticism. For example, in an unpredicated action, on August 23, 1958, the Conference of Chief Justices of the States issued a 30 page document which indicted the Supreme Court's decisions as having seriously eroded the constitutional powers of the state governments, and stated that:

> The overall tendency of decisions of the Supreme Court over the last 25 years or more has been to press the extension of federal power and to press it rapidly . . . (the court) too often tended to adopt the role of policy maker without proper judicial restraint.[1]

Perhaps it is the issue of the control of Communist subversion that intensified the public criticism of the Supreme Court since 1953, although there are other issues involved. However, only the issue of Communist subversion will be examined in this Chapter. But it should be noted that in this narrow field the criticism of the Court has been intense — from the American Bar Association to patriotic societies, groups of concerned citizens have charged the Court with "Coddling the Reds."

Some of the most convincing evidence on the red-coddling issue has been compiled by a Senate investigating committee. In summarizing the conclusion derived from some of these investigations, Senator James G. Eastland (D., Miss.), Chairman of the Senate Judiciary Committee, stated in a

---

*This was a recess appointment, Congress not being in session. The last prior recess appointment was in 1851. President Eisenhower subsequently made two other recess appointments. The significance here, of course, is that the review of the appointment by the Senate is compromised by such a procedure.

speech to the Senate:

". . . Under Chief Justice Warren's regime, the Court has been exp... ...ding its usurpation of the legislative field and purporting to make new law of general application which will be favorable to the Communist position not only in the individual cases decided but in innumerable other cases.

The one area where there seems to be some predictability with respect to the Warren Court's action is where cases involve the interests of the world Communist conspiracy and its arm in this country, the Communist Party, U.S.A.

When delay is necessary to help the Communist cause, the Court delays. . . .

The long-range intentions of the Supreme Court are obscure, as its language in some of these cases also has been. Perhaps we cannot say what the Court is trying to do, but we can see what it is doing: It is moving, step by step, paragraph by paragraph and decision by decision, toward establishment of the Communist conspiracy in the United States as a legal political entity, with just as much right to exist and operate as any political party composed of decent, patriotic American citizens.

When suppression would help the Communist cause, the Court has suppressed. . . .

When pre-emption would help the Communist cause, the Court has pre-empted. . . .

When invention would help the Communist cause, the Court has invented. . . .

When misstatement would help the Communist cause, the Court has misstated.[2]

To examine the credulity of these remarks, it is necessary to review the legislation enacted by the Congress to cope with the domestic Communist threat and the ensuing reviews by the Supreme Court. Basically, the Congress passed two acts for the control of communism: (1) the Smith Act, in 1940, which was directed at subversion by individuals; (2) the Internal Security Act* of 1950 and the associated amendment of 1954, the Communist Control Act, which was aimed at the Communist Party organization and organizational subversion.

The Smith Act was passed in 1940, during a period of cooperation between Hitler and Stalin, to cope with the potential Nazi-Communist threat. This legislation declared as unlawful: the knowledgeable advocation or teaching of the overthrow of any government in the United States by force or violence; the printing, and/or distribution of written ma-

---

*Sometimes referred to as the McCarran or Subversive Activities Control Act.

terial so advocating; the organization of, or knowledgeable participation in, a group which so advocates; or the participation in a conspiracy to accomplish any of these ends. Further, it provided criminal punishment for anyone who "organizes or helps to organize any society, group, or assembly of persons who teach, advocate, or encourage the overthrow or destruction" of government in the United States by force or violence.

The U.S. Communist Party (CPUSA) was founded in 1919, but in 1941 the party was *formally* dissolved and replaced by the so-called Communist Political Association. At the same time the international Commintern for world revolution was also abrogated. After the end of World War II in 1945, the U.S. Communist Party was re-formed along its original lines.

The Truman Administration did not elect to prosecute a case under the Smith Act until 1951, when the *Dennis* case was brought into the courts.[3] Lower court action was reviewed by the Vinson Court and held to be constitutional. Subsequently, the many additional prosecutions against the Communists by the government under the Smith Act were almost uniformly successful. It should be noted, however, that in the *Dennis* case the Court limited its review to the examination of the constitutionality of the Smith Act (disallowing consideration of the sufficiency of evidence presented to justify the findings of guilt under the statute, or considerations relating to the extent of danger posed by the Communist Party). Implicit in the decision on the *Dennis* case, however, was the reliance by the Vinson Court on the "clear and present danger" test — provided in 1919, by Justice Holmes in the *Schenck* case:

> The question in every case is whether the words used are used in such circumstances and are of such a nature as to create a clear and present danger that they will bring about the substantive evils that Congress has a right to prevent. It is a question of proximity and degree.[4]

In other words, what is involved here, in lay terms, is fundamentally a matter of judgement in assessing the danger involved, more than the law.

In 1955, the Warren Court agreed to review the *Yates*

case,[5] which had also been prosecuted under the Smith Act. When the Court rendered a decision on the *Yates* case on June 17, 1957,* it reversed the convictions of five defendants and granted new trials to the other nine. In part, this decision was based on a technicality involving the definition of the word "organize," as used in the Smith Act. The defendants held that the new Communist Party had been "organized" in 1945, and that the statute of limitations for criminal prosecutions had subsequently applied. The prosecution held that the clear intent of the Congress was for a broader definition of the term, taking into account the fact that new cells are constantly being formed and organizers are constantly recruiting new members.**

The second principal basis on which the *Yates* decision was founded was that of the nature and sufficiency of the evidence presented. With the *Dennis* case, the Vinson Court did not question the inherent danger of "teaching and advocating" of overt revolutionary acts. However, in the *Yates* case the Warren Court held that the danger presented by the mere advocacy of the overthrow of the government must represent a "clear and present" danger to allow a conviction—despite the free speech guarantee provided by the First Amendment. Further, it was held that: some evidence of conspiratorial action, other than that of reading Communist books and making speeches should be presented; the government should show some evidence, or testimony by secret operatives (thus exposing them) that a conspiracy was in-

---

*This day was labeled as *Red Monday,* since on the same day a favorable decision to the Communists was also delivered on the *Watkins* case, the dismissal of John Stewart Service by Secretary of State Acheson was nullified, and state legislatures were restricted from investigating Communist subversion. These cases will be discussed later on in the Chapter. It is interesting to note that by this time President Eisenhower had made four appointments to the Court, since the instance of the decision by the Court on the *Dennis* case in 1951. David Lawrence, editor of *U.S. News & World Report,* called these four decisions "Treason's Greatest Victory."

In September 1957, the Communist Party held a rally in New York "to pay honor to the U.S. Supreme Court and its recent decisions."

**There was an immediate reaction by the Congress to adequately define the word organize, but not one of the various bills introduced was passed, perhaps because of the other restricting aspects of the *Yates* case provided by the Court.

volved; and, that the government in presenting its case, should distinguish between "advocacy of abstract doctrine and advocacy directed at promotion of unlawful action."

Now, the historical basis of jurisprudence is right reasoning. Leaving aside the strained reasoning of the "advocacy" vs. "action" issue, *the "clear and present danger" issue and the constitutionality of the Smith Act have not been disallowed by the Court; it is rather that the existence of this danger is not recognized.* Commenting on the Communist threat in 1961, before the Cuban crisis, the assassination of President Kennedy and the substantial involvement in the Viet Nam war, Congressman James B. Utt (Rep., Calif.) remarked:

Russia has been restrained from military action directly against America, simply because of fear of massive military retaliation. Consequently, Khrushchev employs the other weapons more deadly than missiles.

Let us examine that arsenal of deadly weapons employed twenty-four hours a day by the International Conspiracy: (1) propaganda (2) organization (3) infiltration (4) popular fronts (5) deceiving tourists in Russia (6) destroying anti-communists (7) violence and murder (8) communist schools.

America and the Free World are absolutely unprepared to meet this onslaught. Our great military strength will not save us if we are conquered by a war of words.

Let us look at the volume of propaganda in this arsenal of words. The Kremlin uses 150 thousand hours per *week* of radio propaganda in every language; 200 big propaganda films per year; 120 million propaganda books each year (millions of these are carried free in our mails); 2 billion propaganda pamphlets every year; 20 thousand Russian stars sent out every year on propaganda and publicity missions all over the world. Our propaganda is less than 1% of what I have just listed.

How frightened would you be if our military strength was equal to only 1% of that of Russia? One is just as deadly for you and your children as is the other, and yet at this critical time your military establishment has ordered that no one in the military may take part in any anti-communist school or right-wing organization. Our Defense Department has fallen prey to communist propaganda which is out to destroy all anti-communist organizations.

America has never lost a war for lack of missiles, planes, or other weapons. Let's look at our losses and place the blame where it belongs: Yalta — a communist victory because President Roosevelt did not recognize the danger of the International Conspiracy; China — we lost in a torrent of massive propaganda which convinced the world that Mao was an agrarian reformer;

Korea — we had the armaments to destroy Red China. Again communist propaganda convinced England that we should not destroy Red China and England demanded the removal of General MacArthur. It was not missiles that kept President Eisenhower out of Tokyo. It was communist propaganda; Cuba — we did not lose Cuba to the Reds for lack of military power. It was communist propaganda that we would offend other countries if we took the action which we should have taken.

Until this country recognizes that we are losing every engagement to communist propaganda and takes positive action to meet this enemy with the same weapons they use, we will fall like a ripe fruit, without firing a single missile.[6]

Or the reader may consider if the following observation, by a Communist Progressive Labor propagandist, in a publication distributed in the Watts section of Los Angeles and published alongside a map of the Watts and adjoining areas, clearly identifying the adjacent industries, constitutes a "clear and present danger":

These factories are completely vulnerable and can be shut down with a minimum of preparation, personnel and effort. Once the weakest flank of the enemy is discovered, a million ways will be found to focus the full strength of resistance so that every blow drives straight to his heart. . . .

The Black people of South Los Angeles possess a weapon more powerful than twenty-two thousand guns! And the Black people can choose their own time and place for battle.[7]

Nearly three years before the outbreak of the Korean War, a Gallup Poll taken in December 1947, found that 62% of the Americans surveyed were for banning the Communist Party.[8] By 1949, as more and more subversion was uncovered, nine out of ten Americans wanted to register all Communists with the government.[9]

After the Korean War broke out in 1950, the public demanded that the Congress provide more control over the activity of the Communist Party as an organization. The Congress passed the Internal Security Act in September 1950, and it was vetoed within two days by President Truman. In less than an hour, both the House and Senate overrode the veto.* This legislation, following the spirit of the law requiring the registration of foreign agents, specified that:

- Communist party members register with the government, under penalty of fine and imprisonment.
- The Communist Party register as an organization.
- Provided for detention of subversives in camps, during

---

*Voting with the majority were Senator Lyndon B. Johnson and Congressman John F. Kennedy.

periods of emergency.
- Forbade issuance of passports to Communists.

In justifying these measures, the Internal Security Act and the Communist Control Act included the following truisms:

Section 781 (1) of the Internal Security Act of 1950

There exists a world Communist movement which, in its origins, its development, and its present practice, is a world-wide revolutionary movement whose purpose it is, by treachery, deceit, infiltration into other groups (governmental and otherwise), espionage, sabotage, terrorism, and any other means deemed necessary, to establish a Communist totalitarian dictatorship in the countries throughout the world through the medium of a world-wide Communist organization.

Section 841 of the Communist Control Act of 1954

The Congress finds and declares that the Communist Party of the United States, although purportedly a political party, is in fact an instrumentality of a conspiracy to overthrow the Government of the United States. It constitutes an authoritarian dictatorship within a republic, demanding for itself the rights and privileges accorded to political parties, but denying to all others the liberties guaranteed by the Constitution. Unlike political parties, which evolve their policies and programs through public means, by the reconciliation of a wide variety of individual views, and submit those policies and programs to the electorate at large for approval or disapproval, the policies and programs of the Communist Party are secretly prescribed for it by the foreign leaders of the world Communist movement. Its members have no part in determining its goals, and are not permitted to voice dissent to party objectives. Unlike members of political parties, members of the Communist Party are recruited for indoctrination with respect to its objectives and methods, and are organized, instructed, and disciplined to carry into action slavishly the assignments given them by their hierarchical chieftains. Unlike political parties, the Communist Party acknowledges no constitutional or statutory limitations upon its conduct or upon that of its members. The Communist Party is relatively small numerically, and gives scant indication of capacity ever to attain its ends by lawful political means. The peril inherent in its operation arises not from its numbers, but from its failure to acknowledge any limitation as to the nature of its activities, and its dedication to the proposition that the present constitutional Government of the United States ultimately must be brought to ruin by any available means, including resort to force and violence. Holding that doctrine, its role as the agency of a hostile foreign power renders its existence a clear present and continuing danger to the security of the United States. It is the means whereby individuals are seduced into the service of the world Communist movement, trained to do its bidding, and directed and controlled in the conspiratorial performance of their revolutionary services. Therefore, the Communist Party should be outlawed.

The principal decision to date reviewing the Internal Security Act was involved with the requirement for the registration of individual Communists. The test was provided by the refusal of two alleged Communists to register, in compliance with an order by the Subversive Activities Control Board.[10] On November 15, 1965, the Court declared the requirement for personal registration as unworkable. Reviewing the decision, the *New York Times* story stated, in part:

> This (registration) would expose them to prosecution under other Federal laws "in an area permeated with criminal statutes" he (Justice Brennan) said.
>
> Critics of the law have argued that this places the individual on the horns of a constitutional dilemma.
>
> But if he registers he forgoes a court decision on the self-incrimination privilege claim and is subject to prosecution under the Smith Act and other anti-subversive legislation.
>
> Justice Brennan said, in effect, that an individual could not be forced to make such a decision.
>
> Although the opinion did not directly concern the alternate provision of the Act that requires the Party itself to register and to list its membership, it seemed to leave that section hanging by a thread.
>
> Presumably, if party officers register the Party or authorize others to do so, they would forgo the same self-incrimination rights involved in today's decision. . . .
>
> The decision today dismisses the 42 other pending cases against alleged Communist Party members for failing to register...[11]

From this specious reasoning and refusal to admit the nature of the internal Communist threat, the United States entered a final phase in the loss of control of Communist activity. The press treatment of this case was so blase that even Barry Goldwater upheld the Court's action, because of the self incrimination aspect of the case. [12]

On the other hand, there is a somewhat more subtle issue involved which has not been recognized and publicly discussed. It will be recalled that following this decision, Gus Hall, general secretary of the U.S. Communist Party, and other Communist leaders announced that henceforth they would field candidates in future elections.* The unrecognized danger in allowing the Communist party to become politically active was pointed up in the following, somewhat acerbic, letter to Senator Dodd:

December 2, 1965.

The Hon. Thomas J. Dodd
United States Senate
Washington, D.C.

Dear Senator Dodd:

The recent Supreme Court decision releasing Communist Party (CP) members from registering as foreign agents forbodes the elevation of the CP into American political life — or rather the lowering of American politics to the Communist level.

The effects of this decision (the last of a long series of pro-Communist rulings by the Supreme Court) if uncorrected by effective legislation, constitutional amendment and/or executive action may very well negate efforts to resist the onward march of Communism such as the war in Vietnam.

Being engaged in classified defense work, I am most concerned with the potential effect on security. As it stands now, there are a certain number of Communist agents operating with clearance. However, if the CP starts running candidates for political office (as Gus Hall proposes) and as CP activity is increased in colleges and extended down into the high schools what will restrain young minds from falling for the siren-like CP "dogma"? (Certainly not the leadership of the National Council of Churches.)

Assuming the CP becomes established as a minor political party, how can the high school and college student even be expected to discriminate against it? Or with communism in the

---

* The Communist Party ran several candidates in various elections in 1966. Noteworthy of these was that of Herbert Aptheker, who ran for Congress in Brooklyn, and Dorothy Healey who ran for County Assessor in Los Angeles County. A significant point was developed in the Los Angeles race, as Candidate Healey pulled some six percent (86,000) of the vote[13] — thus updating a 1950 estimate by the House Un-American Activities Committee of the number of Communist-subversives in the U.S. as in the order of 1,000,000 or 0.57% of the populace.[14] Of course, the Los Angeles area may have a higher percentage of Communists than the rest of the country, but this difference also suggests a substantial growth for domestic communism during the period from 1950 to 1966.

high schools how can the FBI monitor all the increased contacts of future engineers and scientists with Communist student groups (with FBI undercover agents in the Girl and Boy Scouts)? Clearly, it seems to me, we are faced with a situation in which many young science students will be subverted by Communist dogma. (Although not a science student, Lee Harvey Oswald provides an example.) When this happens a certain percentage of these will undoubtably elect to engage in espionage. According to my crude estimate of agents with clearance, as of now, we cannot hope to maintain effective security after a ten-fold increase in underground Communist engineers with clearance.

Hoping that you will give this matter your gravest consideration, I am

Very truly yours,

Claude L. Strother

Following the reasoning of the High Court, the U.S. Court of Appeals set aside the conviction of the Communist Party for failing to register with the government.[15] Speaking for the three-judge panel, Judge Carl McGowan wrote that the laws passed by the Congress have "exposed it (the Communist Party) in substance to outlawry as well as to an obligation to disclose its records and affairs . . . ", that either approach by the government "was and is constitutionally feasible, but we cannot, because of the Fittn Amendment, safely assume as much in the case of the coexistence of both purposes."

It would seem that the most valuable asset to the Communist Party is that of "respectability;" further, in this attribute lies the greatest danger to the U.S. In other words, if the Communist Party must be outlawed – i.e., banned – to maintain some semblance of industrial security in the U.S., then let it be so!

On Red Monday, June 17, 1957, in delivering a decision on the *Watkins* case,[16] the Supreme Court reversed the conviction of a labor union official who had been convicted in a lower court for contempt of the Congress for his refusal to answer questions by the House Un-American Activities Committee relating to the union official's knowledge as to whether certain persons were members of the Communist Party. Watkins agreed to testify on his knowledge of current Communist party members, but refused to answer questions about former party members, no longer active in Communist work.

One of the most apprehensive aspects of this case was

ιe general, vague admonition to the Congress to instruct and ιhibit a committee, when founded: "on what they are to do ⋅ith the power delegated to them. . . "; to "spell out that ⋅oup's jurisdiction and purpose with sufficient particularity" ⋅o allow a witness to judge the relevancy of the questions). . ; there is no Congressional power to expose for the sake of ⋅xposure . . . there is no general authority to expose the pri- ιte affairs of individuals without justification in terms of the ιnction of Congress." Congressional reaction was, of course, ιtter, and corrective legislation was initiated.

The Jenner Bill, as amended by Senator Butler,[17] would ιve empowered the presiding officer of a Congressional com- ιittee to make a decision on the question of pertinency, ⋅ith provision for referral to the full House or Senate for re- ⋅ew. However, before the measure could be enacted, the ⋅ourt retreated from its position in the *Watkins* case, by the ⋅ecision given on the *Barenblatt* case.[18] In rendering this de- ⋅sion it was stated, referring to the House Un-American ⋅ctivities Committee, "comes to us with a 'persuasive gloss ⋅f legislative history' . . . which shows beyond doubt that in ⋅rsuance of its legislative concerns in the domain of 'national ⋅curity' the House has clothed the Un-American Activities ⋅mmittee with pervasive authority to investigate Commu- ⋅st activities in this country . . . So long as the Congress acts pursuance of its constitutional power, the judiciary lacks ⋅e authority to intervene on the basis of motive which ⋅urred the exercise of that power."

The net effect of the *Barenblatt* decision was a "veto" ⋅ the *Watkins* decision. A similar situation occurred in the in- ⋅ance of the *Sweezy* case,[19] which was reversed by the *⋅phaus* decision. The issue involved in these two cases was ⋅e refusal by the defendants to supply information on pos- ⋅ble Communist connections of their associates. The details ⋅ the issues are reviewed in summary form by Pritchett.[20]

In the *Slochower* case,[21] the Court annuled the dismissal ⋅ Harry Slochower, a professor at Brooklyn College, because ⋅ had refused, under the Fifth Amendment to testify before ⋅ Senate committee as to his political as⋅ ⋅ations prior to ⋅41. The New York City Charter had provided for the auto- ⋅atic firing of any employee who used the privilege against ⋅lf-incrimination to avoid answering questions about his ⋅nduct.

A decision on a similar issue was provided in the *Nelson* ⋅d *Globe* case.[22] Two social workers in Los Angeles County, one with permanent and the other with temporary status, had been dismissed because they invoked the Fifth Amendment and refused to answer questions by a Congressional committee about alleged subversive activity.

A California statute makes response to such investigations obligatory, under "pain" of instant dismissal. The Court upheld the discharge of these two social workers, despite the action taken in the *Slochower* case, by the contorted reasoning that the California law provided for dismissal on the basis of any employee refusing to give any sort of information.*

In June 1957, actually two weeks prior to Red Monday, the Court handed down a decision on the *Jencks* case.[23] The case involved an official of the Union of the Mine, Mill and Smelter Workers, Clinton E. Jencks, who was prosecuted for perjury in filing an allegedly false non-Communist affidavit under the Taft-Hartley Act. The Government case was based on the testimony of two undercover agents, who testified as to Jencks' alleged Communist activities.

The council for the defense requested that the Government attorney make available to the Court the original reports of their agents to the FBI, to allow the Court to check them against the open Court testimony. With a single exception, the High Court held that the defense be allowed to inspect relevant reports of witnesses to the FBI, because only the defense attorney could know what was important in the case. Giving a token recognition to the existence of a national security problem, the Court gave the Justice Department an option: "The criminal action must be dismissed when the Government, on the ground of privilege, elects not to comply with an order to produce, for the accused's inspection and for admission in evidence, relevant statements or reports in its possession of government witnesses touching on the subject matter of their testimony at the trial."

In a single voice of reason, Justice Clark dissented. He declared that the Court had opened a "veritable Pandora's box of troubles. . . . Unless the Congress changes the rule announced by the Court today, those intelligence agencies of our Government engaged in law enforcement may as well close up shop, for the Court has opened their files to the criminal and thus afforded him a Roman holiday for rummaging through confidential information as well as vital national secrets."

---

*Chief Justice Earl Warren, a Californian, did not participate in this case.

In *Pennsylvania v Nelson*,[24] the Court made one of their most effective decisions in limiting the control of Communist activity. Steve Nelson had been convicted by a County Court on a charge of sedition against the United States, but the State Supreme Court of Pennsylvania reversed the conviction on the grounds that the Congress had superseded state legislation on sedition by passage of the Smith Act. The High Court held that the Federal interest in national security was so dominant that the Congressional action in providing the Smith, Internal Security, and Communist Control Acts had pre-empted the State enforcement activity — which might present a "serious danger of conflict with the administration of the Federal program."

As a result, the criminal anarchy laws, the criminal syndicatist laws, etc. — dating back to the assassination of President McKinley at the beginning of the century, and generally called anti-sedition statutes — in some 42 states were invalidated.[25,26]

Three dissenting Justices objected that they could find no Congressional intent to pre-empt the state control of sedition, or see any "clear and direct" conflict between state and Federal legislation in the area. In his dissent Justice Reed quoted from the *amicus curiae* brief of the Justice Department: "The administration of the various state laws has not, in the course of the fifteen years that the Federal and state sedition laws have existed side by side, in fact interfered with, embarrassed, or impeded the enforcement of the Smith Act."

In article 3231 of Title 18 of the U.S. *Code* — the title under which the Smith Act and other Federal criminal laws were collected — the Congress had specified that: "Nothing in this title shall be held to take away or impair the jurisdiction of the courts of the several States, under the laws thereof."

Following this decision on the Nelson case early in 1956 the Court then proceeded to, in effect, nullify the Smith Act, the Internal Security Act and the Communist Control Act in the various decisions subsequently handed down, as discussed above.

Following the instruction of the Internal Security Act, the State Department refused passports to Communists or adherents to the Communist Party line.* This policy was brought before the Supreme Court in the *Kent v Dulles*

---

*This policy had actually been initiated following the Communist Revolution in Russia.

case[27] in 1958. The State Department had denied Rockwe
Kent and Walter Briehl passports to travel abroad, because c
their connections and associations with the Communist Pa
ty.* This was sustained in the lower courts but the Suprem
Court held that even Communists must enjoy the privilege c
travel.

Communists consider their printed propaganda leaflet
newspapers, magazines, books and other material as the
most important and effective tools for agitation and subve
sion. Through the dissemination of this material, both in th
United States and the other parts of the Free World, th
party indoctrinates its members and spreads propaganda us
ful in the recruiting of new members. Much of this type c
propaganda distributed in the U.S. is printed abroad.

Recognizing this danger, the Congress enacted Sectio
305(a) of the Postal Service and Federal Employees Salar
Act of 1962, which provided, in part:

> Mail matter, except sealed letters, which originates or which
> is printed or otherwise prepared in a foreign country and which
> is determined by the Secretary of the Treasury pursuant to rules
> and regulations to be promulgated by him to be "Communist
> political propaganda" shall be detained by the Postmaster Gen-
> eral upon its arrival for delivery in the United States, or upon
> its subsequent deposit in the United States Domestic mails, and
> the addressee shall be notified that such matter has been received
> and will be delivered only upon the addressee's request. . . [28]

The Post Office maintained several screening points fo
checking unsealed Communist political propaganda arrivin
in the United States from abroad. It would notify th
addressee of the arrival of such material and, unless deliver
was requested, the propaganda would be destroyed.

Mail delivery of Communist propaganda was (and stil
is), in effect, free — since by reciprocal agreement interna
tional mail is delivered within each country on a courtes
basis. However, the amount of printed material adverse t
communism and supporting capitalistic enterprise delivere
free in Russia is nil.

The requirement for request for delivery was littl
enough protection from the Communist propaganda mill, bu
in the *Lamont* case[29] the Supreme Court refused to uphol
the right of the Postmaster General to intercept the mas
mailings of Communist propaganda. The unsuspecting Ameri

---

* Both men refused to submit affidavits regarding past or present mem
bership in the Communist Party.

can public is now subject to being harrassed by material designed to create, foment, and direct: social, racial and religious disorders — for background support of the Communist causes.*

On April 18, 1966, the Court, in another 5-4 split-vote, relieved Mrs. Barbara Elfbrandt of the obligation to sign the loyalty oath required by Arizona's Amended Communist Control Act of 1961.[30] The act subjected anyone to liability to prosecution for perjury and dismissal who, after taking the oath, then knowingly remained or later became a member of the Communist Party or any other organization advocating the overthrow of the Arizona Government.

Mrs. Elfbrandt, and her husband Vernon, had continued to teach in the Tucson schools without salary from 1961, since the law did not specifically require dismissal for those refusing to take the amended oath, but only the suspension of payment. Mrs. Elfbrandt, although a Quaker, did not base her objections on religious grounds.

The position of the majority in the Elfbrandt case was that membership in a subversive organization, such as the Communist Party, could not be used as a criterion for loyalty, inasmuch as Party membership might not, it was suggested, necessarily imply belief in or support of the Party's illegal aims.

In similar decisions made since 1969 the Supreme Court has also struck down loyalty legislation in Florida, Washington State, New York, Maryland and Texas. The trend of the Court's action is to disallow an oath affirming non-membership, but allowing a positive affirmation of loyalty. Apparently the positive oath cannot be used as a basis of prosecution for perjury if it turns out that the individual signed the oath while belonging to a subversive organization.[31]

On January 23, 1967, the Court ruled, in a 5-4 decision, that the State of New York's Feinberg law violated the First Amendment.[32] The decision invalidated a series of New York anti-subversion and anti-sedition acts, dating back to 1917. Among the provisions involved was the requirement for loyalty oaths for teachers and college professors, and the barring of employment by the state persons who willfully and deliberately advocate, advise, or teach the doctrine of forcibly

---

*For a full account of the Communist attack on America via the postman, see *Attack By Mail,* by Edward F. Hunter, The Bookmailer Linden, N.J.

overthrowing the Government — as would be expected by Communists. The decision, according to Justice Brennan, was based, in part, on a teacher's inability under the law to inform his class about the precepts of communism or the Declaration of Independence. Justice Clark rejected these dangers as "horrible hypotheticals" and further commented that the majority had "swept away one of our most precious rights, namely, the right of self-preservation. Our public education system is the basis of our democracy. The minds of our youth are developed there, and the character of the development will determine the future of our land. Indeed, our very existence depends upon it."

Although the Feinberg Law was passed in 1949, the State of New York withheld enforcement until the constitutionality could be determined by the High Court. When this was accorded by the Vinson Court, in 1952, the law was then put into operation. Between 1952-1958, some 375 teachers and other New York employees were then dismissed or "terminated their services" as a result of inquiries based on this act.[33]

Three months after the Court's decision on New York's Feinberg law, the American Civil Liberties Union filed a suit in the California courts, in behalf of an American Friends Service Committee official, to challenge the loyalty oath there.[34] On December 21, 1967, the California State Supreme Court, following the High Court's precedent, ruled that prospective public employees in the State need not declare that they are not members of an organization (such as the Communist Party) advocating the overthrow of the U.S. Government "by force or violence or other unlawful means."

Although the admission of Communists to the practice of law may be considered as representing only an indirect security problem, it is probably worthwhile to mention the *Schware* v. *New Mexico*[35] and *Konigsberg* v. *California*[36] cases. Decisions on both cases were given in 1957, and resulted in the admission of alleged Communists to the Bar.

Before discussing the decisions of the Court relating to Govermental, Military and Industrial Security programs relating to the clearance of personnel for the handling of classified material and for loyalty, it will be helpful to briefly review the background involved.

The Federal Government had a fairly rigorous loyalty program, dating as far back as the Civil War, but the basis for the prevailing system was set up by the Hatch Act in 1939.

This legislation forbade Federal employment to members of a party or organization "which advocates the overthrow of our constitutional form of government." (However, it was not properly enforced to screen out Communists during World War II.)

Following the outbreak of the cold war, the matter of security and the pressing need for an effective loyalty program was recognized and the Military and the State Department both organized new security programs. To provide a common plan, President Truman established the Employee Loyalty Program by Executive Order (E.O.) 735, on March 31, 1947. In support of this program a Loyalty Review Board was established, empowered to conduct hearings on appeal from employees faced with dismissal because of "loyalty risk." (Its limited effectiveness was discussed in Chapter 4.)

In August 1950, during the Korean War, the Congress effected a dual system with the passage of Public Law 733, the Summary Suspension Act. By this Act the heads of eleven Federal agencies were empowered to suspend an employee "in the interest of National security."

This dual system remained in effect until May 1953, when President Eisenhower set up a single security program with the issuance of E.O. 10450. At this time the provisions of the Truman Loyalty Program were terminated and all of the Executive agencies were brought under the provisions of Public Law 733. Interdepartmental avenues of appeal were eliminated and final authority for approval of clearance rested with the executive department head, i.e. Secretary of State, Defense, etc.

Basically, the new system was designed to identify and terminate "security risks," as opposed to the (more timorous — and also more unfair) concern with identifying "loyalty risks" under the Truman Administration. Among the grounds for dismissal provided by the new system were: excessive use of alcohol, sexual perversion, drug addiction, or mental illness or instability. As a result of this change in the period from May 28, 1953 to June 30, 1954, some 7,000 Federal employees were fired as "security risks" or resigned because of adverse information in their files.[37] However, this improvement was more in the nature of a step in the right direction, since as discussed in Chapter 4 review and investigation of security by the Congress was effectively stopped.

With this background on the Government security program, the actions of the Court relating to the Federal security program and the similar Military and Industrial Security programs can be discussed.

In 1956, the Government's security program came under the review of the Warren Court, in the case of *Cole* v. *Young.* On June 11, the Court ruled that only those Federal employees who held sensitive positions could be fired as security risks. Kendrick M. Cole was employed as a Federal Food and Drug inspector in New York. In November 1953, he had been offered the opportunity by the Government to comment on accusations of association with persons "reliably reported to be Communists" and attending meetings and giving funds and support to a group which was on the Attorney General's list of subversive organizations. Following his response of charging invasion of privacy and refusing to comment, he was fired by the Secretary of Health, Education and Welfare, Mrs. Oveta Culp Hobby. (He did ask for a hearing two weeks after the initial confrontation but this request was denied.)

The dismissal was taken into the courts and eventually selected for review by the Supreme Court. The Court held that President Eisenhower had not followed the direction of Congress in setting up a security program applicable to all Government employees. In reporting on the decision the *New York Times* noted:

> The decision was widely regarded as a major blow at the Administration's security regulations. Published statistics indicate that about half of the "risks" dismissed under the program held non-sensitive positions.[39]

As a result, the Government was forced to re-employ some 300 people previously discharged as security risks. Justice Clark, in speaking for the dissent noted that:

> We believe the Court's order has stricken down the most effective weapon against subversive activity available to the Government. It is not realistic to say that the Government can be protected by applying the Act to sensitive jobs. One never knows just which job is sensitive.

> The plain words of the Section 1 make the Act applicable to "any civilian officer or employee," not as the majority would have it, to "any civilian officer or employee in a sensitive position."

> The President's standard is "complete and unswerving loyalty" not only in sensitive places but throughout the Government. The President requires that every employee give no less.

On Red Monday, June 17, 1957, the Warren Court, in the case of *Service* v *Dulles*,[40] reversed the ruling of a lower court which had upheld the summary dismissal of John Stewart Service by Secretary of State Dean Acheson.

The matter of Service's loyalty had been made a matter of question because of the notorious Amerasia case.* In this instance Service was arrested and charged with violating the Espionage Act, but a grand jury cleared him and he was reinstated to active duty in Government service. His loyalty was subsequently reviewed some six times by various State Department Loyalty Boards, but in 1951, under the newly revised security procedures, Service's record was "post audited" by the Loyalty Review Board of the Civil Service Commission. This board found "reasonable doubt" of his loyalty, and Secretary Acheson dismissed Service on the following day.[41]

The High Court ruled that Acheson had the discretionary power to discharge Service, but he had used the wrong procedure. The case was remanded to the district court for further proceedings, and Service was subsequently reinstated as a Foreign Service Officer.

On June 29, 1959, the Court handed down the decision on the *Green* v. *McElroy* case,[42] which Justice Clarke, in dissent, characterized as relating to whether a citizen has a "constitutional right to have access to the Government's military secrets."

William L. Green was a highly paid aeronautical engineer for a firm whose major business was in defense contracts. When Green was denied clearance by the military because of alleged past associations with Communists, it was necessary for the firm to terminate his employment. The Court ruled that a person so accused must be allowed to confront those who had witnessed against him — in effect nullifying the Industrial Security Program.

In dissenting, Justice Clark noted that the Court's language adversely influenced the status of the Government Security Program also, as there was no provision for confrontation in the Government Program either.

Before the Congress could react with corrective legislation, President Eisenhower re-instated the Industrial Program, with minor changes, on February 20, 1960, by Executive Order 10865. In response, Justice Warren cautioned that any authorized program must contain some provision for confrontation and cross-examination. In the Eisenhower order the witness was relieved of exposure and cross-examination

---

*See Chapter 4, p. 43.

upon certification by the head of a Department that said individual was a "confidential informant who had been engaged in obtaining intelligence information for the Government."[43]

On May 16, 1966, the Court agreed to rule on what kind of Communist Party members are forbidden to work in defense plants. The issue involved was the Government's case against Eugene F. Robel, a shipyard employee in Seattle.[44]

The Government charged that Robel was aware of the nature of the Communist Party, but the Seattle Court dismissed the indictment on the grounds that the Government did not charge Robel with being an "active" party member, or that he intended to participate in the illegal aims of the Party. The Justice Department then appealed the case to the Supreme Court. On December 11, 1967, the High Court ruled in favor of Robel. Justice Warren stated that the exclusion of Communists from defense work, based on the Internal Security Act of 1950, violated the First Amendment.

Three days later, in passing an amendment to the Internal Security Act written to revitalize the Subversive Activity Control Board, the Congress added a section to again bar the employment of Communists in defense plants. When the Board has finally determined that any group is a Communist-action organization, the legislation provided that it shall be unlawful for any member of such a group:

> . . . "in seeking, accepting, or holding any nonelective office or employment under the United States, to conceal or fail to disclose the fact that he is a member of such organization; or
>
> "(B) to hold any nonelective office or employment under the United States; or
>
> "(C) in seeking, accepting, or holding employment in any defense facility, to conceal or fail to disclose the fact that he is a member of such organization; or
>
> "(D) if such organization is a Communist-action organization, to engage in any employment in any defense facility; or
>
> "(E) to hold office or employment with any labor organization, as that term is defined in section 2 (5) of the National Labor Relations Act, as amended (29 U.S.C. 152), or to represent any employer in any matter or proceeding arising or pending under that Act.[45]

No doubt, this legislation will remain in effect until a trial case can be carried up through the lower courts. Then, following prior action, perhaps the Court will conclude, a year or two hence, in removing this stop-gap restriction against employment of Communists in defense work, that the

security problem has after all become an academic one —
inasmuch as security of defense secrets is no longer a realistic
goal (what with undesirable, but uncontrollable in a legal
sense, influences on campus and elsewhere in our society
which tend to produce a substantial number of activists in
the engineering community constituting the major source for
defense workers) *so that preoccupation with restriction of
interchange of technical information, even though related to
military applications can only be considered as a myth and
so should not be a further concern of the Court.* Moreover,
the Court might very well observe that the maintenance of
defense secrets contributes unduly to international tensions.

It hardly seems necessary to discuss the notorious spy
trials, and the dismissal of some of the open-and-shut cases,
because of adverse court rulings.

Although not reported in some leading newspapers, on
January 16, 1968, Justice Douglas delivered the opinion
rendered in the case of *Schneider V. Smith,* relating to the
employment of Communists by the merchant marine. Herbert
Schneider had been denied a license to work as a merchant
seaman by the Commandant of the U.S. Coast Guard, Willard
Smith. The basis for denial was Schneider's affirmative answer to a question asking if he had, in the past, belonged to
any of the organizations listed by the Attorney General as
subversive. Also, he refused to supply details relating to
activity and associations during periods of memberships in
these organizations.[46]

The Court held that the standing legislation, the Mag-
nuson Act, did not provide authority for a screening process
for the merchant marine. The *New York Daily News,* however, did note this decision, and commented:

Score another Red win in the Earl Warren Supreme Court.
This one concerns the U.S. merchant marine.

Having recently thrown defense-plant jobs all but wide-open
to subversives, the high court ruled Tuesday that the government
had no right to set up a screening program against subversives
wanting jobs in the merchant marine.

Some delicate hair-splitting was performed in the opinion,
written by the ineffable Justice W. O. Douglas, but the net effect
of the decision is to compel the government to wait virtually
until a Red-sabotaged merchant ship starts to sink before nailing
the Red sailor who did the sabotaging.[47]

The editorial concluded with a strong recommendation
for positive action.

In continuing his crusade for the adoption of effective

control of Communist subversion, Senator Eastland presented to the Senate, on May 2, 1962, a summary of the cases related to the Communist problem on which the Supreme Court had handed down decisions. Significant sections of his speech are :

My voice has been raised time and time again in viewing with alarm both the language and effects of decisions by that body that transgress constitutional principles, established precedents, and threaten fundamentally the basic security of our country from the onslaught of the Communist conspiracy from without and within. In 1958 I had prepared charts and statistics concerning the attitudes and decisions of individual members of the Supreme Court in cases that involved one aspect or another of the Communist conspiracy. The rule of thumb applied to determine the results of the survey is simple. If the decision of the individual judge was in favor of the position advocated by the Communist Party, or the Communist sympathizer involved in the particular case, it was scored as pro, meaning pro-Communist. If the judge's decision was contrary to this position, he was scored as con − or contrary.

Since 1919 through June of 1961, the U.S. Supreme Court rendered 115 decisions involving Communists or subversive activities in cases where the position of the individual judge could be determined.

In 24 years − 1919 to 1942 − the Court decided only 11 cases in this category. Of these 11, the first 7 were decided against the Communist position and in favor of the Government.

Since 1943 down to June 1961, 104 cases involving communism or subversion have been decided where the position of the individual judge could be ascertained.

Madame President, I ask unanimous consent that a chart containing a detailed breakdown of the cases to which I have referred be printed at this point in the RECORD.

There being no objection, the chart was ordered to be printed in the RECORD, as follows:

Mr. EASTLAND. Madame President, from 1943 through 1953, a total of 34 cases in the described category were considered. A majority of the Court voted in favor of the position advocated by the Communists in 15 cases, and held contrary to what the Communists wanted in 19 cases.

Earl Warren took the oath of office as Chief Justice in October 1953. In the 7½ years since he has been Chief Justice the Court has heard the enormous total of 70 cases or more involving Communist or subversive activities in one form or another. Forty-six of these decisions have sustained the position advocated by the Communists, and 24 have been to the contrary.

In regard to decisions involving subversive activities, the balance of power on the presently constituted Court has been frightfully narrow. Justice Stewart was appointed to the Court in October 1958. He did not participate in any of the cases contained in the original tabulations. He has participated in 20 of the decisions now under discussion since that time. In 12 of these 20 decisions, he was the swing man in a 5-4 decision contrary to the position advocated by the Communist Party. If these 12 decisions had been on the "pro" side, the box score of the Warren Court would stand at 58 pro-Communist decisions and only 12 taking the contrary position.

Now let me turn from the composite results of the opinions to the box score registered by the individual judges. Hugo Black is the senior judge on the Supreme Court. He has been on the Court since August 1937. As to cases involving communism or subversive activities, it is impossible for a man to demonstrate greater consistency than he has evidenced. Over this span of 24 years, he participated in 102 decisions where his position could be ascertained. He supported the position urged upon the Court by the Communist Party or its sympathizers exactly 102 times. His support of decisions contrary to the position urged by the Communists is zero.

Justice Douglas participated in a total of 100 cases. Out of this total he reached a conclusion favorable to the position urged by the Communists 97 times and held to the contrary 3 times.

Chief Justice Warren participated in 65 decisions. His box score is 62 pro and 3 contrary.

Justice Brennan has participated in 51 cases. His score is 49 pro and 2 con.

Justice Frankfurter participated in a total of 103 decisions. His record reveals 69 votes pro and 34 votes con.

Now the pendulum swings to the judges who have opposed the position urged by the Communists more than they have supported it. Justice Clark has the longest record of vigorous opposition to the position favoring communism or subversive activities. Out of a total of 82 opinions, he has been on the pro side only 21 times and contrary 61.

Justice Harlan's decisions total 65 — 30 pro, 35 con.
Justice Whittaker, 42 decisions — 12 pro, 30 con.
Justice Stewart, 20 decisions — 6 pro, 14 con.

One of the results of these red-coddling decisions was a ourt order upholding university professorships for Com- unists, issued on October 20, 1969 in the Los Angeles uperior Court by Judge Jerry Pacht — a liberal appointee of rmer Governor Pat Brown. The issue developed when ngela Davis, a militant Negro and former student of Herbert arcuse, announced she was a Communist — just following r appointment as a professor at the University of California Los Angeles. The *Los Angeles Times* commented, melling unmistakably like a carefully contrived plot" (to place an admitted Communist in the California University system). Other University Communists may now "surface," and the Communist Party can move more into the open.

Although Mr. Nixon could, in the course of time, effect reversals to many of the pro-Communist decisions of the Court by making new appointments to the bench, the matter is too urgent for such a long-range solution. Also, the correction of such an interlocking chain of decisions really calls for legislative action.

In 1969, a lengthy (123 page) bill entitled, "Internal Security Act of 1969" (S-12) was introduced in the Senate. Reportedly this bill has Administration backing. However, the Red lobby is so strong in Washington that the passage of a substantive version of this bill would seem highly problematical.

What is really needed to bring about corrective legislation is polarization of public opinion on the issue of the rapid growth of domestic communism, the success of Communists in Washington in heading off effective military action in Vietnam and otherwise undermining the structure of American society. Given this, there would be no difficulty in passing what is really needed to correct past Court decisions and to provide positive control of the Reds — a Constitutional Amendment. Alternately, the Congress

TIME REQUIRED TO RATIFY CONSTITUTIONAL AMENDMENTS 11-24

Amend. No.	Proposed	Ratified	Months in Approval
11	Mar. 1794	Feb. 1795	11
12	Dec. 1803	July 1804	6
13	Jan. 1865	Dec. 1865	11
14	June 1866	?	—
15	Feb. 1869	Feb. 1870	12
16	July 1909	Feb. 1913	53
17	May 1912	Apr. 1913	11
18	Dec. 1917	Jan. 1919	13
19	June 1919	Aug. 1920	14
20	Mar. 1932	Jan. 1933	8
21	Feb. 1933	Dec. 1933	10
22	Mar. 1947	Feb. 1951	47
23	June 1960	Mar. 1961	9
24	Aug. 1962	Jan. 1964	17
		Average	17

could increase or reduce the number of Judges in the Supreme Court, or limit their tenure. Also the Congress could withdraw certain types of cases from the Court's jurisdiction.

Because of the many issues involved, and the long series of related decisions, it would seem that the most forthright approach would be a constitutional amendment. Legislation, if enacted, is subjected to Presidential and Court review – the latter extending many years into the future. Although the question of the time required to pass an amendment might seem critical, the preceding table shows that the average time for passage of the existing amendments has been 17 months.

Frequently, in computing averages, data samples which are excessively out of the norm are rejected. If the 16th and 22nd Amendments are not included, the average time for the ratification of the other amendments is 11 months.

This amendment might very well be entitled the National Security Amendment – or even The National Survival Amendment, were it not inappropriate to do so. The following items are offered for consideration in developing such an amendment:

- Communist Party and satellite groups banned.
- Require all Federal Government employees to be cleared to equivalent of the Secret level, including supporting personnel of the Congress and the Supreme Court, State, CIA, NASA, Foreign Service, Health, Education and Welfare Department, U.S. U.N. staff, etc.
- Bar "former" Communists from responsible positions in unions, industry and the professions.
- Registration of all "former" Communists.
- Activation of the confinement camps provided for under the Internal Security Act.
- Withhold passports from "former" Communists.
- Federal support and encouragement of State security programs.
- State autonomy in requiring loyalty oaths, investigating and selecting state employees.
- Prohibition of employment of homosexuals by the Federal Government.
- Delivery of Communist propaganda in the mails placed on a par with that accorded U.S. mail in the Red bloc.
- Bar reference to international agreements, such as the U.N. Charter or disarmament treaties, in rendering Court decisions.
- Limit of exchange of diplomatic personnel between the

U.S. and nations of the Red Bloc to an equal exchange basis, including UN personnel.

- Clarify status of various sections of the Smith, Internal Security and Communist Control Acts, to comply with the Amendment.
- Testimony of confidential witnesses and various types of recorded conversations allowable in cases involving Communism.
- Transfer of the security, investigating function of the FBI to the responsibility of the Congress, provide for a director of this group appointed by the Congress, and authorize this group to investigate and issue clearance for *all* Federal employees as well as all industrial jobs requiring security clearance.

The second and last items require explanation. At the present time the office assistants of the members of Congress are considered as temporary employees, and therefore are not required to be subject to security clearance. The same situation applies to the Supreme Court, where each justice selects one or two graduating law students for one or two year terms, following which they are replaced with new graduates. Since the positions are temporary, and since the Court is still following the same procedure of the preceding century in this regard, the positions do not require formal clearance or loyalty investigation. These young men prepare briefs of cases submitted and otherwise assist in the selection of the cases to be heard by the Court. In some instances there have been indications that they have contributed substantially to the writing of the decisions handed down.[48]

The alarming direction in which this uncontrolled situation is developing is shown by the following editorial from the *San Diego Union,* July 23, 1966, at which time it appeared that a prominent Berkeley activist was to be selected as a clerk:

TIGAR IN THE COURT*

The selection of Mike Tigar as a law clerk to Supreme Court Justice William Brennan is an example of poor judgment, which unfortunately also raises questions of national security.

The title "law clerk" is misleading because it connotes an image of an innocent errand boy or aide. To the contrary, the post is a highly important part of the Supreme Court decision-making process.

---

*Editorial, *San Diego Union,* July 23, 1966. Reprinted by permission.

As a clerk to Mr. Brennan, Tigar will research many of the cases for his superior, recommend cases he thinks should be reviewed, brief the justice and assist in writing opinions.

It is reported that Tigar received recommendations for the position from the faculty of Boalt Law School of the University of California at Berkeley on the basis of academic standing. In selecting his clerk, however, Mr. Brennan also should have sought advice of the House Committee on Un-American activities.

The committee reported Tigar was among young radicals who organized in 1964 the founding convention of the W. E. B. Du Bois Society, which has been labeled a Communist operation by the Federal Bureau of Investigation and the attorney general.

He has also led a U.S. leftist group abroad, was a prime mover in the so-called "free speech" movement at the University of California at Berkeley, participated in the so-called "Fair Play for Cuba Committee," wrote for two Communist publications while a student, and was "legal" adviser to Bettina Aptheker, a professed Communist.

Because his activity leaves little doubt of the kind of influence Tigar will try to exert on the highest court in the land, he should be discharged as soon as possible.

Fortunately, Tigar was not allowed to take this position — no doubt public pressure, such as this editorial, was effective. *There was no legal reason why he could not have been given the position.*

As to the last item, transferring the responsibility for clearance to the Congress, under the current security program the final authority for issuance of clearance rests with the administrative heads of the various executive departments. Clearly, this individual cannot always be wholly impartial. For example, there have been charges in the past, that an incoming Secretary gave a number of personal acquaintances "quickie" clearance, prior to the completion of the required security questionnaire by the individuals.

The issue of Congressional investigation of Executive personnel in the past was, obviously, in part, political. With provision for Congressional control of the issue of clearance, the need for investigation of improper appointments is obviously eliminated. Moreover, the duplication of effort and patchwork administrative structure used in the security program is inefficient and costly. One estimate of the industrial security program, circa 1960, was in the order of two to five billion dollars per year.[49] No doubt a marked reduction in cost could be effected by a well organized program.

There is another critical reason for isolating the entire security program from the control of the Executive Department. This involves the maintenance of the obviously sensitive investigative records. There have been some alarming reports that valuable files are being destroyed; for example, reportedly the Office of Security of the State Department ordered its Field Agents in the United States to destroy by burning "all completed investigation reports, index cards, and all accumulated administrative material . . . with the exception of field personnel files, current instructions, and the Office of Security Handbook."[50] Further, it developed that in this order for destruction there were included some vital and absolutely indispensable "working tools" of Field Agents and Resident Agents; these records were the "Main Indices, Cross-Reference File, Subversive Organization Index, and Source of Information File."[51]

It does seem that unless corrective action to support the security program is effected soon, the point in time will be passed by at which such action would have been useful. But given a substantive movement to enact such an amendment as proposed here, it would be important to work for a comprehensive and effective measure. A characteristic last-ditch Communist technique is to support such efforts that restrain their activity the least. There are no principles involved in their thinking — only a calculated weighing of the issues at hand.

CHAPTER 14

DISARMAMENT AND GRANDEUR CONTROL

The objective in considering disarmament is simply that of peace. Those who work for unilateral disarmament, strategic surrender*, or otherwise seek to reduce the military capability of The United States are perhaps correct in their judgement, that an unarmed America need not fear a thermonuclear attack — immediately following disposal of armaments.

However, most Americans think of an expanding, developing society which continues to provide more and better goods and services, as a by-product of the industrial-technological development. This is now a frimly fixed way of thinking, and it hardly seems *politic* to propose a retrenchment of outlook.

In this Chapter it is hypothesized that the two goals, disarmament and affluence, are incompatible. In other words disarmament can be successful as a policy only if it is accompanied with sharply depressed living standards.

The basic objectives of the governments of the Communist nations are: to maintain control, effect continuing territorial expansion, and provide for the more essential needs of the populace. It is well known that internal control in Communist countries is maintained by total brutality, if need be. But what is perhaps not so obvious is the likelihood that, were the entire Free World living under the same, or lower, economic conditions that prevail in the Communist World, the problem of internal control by the Communist governments would be considerably simplified. With lower standards prevailing elsewhere, the Communist rulers would not have to maintain the Communist system by force.

That the difference in opulance between various Free World countries may even be a rather natural irritant, is borne out by the developing situation between the United States

---

*Here defined as disarmament by planned weapons obsolescence.

and Western Europe. Following World War II, while Europe was struggling with recovery, the U.S. launched into extensive research and development programs, largely sponsored by the government. Today, the U.S. is spending about $15 billion per year on government sponsored R & D, and approximately $5 billion per year on industrial R & D activity..The combined funds spent in Western Europe are perhaps not quite half this amount. As a result the United States has developed a superior technological capability in many areas, such as atomic-reactors, computers, electronics, etc. This situation has led to the U.S. being accused by some West Europeans of "technological imperalism." [1] It may be expected that minor frictions of this nature with Western Europe will be eventually abated via infusion of processes and techniques, through normal commercial and engineering channels.

However, an entirely different set of circumstances applies in the case of the Communist bloc. If West Europeans are envious of American achievement, how much more so are the Communist leaders? In fact, it would seem that we may have taken a questionable course in trying to build cultural contacts with the U.S.S.R. Perhaps the easiest way to insure the absence of inharmonious relations would be by maintaining no relations. At least the problems in maintaining domestic control within the Communist bloc would be facilitated if the people had essentially no knowledge of the way of life in the Free World — witness Czechoslovakia.*

It would seem that as the American way of life becomes even more posh, from the continuing developments in automation and other technological advancements, the pressure

---

*Some Western liberals have held that as the Communist World "matures" it will evolve toward capitalism and that therefore the U.S., and other Free World nations, should promote trade to aid the Communist economy, thus speeding up their arrival at a state of maturity. It could be reasoned that such trade was a form of "economic-aggression," designed to advance capitalism in the world, by taking advantage of a (temporary) weakness in their system. Perhaps the Communists should be accorded the opportunity of maximum freedom for internal development, without outside (economic) penetration. After all communism is more than an economic system. It also embraces a sort of a crude humanism and an *anti-religion* (sometimes referred to as a "big hate"). Further, this claim that communism *may* mature toward capitalism (just opposite to Communist theory) involves an assumption that communism would not collapse of its own accord, if left alone, while as a matter of fact the U.S.S.R. has chronic farm management problems and serious industrial problems.[2]

created by the "cultural-gradient" between the Communist World and the Free World, might be expected to increase in proportion. A continued policy of Spartan limitation of consumer wares and maximum military developments by the Communists should be expected to add to this chasm between the two worlds.

In general, history has shown that opulent civilizations have maintained strong military forces. Yet, in the current decade, the U.S. has given unparalleled consideration to disarmament and even taken preliminary steps in unilateral disarmament. Strange to say, unilateral disarmament might be sound if, at the same time, there were effected a sharp depression of living and cultural standards. It is hard to visualize how such a condition could be brought about, but it might be interesting to speculate on the effect produced in the world arena by a rapid U.S. economic and military retrenchment, coupled with a gross reduction in the American living standard. Nevertheless, that such a development is unlikely seems clear, unless the beatnick, hippy, anarchist and other iconoclastic elements actually realize their objectives.

What does seem uncertain is the continuing superiority of the military position of the United States. There are strong pressures for continued unilateral disarmament and strategic surrender — despite increasing Communist aggression as evinced by the war in Vietnam. And at the same time there is no policy for dispersing people and industries — long recognized as urgently needed by Congressional committees.[3] On the contrary, all the planning seems to be centered on urban renewal and other steps designed to concentrate more and more of the U.S. populace in super-cities.

To place the Communist threat in proper perspective, it is necessary to consider in addition to current aggressions, the cumulative positions of the opposing forces over the next 20 to 40 years.

Visualize, then, a steadily growing Communist military capability (worst possible conditions to be conservative — as realistic military projections must be) coupled with a carefully curtailed living standard, *for a dispersed society* not unwilling to risk suffering a high casualty level. On the other hand, visualize a gay and glittering American society — with a gradually declining defense capability — centered in vertical cities, and intensely preoccupied with the vicissitudes and indulgences of a pom-pom life.

If the reader will allow these rather gross assumptions

and over simplifications, then consider whether such a disparity between the U.S. and the Communist bloc, as it progressively increases over the accumulating years, would be allowed to increase indefinitely. *According to their rules, why should it? In this type of situation the aggressor would be in a position to obtain control by use of the "diplomatic suggestion box."* A hint passed along to the President, that if Mr. Smith replaced Mr. Jones as the head of the Department Defense or State, relations could be so much more cordial. Once this first step is achieved, then takeover can follow a standard scenario – unless the victim country becomes emotional and decides to fight, as the Carthaginians did, a few years too late.*

In a panoramic examination of the arms-limitation drives (centered primarily on the U.S. and N.A.T.O.), it is just inevitable that every dolsc, every Communist-subversive group, and most fellow-travelers, will be working in support of these movements to their maximum capacity. And it sometimes seems problematical whether we can, or rather, will, succeed in effectively resisting the sly steps designed to gradually effect a Communist system here – by unilateral disarmament and subversion.

Consider then, the possibility that the U.S. becomes a Communist state – thus accepting the loss of independence, enforced atheism, poor standards of living, low industrial and

---

*The Carthaginians were rich and powerful, but desired peace above all, so that they could continue their way of life. But Rome desired the destruction of Carthage. First the Romans demanded tribute, which Carthage agreed to pay annually. Rome next demanded the destruction of the Carthaginian fleet (to insure peaceful intentions). Then Rome demanded hostages, which Carthage supplied. Finally, Rome demanded surrender of all arms, and reliance on Roman soldiers for their protection. Carthage obeyed. In the end, Carthage was notified that she was to be destroyed. They then elected to fight – bravely, desperately, skillfully, and uselessly.

Some of the stalwart Tibetians are now engaged in such a struggle. They admit that it is a war of extinction; but there is no alternative, which they can accept.

As Winston Churchill said, "Still if you will not fight for the right when you can easily win without bloodshed; if you will not fight when your victory will be sure and not too costly; you may come to the moment when you will have to fight with the odds against you and only a precarious chance of survival. There may even be a worse case. You may have to fight when there is no hope of victory, because it is better to perish than live as slaves."

agricultural efficiency, and other manifestations of grandeur limitation characteristic in Communist states. Would this avert a holocaust? Since the answer to this question can only be speculative, the following scene from George Orwell's vivid projection is as good as any:

> Winston could not definitely remember a time when his country had not been at war, but it was evident that there had been a fairly long interval of peace during his childhood, because one of his early memories was an air raid which appeared to take everyone by surprise. *Perhaps it was the time when the atomic bomb had fallen on Colchester.*
>
> ... Since that time the war had been literally continuous, though strictly speaking it had not always been the same war ... At this moment, for example, in 1984 (if it was 1984), Oceania was at war with Eurasia and in alliance with Eastasia. In no public or private utterance was it ever admitted that the three powers had at any time been grouped along different lines. Actually, as Winston well knew, it was only four years since Oceania had been at war with Eastasia in alliance with Eurasia. But that was merely a piece of furtive knowledge which he happened to possess because his memory was not satisfactorily under control.[4] (italics added)

Regardless of the uncertainty inherent in this fictional account, it will be assumed that the reader is not interested in peace-through-communism but is, on the contrary, primarily concerned with freedom from communism. This being the case — and if the hypothesis presented at the outset of the Chapter, that disarmament requires an accompanying depression is acceptable, as a hypothesis — then it is essential that the "accomplishments" and the failures of the disarmament movement be briefly reviewed, to place in proper perspective possible threats to the United States being effected by arms limitation.

Following preliminary discussions between the Foreign Ministers of Russia and Great Britain and the U.S. Secretary of State, on disarmament and control of atomic energy, the United Nations General Assembly established the International Atomic Energy Commission, on January 24, 1946. The first American representative on this Commission, Bernard M. Baruch, submitted, on June 14, 1946, the Baruch-Lilienthal plan for control of all atomic-energy activities (those potentially dangerous to world security). This plan called for the United Nations seizure of existing bombs and prohibition of further manufacture of such devices, and further suggested total disarmament in graduated stages.

On July 19, 1946, the U.S.S.R. presented their proposal, which called for similar control in the atomic-devices area, but differed in that inclusion of conventional arms was to be omitted and the controlling authority would be the U.N. Security Council (subject to Russian veto) rather than the U.N. General Assembly as called for in the Baruch-Lilienthal plan. Congressional opposition and Soviet intransigence limited efforts to compromise the two plans, and as the Russians became an atomic power (and were closing the weapons-technology gap with the U.S.)*, they lost interest in these discussions.

In the post-war period the U.S.S.R. retained most of its war-time mobilization, while the U.S. and its Allies quickly returned the majority of their troops to civilian life. This allowed the Soviets to assure their control of Eastern Europe and, in addition, to threaten the take-over of the remaining sector of Free Europe – then in an impoverished condition as a result of the destruction and disaster of the war. This threat of further aggression arose because of the value of the still intact industries, remaining resources, the talents of the European people, and the valuable land. As a result, the United States bolstered West European defenses by establishing the Marshall Plan for aid and cooperated in establishing the North Atlantic Treaty Organization (NATO). Although life in West Europe was not very "grand" at that time, it was, in the main, far above that in the U.S.S.R. However, the demonstrated interest of the U.S. in European freedom, coupled with the atomic-monopoly then prevailing, was adequate to deter Russian expansiveness.

At the end of the war, the Russians collected every German scientist and engineer they could find in the East Zone

---

*Facilitated greatly by Communist spies working on classified projects in the U.S., Canadian and British Defense establishments, such as Allan Nun May, Julius and Ethel Rosenberg, Morton Sobel & Klaus Fuchs. Also at the same time, many U.S. scientists opposed efforts to continue research and development on advanced atomic weapons. One of the leading exponents of this policy was J. Robert Oppenheimer, who opposed the development of the hydrogen bomb. As a result of his intense activity against the development of the H-bomb, monthly donations to the Communist Party, frequent contact with Soviet agents, etc., his security clearance was revoked in 1954. On December 2, 1963, President Johnson presented Oppenheimer the $50,000 tax-free Fermi Award, in a transparent attempt to erase what had been a grave security problem. (See *U.S. News and World Report* June 11, 1954, and June 25, 1954.)

that had been connected with the V-II ballistic missile and shipped them off to Russia and Siberia. There they were divided into small isolated groups and *directed* in the continuance of their work. At the same time, the Americans also managed to enlist the aid of some of the German scientists from the V-II center at Pinemunde. These men were brought to the States with their families and assisted in the test firing of some "liberated" V-IIs. They subsequently provided vital assistance in the development of the REDSTONE and ATLAS missiles and then participated in a variety of other missile and space projects.

Both the U.S. and the U.S.S.R. were engaged in ballistic missile research, development and test work. However, the Russians plunged right ahead with the development of the "giant" boosters required for an intercontinental missile. Also, they were at the same time proceeding at a maximum pace on the development of an atomic bomb and then a hydrogen bomb. The U.S. had at that time suspended further development in atomic weapons, *despite the fact that the use of the hydrogen bomb was absolutely essential for a practical intercontinental missile.*

Further, shortly after his re-election in 1948, President Truman, and his Secretary of Defense, Louis Johnson, severely cut back the defense budget. As a result, the promising work on an ICBM being carried on at the Consolidated Vultee Aircraft Corp., San Diego, Calif. (now the Convair/Astronautics Division of General Dynamics) was cancelled. Because of the successful test results obtained before contract closure, and because of the vision of the Convair management, this project was carried on by means of company funds (necessarily on a much more limited scale).

It was not until after the Korean War, and the change of command ushered in by the Eisenhower Administration, that this project was restored to the all-out status it merited. But it should be realized that, in the ICBM race that was to ensue in the late fifties and early sixties, the *character* of these men at Convair, a few years before, had provided the necessary sustenance to the "infant" missile program which allowed it to pull up sharply and to forge ahead. Otherwise it might very well have not been possible for the U.S. to have entered the ICBM race * Given an intercontinental missile, a hydrogen type warhead had to be added, as the larger (over a Hiroshima type A-bomb) explosive capability is required to compensate for the limited impact-accuracy of the ICBM. Yet the capability of the U.S. to provide the required H-bomb also came about because of efforts of a few men of resolute character.** One of these was Lewis Straus, the one conservative Republican member of the five men, Atomic Energy Commission (AEC), appointed in 1946 by President Truman because of his outstanding military and administrative background.

In reflecting on the plight of the United States following the announcement of "Joe One," the first Russian atomic-bomb explosion, in September 1949 (which everyone predicted would require 20 years), Commissioner Straus recalled a long-forgotten proposal, prepared in 1945, to develop a "Super" weapon. This super bomb would be as much as one-thousand times more intense than bombs of the Hiroshima—"Joe One" category. Upon finding nothing but opposition to development of the "Super," or hydrogen-bomb, within the AEC, Straus bypassed the Chairman of the Commission, Mr. Lilienthal, and appealed to Senator Brien McMahon, Chairman of the Joint Senate-House Committee on Atomic Energy. With the testimony of the originator of the theoretical model of the bomb, Dr. Edward Teller (sometimes referred to as the "father" of the H-bomb), Straus was able to promote consideration of "Super" by the military, the State Department and by the President. About the discussions that ensued, authors Sheply and Blair stated:

> Before the struggle ended, it set Democrat against Democrat, Republican against Republican, and reached into the Pentagon to influence almost every question of military strategy that arose. It evoked angry discussions inside the Joint Committee,

---

*If the Eisenhower Team had subjected the ICBM project to cost-effectiveness in 1953, they might have sought disarmament negotiations as an alternative at that time. Actually the proposed schedule was telescoped several times, working down from ten to two and one-half years. And this was achieved by 80 to 100 hour work-weeks, for months on end, for engineers, administrators, mechanics and technicians.

**The story of U.S. atomic policy in the 1946-52 period is too much of a maze to be discussed in any detail here. The reader is referred to an excellent book entitled, *The Hydrogen Bomb*,[6] for a good background survey of events during this period.

and some Democratic members even talked of bringing impeachment proceedings against the President of the United States, Harry Truman, if he failed to give the go-ahead signal on the super. It created bitterness in the political and scientific communities that would rankle for years.[7]

One of the major aspects of the problem was whether the Russians might also be working on the H-bomb, as well as the A-bomb. On January 29, 1950, four days before President Truman announced the decision to develop the H-bomb, Klaus Fuchs, a naturalized British scientist who had attended the reviews of the H-bomb theory at Los Alamos during World War II, confessed that he had been a Soviet spy.[8]

Thus the Truman Administration was forced to undertake development of the H-bomb and to abandon the abortive Defense economy program.A few months later the start of the Korean war effectively *buried* the post-World War II disarmament movement.

With the advent of the Eisenhower Administration the United States was to experience one of the greatest leaps forward in relative military power in its history. Although politically Mr. Eisenhower may have not been as intense as some people desired, in the military area *General Eisenhower organized the tremendous technological-military program which was to sweep the U.S. forward and to avert, for a time, its lapsing into a second-rate power.*

In addition to the development and deployment of the ATLAS, POLARIS*, MINUTEMAN, NIKE-AJAX, the TARTAR-TERRIER-TALOS Guided Missile Ships and other new missile systems, General Eisenhower called for many other new improved aircraft and naval units following established designs. It may well be that in the crucial years to come, the Eisenhower years will be considered as a zenith, from which time America began to wane, as various restraints were *phased* into defense management. It is certain that the defense-security now enjoyed, is due, in the main, to weapons implemented during the Eisenhower years.

In March 1958, the Soviet Union, after finishing a series of atmospheric tests, announced that they were halting all

---

*Development in the time period achieved was largely due to the resolute action of Navy Captain H. G. Rickover. He slashed through AEC bureaucratic opposition during 1946-48, and finally obtained authorization for the development of an atomic-reactor, such as would also be useful for submarine power. Oppenheimer had dismissed the possibility of a nuclear power reactor for ships as so much hogwash.[9]

testing of nuclear weapons and called on other nations to also cease testing. State Department officials called this plea a fraud, but countered with a suggestion for an orderly approach to a test ban. On October 31, 1958, representatives from the U.S. and the U.S.S.R. met at Geneva for the first test-ban discussions and agreed to suspend all testing—i.e., atmospheric and underground, despite the fact that underground tests cannot be detected at large distances — while the talks continued.

Of course, one of the prime arguments for this suspension was the gradually increasing, world-wide level of strontium-90 and other, shorter life fallout elements. There was much agitation for test suspension from various scientific groups, despite the fact that the increasing radioactive fallout level could have been sharply reduced by eliminating fission-fusion-fission tests and making only fission-fusion tests in the atmosphere.* This practice was later followed by the Russians with their 50-megaton test — which was estimated to have been capable of producing a 100-megaton yield, had the bomb been cased with uranium-238 instead of some such material as lead.

While visiting the United States as a guest of President Eisenhower, Khrushchev spoke to the United Nations on September 18, 1959, and called for world-wide disarmament. He ignored the prior U.S. proposals, which had included inspection and controls. From this, five Western powers and five Communist powers met in Geneva on March 15, 1960, for general disarmament talks. These were separate from the test-ban discussions, also still in session at Geneva. On September 23, 1960, the Soviets, in another propaganda maneuver, formally presented the Khrushchev plan for disarmament to the U.N.

Throughout 1959, 1960, and 1961, the U.S. continued to suspend nuclear testing, despite strong Congressional concern over the possibility of jeopardy to our security from this policy. But on August 30, 1961, the Soviet Union abruptly announced it would resume testing in the atmosphere. They then conducted a massive series of tests, including the 50-megaton explosion.

In March 1962, President Kennedy announced a resump-

---

* The fission-fusion-fission is sometimes referred to as a "dirty" reaction and the fission-fusion is called "clean" because of the lesser amount of fallout produced.

tion of U.S. testing, although offering to suspend the planned tests if the test-ban treaty, still under discussion in Geneva, were signed first. As the Russians did not comply, the U.S. resumed testing as planned on April 26, 1962.

Although both parties had resumed testing, the treaty talks were continued, as were the separate disarmament discussions. In the disarmament talks the Soviets called for a test-ban treaty, as a part of an over-all disarmament plan to be supervised by U.N. inspectors — composed of local (or national) units until such time as these units were turned over to U.N. control (if ever).

In the ensuing test-ban discussions, the U.S. suddenly abandoned its previous position requiring inspection and controls and agreed to sign a limited treaty, which would allow only underground tests (and atmospheric tests not spreading radioactivity outside national territory). Although this appeared to solve the fallout-contamination problem, which had figured so much in the public discussion involved, the primary concern of the State Department was in reaching some type of limited accord with the Soviets.[10] The fallout problem could have been solved by a much more limited treaty, or moratorium, in which all parties agreed to test only "clean" rather than "dirty" weapons. The results could have been easily extrapolated to obtain the desired weapons-effects information. On July 25, 1963, Averell Harriman signed a draft of the test-ban treaty with the British and Soviets in Moscow. After serious deliberations in the U.S. Senate over the resulting effect on national security and testimony from many sources,[11] the Senate approved the treaty on Sept. 19, 1963.

As indicated in Chapter 12 this treaty seriously compromised the U.S. position on ABM technology and on peaceful use of atomic explosives for such applications as paralleling the Panama Canal.

With the advent of the Kennedy administration, a quiet but intense movement was initiated for international disarmament and, failing that, unilateral disarmament — or at least unilateral arms limitation. Even before the new Administration was to step into office, a meeting of the Conference on Science and World Affairs (COSWA), more commonly known as the Pugwash Group*, met in Moscow, Russia on November 27, 1960. Among the American delegates were Jerome B. Weisner, Walter W. Rostow and Paul Doty.

The Kennedy Administration, after having won a close election victory on an imaginary missile-gap, immediately started various programs intended to reduce East-West armament differential and political tension. A cardinal step of this overall program was the establishment of the Arms Control and Disarmament Agency (ACDA), as a part of the State Department — but with some vague extra powers, intended to limit Congressional control.

President Kennedy, in a special message to Congress on January 23, 1961, asked for the establishment of the ACDA. The formation of this Agency was strongly supported by many prominent figures of both parties (mostly members of the Council of Foreign Relations) and even former President Eisenhower wrote a letter of endorsement. On September 23, 1961, three weeks after the Soviet Union had announced the resumption of atmospheric testing, the House of Representatives authorized the final version of the Arms Control and Disarmament Act of 1961 (HR 9118, Public Law 87-297).

On September 25 following, Adlai Stevenson presented to the United Nations General Assembly an American plan for total world-wide disarmament. This plan, very similar to the plan submitted by the Soviet Union on September 23,

---

* The Pugwash conferences were started in London in 1955, under the sponsorship of the "Parliamentary Association for World Government." The initial sponsors were such neo-Communists as Bertrand Russell and Cyrus Eaton. The emphasis of the group has been on world affairs and social sciences, especially disarmament. But the membership is generally composed of members whose profession is in the exact sciences. Of a list of 38 known American members with some type of professional standing: eight were physicists, eight in the biological sciences, four in psychology or psychiatry, three from "think factories," two were geological specialists, one each in economics, anthropology, law, arts and sciences and the specialty of the remaining nine was not identified.

One Pugwasher, Sir Mark Oliphant of Australia, advocates a course of action which concurs, in effect, with the tenets of this Chapter. He suggests that an objective study be undertaken, and that from that the World's population be provided with a minimum standard of living, with little but equal for all. Although this would eliminate various cultural-gradients existing through the world, the problem of convincing the haves of the merit of this course is paramount. They tend to the view that high-grandeur comes from know-how and other non-material attributes, rather than resources.

1960, called for creation of a United Nations peace force, transfer of control of U.S. nuclear weapons to the U.N., restriction of military establishments — *and disallowance of the development of defenses against weapons of mass destruction.* *

The ACDA has continued to handle international discussions on arms limitations, such as negotiating for the non-proliferation treaty, ostensibly designed to halt the spread of nuclear weapons. It should be noted that this treaty actually will only prevent other participating nations in the Free World from acquiring nuclear weapons, or from developing anti-balistic missile defenses to protect themselves against nuclear blackmail and/or attack.

Also the ACDA, while continuing negotiations with the U.S.S.R., has announced (and perhaps influenced) a U.S. policy of refusing all future assistance to non-nuclear NATO allies in the building of atomic submarines or nuclear-powered naval surface vessels.[13]

The ACDA was specifically forbidden by the Congress from spending money to plan the surrender of the United States. However, such a study was, apparently, performed by the North American Aviation Corp., under Contract No. AF 49(638)-1411, with the Air Force.[14] The entire report on this study contract was never made public—only the briefing charts, and that by an unauthorized release (although the released material was unclassified). Consequently, it is not clear, since some of the steps for disarmament seemed entirely naive, that this was not a poorly prepared leak, intended to spoof the Communists.

Since 1960, however, many studies and plans have been generated for general disarmament, and for disarming the United States — on a unilateral basis, if necessary. One of the more significant disarmament studies was provided by

---

This plan received much criticism at the time it was released. Some Congressmen were impelled to inquire as to who is spoofing whom? The plan was initially published by the Government Printing Office as Pub. 7277, entitled, "Freedom From War: The United States Program For General and Complete Disarmament in a Peaceful World." It is now listed as being out-of-print; however, numerous patriotic groups have reprinted it, apparently as a "horrible example."[12]

Walt Whitmen Rostow, who held various positions in the State Department and on the President's staff during the Kennedy and Johnson Administrations.* As reported in a survey article in the *Chicago Tribune* — the full study was never released to the public — the Rostow study called for:

- Selling (indoctrinating) the American people on cooperation with Communism (largely by widespread use of the word "modernization").
- Economic detente between capitalism and communism.
- Eventual "evolution" of a representative process of government out of existing Communist dictatorships.
- A no-win (over communism) and end of nationhood policy (for the U.S.).
- Exploitation of common interests between the Free World and the Communist bloc.
- Ignoring pleas of allies, or of the American public, in any crisis with Russia (to avoid embarrassing the Soviets, in the eyes of the world, by exerting any type of pressure on them).
- Recognition and support of all East European satellite governments (apparently including eventual recognition of the present East German government).
- Denial of foreign aid, to further the "common interest" of the Free and Communist Worlds (such as happened with Laos).
- Absorption of the U.S. public with a surging economic growth, to minimize possible criticism of these policies and to allow support of liberal trade allowances to the Communist bloc.[16]

Perhaps the most notorious of the disarmament studies (which came to public view) was the so-called Phoenix Study, the full title of which was *Common Action for the Control of Conflict: An Approach to the Problem of International Tension and Arms Control.* This report seemed to parallel and supplement the earlier study by Rostow and is also a "classic" of the dolsc-Left in their campaign to disarm the U.S. As condensed in several issues of the *U.S.A. Reports* the points of the Phoenix Study were:[17,18]

- Immediate, unilateral disarmament of the U.S., without even an informal commitment from the U.S.S.R. to do likewise.

---

*As a special assistant to President Johnson, Rostrow was responsible for planning the conduct of the Vietnam war; he vigorously opposed action to close the Haiphong Harbor, but constantly recommended that the number of American troops in Vietnam be increased. [15]

- Economic, industrial and agricultural aid to the Soviet Union.
- The President should seek "tacit" agreements with the U.S.S.R. relating to interdependence, disarmament, restraint of allies — but not try to bind them with open, formal agreements (thus avoiding the requirement for Senate approval).
- The U.S. should endeavor to restrain its allies and hopefully the U.S.S.R. would reciprocate — *but the U.S. should tolerate a dual policy of collaboration and conflict, in the hope of averting an all-out holocaust.*

It is clear that there is a common theme in these two studies. In some respects they make the same points, but the Phoenix Study seems to apply to a second phase effort. Passing over the question of possible motivation of the people involved in and supporting these studies and considering, first, only the *alleged* effects to be produced by application of the policies espoused one might reach the following conclusions from a basis of common sense:

- The U.S. would not be in a position to re-coup the strong, secure place in the world it had during the Eisenhower Era, if these policies did not produce the desired response by the Communists.
- U.S. allies would vanish.
- What is proposed is sheer economic aggression against the Communistic system.
- Communist acceptance of this aggression without resistance is assumed.
- Communism is devoid of moral scruples: the Communist states should be expected to fully exploit such naive relationships.
- The Vietnam war seems to fit nicely into this overall pattern — i.e., Communist expansionism is being curtailed by "wrist slapping" (no-win) action while the Administration proposes expanded trade* with the Communist bloc.

And if the hypothesis relating to disarm, ment and grandeur control is allowed, the following observations may be added:

- Stimulating the domestic economy and at the same time

---

*The Rostrow and Phoenix reports proposed that large increases in East-West trade be established, proportedly to influence the evolution of communism into capitalism.

reducing armament (via strategic surrender) is the worst possible policy to follow.

- Although the objective of raising the grandeur level within the Communist nations is included, there is no assurance that the economic benefits derived would not be effectively directed into arms increase.
- Reduction of defense levels to those on a par with Communist forces invites the Communists to increase their strength, whereas a manifestly superior level of forces in the Free World discourages Communist aggression, and directs their attention to internal growth, and development of resources they have within their own geographic boundaries.
- Higher living standards in a glittering but weak Free World provides a natural irritant to the Communist bloc, which invites aggression.
- Aid (tribute) to the Communist bloc supports their inefficient economy and discourages natural pressures within the bloc to bring about more efficient production by decentralization of authority.
- A policy of arms-parity, or detente, encourages "brushfire," or "people's wars of liberation" in troubled areas of the world.
- In a weak and poorly armed nation, the government is forced to discourage the advancement of the standard of living, to equalize the grandeur-gradient between itself and its stronger "neighbor."
- Under circumstances of planned, progressive unilateral disarmament, the country so disarming should also plan to gradually become a have-not nation.
- A weak nation cannot ignore trade "invitations" from a superior power (tribute) when the superior power is a pre-eminent Communist nation (this is well borne out with the trade structure within the Red World, between the U.S.S.R. and the satellite countries of East Europe).

A corollary of the disarmament and grandeur hypothesis states that: *a strong defensive position coupled with a formal, aloof and non-too-accessible foreign policy effects a respectful and considerate attitude on the part of the Communist bloc.* In other words, the way to win the respect of a Communist government is with power. There is no other significant factor.

This corollary introduces the positive side of the Disarmament and Grandeur Control hypothesis. For there are four associated factors, which if recognized and well practiced in Free World affairs, under American leadership, could very well not only stem the tide against looming engulfment into communism but might very well lead to the gradual decline and fall of the Red World:

- History has shown that the mantle of legitimacy and respectability moves to the powerful and prosperous.
- American drive for preeminence as a strong, capitalistic nation will attract support in the Free World.
- Outstanding superiority of the Free World nations, in both an economic and military sense, will effect a feeling of despair in the Red World and cause demands for reforms of repressive central bureaucratic control.
- An increasing low level of living in the Communist bloc (produced by stopping Red trade) will further discredit communism.

That these relationships have been, at least subjectively, recognized by historians and statesmen for hundreds and thousands of years, seems obvious. Yet the newness of the technological explosion, giving such developments as television, jet aircraft satellites, space exploration, and thermonuclear weapons seems to have overawed, or hypnotized, impressionable diplomatic and governmental personnel into thinking that the basic nature of modern (Communist) man is not the same as that of Tamerlane, Genghis Khan, and Alexander the Great. Moreover, these conquerors of bygone eras were inhibited to some extent by native superstitions and animistic religions, and additionally constrained by the limits imposed by transportation and communication, whereas the Communist mores have been carefully contrived to synthesize a totally unscrupulous, crafty and ruthless man and man-army-machine complex. Further, in ancient times, a despotic empire generally fell apart upon the death of the founding-conqueror — but the Communists seem to be evolving a method of effective power transfer.

The ascendency of the Free World should be based on the superior free-enterprise production capability possible under capitalism. *Economic warfare should be used to gradually wither away the economy of the Red bloc so as to render the Communists incapable of continuing their program for world conquest.* Why should the United States assist the Soviet Union in the construction of an automobile plant, and as a direct or indirect result, aid in the transport of armaments to the Arabs in the Middle East, to the North Koreans, and to the North Vietnamese? The initiation of any such program would produce a paroxysmal propaganda outburst from the Reds. Chief among their propagandistic outbursts would be the accusation of Western transition into fascism. This is the "maximum epithet," universally used for vilification by the Communists against anyone they wish to attack. It is therefore important to briefly review the background and nature of fascism. There has been too much confusion in this matter of political labels. A lot of newsprint has been consumed identifying various Fascist governments as being on the right, or of being conservative. The customary representation of political structure is antiquated. This system of division separates political systems into a line spectrum, ranging from, say, the monarchy on the right, to socialism on the left, and communism on the extreme left. This organization is not only crude, but in many respects is entirely misleading. For example, it does not even satisfy a simple, nevertheless sage, Oriental truism that extremes are equal. *A more meaningful arrangement would place governments in a grouping in accordance with the free-will of their citizens, or conversely of the personal powers and tenure of the governmental leaders.* *

Regardless of organization of political systems, the close similarity between fascism and communism should be recognized. This is readily apparent from a critical review of European Fascism.

The Italian Fascist dictator, Benito Mussolini, was named

---

*This confusion is shown by the Far East correspondent Robert S. Elegant, for example, in speaking of U.S. policy toward Red China, "An ancillary purpose is to encourage the development of *liberal communism.*" (italics added) In the article he also defined liberal communism as being of the Russian variety, while the Red Chinese variety was classified as "orthodox."[19] To be quite logical and orderly in the use of terms, the Red Chinese brand of communism should be called ultra-liberal, or alternatively the Russian brand could be called reactionary communism (something like fascism) and the Red Chinese variety called liberal communism.

after the Mexican revolutionary Benito Juarez by his anti-religious, Socialist father. In his youth Mussolini was a Socialist activist and his companions were Socialists and Communists. However, following World War I, he cleverly exploited fears of the Communists by the industrialists and landowners to obtain political rule over Italy. Once in power, Italian Fascism retained its Socialist roots, according to their *leitmotiv* "for the Fascist all is in the State, nothing exists outside the state." [20]

In Germany one of the root sources of fascism was an anti-capitalist, anti-Semitic Christian Socialist Party, started by Karl Lueger in the last century. Before World War I, a similar group called the *Deutsche National Sozialistische Arbeiterpartei* (German National Socialist Workers Party) was founded. Adolph Hitler chose a similar name for the movement which he used to eventually seize political power — The *National Sozialistische Deutsche Arbeiterpartei*. (Later the term Nazi came into use in the United States.)

In the 1920s, many of the Nazi party members were recruited from the ranks of the Communists and the Communists were also active in recruiting restless Nazis. Hitler accepted many Communist methods, but also obtained support of conservative and business groups by purporting to offer protection from the evils of communism. On the other hand, he gained wide support from the masses with vague promises of an anti-capitalist order. Even the Nazi flag was an adaption of the Red flag of the Revolution. After seizing power, Hitler was careful to avoid offending big business, but examination of documents found after 1945 showed gross inefficiencies, especially after 1938, when key members of the Civil Service staff were replaced with party functionaries. [21]

The underlying political nature of German Fascism is clearly described in quotations from Hitler related by Hermann Rauschning:

> There will be no license, no free space, in which the individual belongs to himself. This is Socialism . . . Of what importance is it that if I range men firmly within a discipline they cannot escape? Let them own land or factories as much as they please. The decisive factor is that the state through the Party is supreme over them regardless whether they are owners or workers. Our social-

ism goes far deeper. It does not alter external conditions; it establishes the relation of the individual to the state . . .

Why need we trouble to socialize banks and factories? We socialize human beings. 22

In terms of economics, the people can benefit most under a regime with the highest production efficiency. Highest efficiency will result when the proper amount of control is provided at each stage of the industrial process involved. Any organization of excessive size will tend to group too much power at the top. Realizing this, many large corporations limit the size of any one plant and continue expansion by adding more small or medium size plants in different locations. Fascist governments, although socialist orientated, operated on a franchise basis; favored companies were granted monopolies in certain industries. And in Red China over 300,000 families have survived as capitalists and live in a comfortable oasis, even through the fury of the Cultural Revolution. They enjoy the protection of the government and receive a fixed percentage income and may have large houses with servants. 23 No doubt, the Communists will plan to use the power of franchise in the terminal phase of the subjection of Western capitalism.

In coping with communism, the basic advantages of the capitalist economy should be stressed. Economic walls should parallel the Iron and Bamboo Curtains. It should be accepted that increases in the cultural gradients between the Free and Red Worlds would increase tensions, unless outstanding military capabilities in the Free World are developed in step with general economic advances.

If the true nature of the Communist dynamic is not acknowledged, the United States may very well slide into a synthesis with communism. The leftward movement in this country has been noted by David Brinkley, although exception must be taken to his view that really basic changes are being allowed to develop within the U.S.S.R. and Red China:

It seems to me that sometime we're going to meet the Communists somewhere in the middle. We're moving to the left and they (the Communists) are moving to the right, and the differences are becoming smaller every day . 24

Assuming that the United States is able to resist the slide into some form of socialism via the "welfare caress," and that meaningful consideration is to be given to changes which could develop, or be encouraged to develop, within the Red World, it will be essential that the similarity between fascism and communism be fully appreciated. A leading economist, Friedrich A. Hayek, has noted that:

> Few recognize that the rise of fascism and Nazism was not a reaction against the socialist trends of the preceeding period *but a necessary outcome of these tendencies*. . . "Conservative socialism" was the slogan under which a large number of writers prepared the atmosphere in which National Socialism succeeded . .
>
> Not that communism and fascism are essentially the same. Fascism is the stage reached af er communism has proved an illusion. [25]

The Russians will attempt to repeat their successes in trapping the United States into the nuclear-test and space-weapon treaties, at the Strategic Arms Liberation Talks (SALT) scheduled to continue in 1970, by stopping U.S. deployment of the ABM system. Since the Reds were unsuccessful in stopping the ABM in the U.S. Senate, they must now resort to negotiations with the Executive Department. It is interesting to note that the Russians held back on formally agreeing to this conference until Senator Edward Kennedy's campaign to stop the ABM was defeated in the Senate.

One of the key policy, planning, and public relations organizations the Reds have working for them in Washington on issues such as the ABM is the "think-tank," Institue for Policy Studies (IPS). This radical organization is interwoven with similar organizations (through common membership) such as: the National Conference on Military Priorities, the Congress For Peace Through Law, the Center for the Study of Democratic Institutions, the National Mobilization to end the War in Vietnam, and the Council for a Liveable World. The latter organization — which ranked third in expenditures filed for lobbying in 1968, topping even the American Legion and the American Medical Association — was described by a Senate Committee as aspiring to "turn this country into a fourth-rate power at the mercy of the international wolfpack." Lamentably, these dolsc groups are liberally funded by tax-free foundations. For example, the IPS has a budget of $400,000 a year. Financing has come from the Ford Foundation, Edgar Stern Family Fund, Samual Rubin Foundation, Irving Lauch, the Institute for International Order, Milbank Foundation, James P. Warburg, Field Foundation, Cudahy Fund, Edwin James Foundation, Jenifer Cafritz, Walter E. Meyer, Michael Gellert and the National Board of Missions for the Presbyterian Church. [26]

Another objective of the dolsc-Left is the elimination of Government defense research in the university laboratories. "We are not asking you to stop defense research, we are going to stop it," students told MIT officials, for example. Their objective is not only to stop the research, but to keep the student-engineers from exposure to the defense establishment. The young engineer is then more likely to seek a non-defense position after graduating. [27]

Actually, dissent, anti-militarism, rioting and subversion has flourished so much in the 1960's that survival in the 1970's hinges both on regaining internal control and — now, at the last possible hour — facing reality on the international scene.

CHAPTER 15

EPILOGUE

As recognized by philosopher-historian Will Durant, one of the most significant developments in Europe in the last century has been the falling away from the Christian religion. At the same time, there has been unleashed in Europe an iconoclastic force which is engulfing that continent and sweeping throughout the world. Established cultures and traditions everywhere have not been able to withstand at least some penetration by the exponents of the Red doctrine of revolution. And over one-third of the world's population has been enmeshed in what could only be gratuitously called an industrialized serfdom.

Whether one's philosophical views are fundamentally based on the classical Judeo-Christian heritage or are more generalized after the nature of Carlyle's *Sartor Resartus,* in which he pictured civilization as an evolutionary struggle between the Everlasting Yea and the Everlasting Nay, the refined wisdom of thousands of years of civilization must be supported.

Yet the Communists seek to destroy all standards of ethics, supporting only the personal rule of a privileged elite class of amoral brigands. Purporting to base their rule on a simplistic patchwork of Marx, Lenin and others, they have established a morbid humanistic cult which even they do not understand. The specious rationale of Marx was based on the goal of developing a perfect man in an Atheistic society through the elimination of the "evils" of capitalism and the "opiate" of the Church. Yet, he apparently never presumed to recognize the question of why Atheists should seek perfection and the elimination of capitalistic "evils." The mentality of the Communist leadership is similar to that of the religious cultist: they are free to believe what they want to believe. There are few restrictive dogmas in communism, and even history can be adapted to support current purposes.

241

Propaganda based on unreason and distortion generated in pseudo-scientifically operated psychological welfare centers in Moscow and Peking is directed into every country. The influence of this Red cult of unreason is primarily channeled into the colleges and universities. However, in the United States it has also penetrated extensively into the world of the mature "intelligentsia," as noted by Theodore White in his book, *The Making of a President, 1968,* and in other writings. White comments that, "The root of the problem is something I call the new intolerance. In the new intolerance, the U.S. Government is the master of all evil, the chief world agent of repression; the 'establishment' is as corrupt as the Romanov dynasty; and the spokesmen of the new intolerance are infused with a morality so stark that any deviation from their morality is heresy . . . a 'new avantgarde' now dominates the heights of national communication, which has come to despise its own country and traditions."[1]

But, more than the development of cultish unreason in America is the decline of a moral sense of values. Can America survive as a secular society? Certainly a hedonistic society – the increasing empathy extended to pot, porn and homos by establishment society is becoming more and more apparent – cannot stand secure from the international Red wolf pack! Is there an inner core of strength in America which will lead to a great national awakening, or has this country reached a plateau from which it should expect to fall away into a Spenglerian decline?

The one factor which could revitalize this country is an appreciation of the connection between the situation in the Middle East and in Vietnam. According to Anatoly V. Kuznetsov, a defecting Soviet writer who had close contact with the Russian leaders, the U.S.S.R. plans to keep the United States bogged down in Vietnam to break the will of the American people to oppose Communism in the future. [2] The Soviet leaders agree that the U.S. is the only nation which *could* keep them from realizing their goal of world domination in their lifetime. When will those who are so indifferent to the fate of Vietnam awaken to the peril that faces Israel?

According to Max Lerner, Mr. Nixon's Rogers-Kissinger team entertain thoughts about frightening Russians by cozying up to the Red Chinese.[3] Although never admitted, what the Red Chinese need most is American trade. As Red China's military prowess increases, Israel's peril will increase in proportion — for the apparent course of China's expansion includes Africa. Although the Soviet Union might be willing to cede the southern half of Africa to the Chinese during the Red colonization of that continent, the Russians will feel that their control over the northern half is vital to their interest. To insure positive military control over northern Africa, Russia needs surface access through Turkey (or Iran), Iraq, Syria and Israel. *If NATO is broken up, Israel alone will block the Soviet military road into Africa. And as the West German Government continues to move toward reunion with the East, the future of NATO wanes.*

If the course of communism *viv-a-vis* the Free World were charted from current indicators, in a few years victorious world communism would reign supreme. If they should inadvertently trigger a nuclear holocaust a few years hence, they might survive as the dominant world power — considering the trends of military programs in the U.S. and in the Red bloc. Because the Free World countries are always on the defensive, the communists continue to gain control of more and more territory. Projecting a continuation of past policy in Washington and other leading Free World capitols, the logical conclusion is that of a gradual expansion of communism throughout the world — since they obtain a net gain from most of their aggressive actions.

Can America influence a change in the course of victorious world communism? In reflecting on the probable future course of events to be expected, the discerning individual will admit that the American Ship of State still has the same crew of pilots and navigators (at the State Department) which has set the course for: the loss of the mainland of China to the Communists; the Korean war; the co-existence mirage; the neutralization of Austria; non-support for the Hungarian Freedom Fighters; forcing France and England to turn the Suez over to Egypt; a Communist Cuba; war in Vietnam and other catastrophies too extensive to list. He will also consider that only America's stand as *the* greatest world power can deter Red aggression — but that it is increasingly clear that American strategic policy is following the same course taken by Great Britain. As a result, he will conclude by projecting past and current policy that, in a few years, the United States will become a second-rate power — thus opening up the remainder of the Free World to Red colonization. He should understand, however, that such a condition would not immediately precipitate a Red attack on the U.S. but rather accelerate the revolutionary effort already under way for a take over from within. In other words, the present course of events suggest eventual expansion of communism throughout the world by revolutionary take over: the Free World is not supporting the military and political programs needed to resist nuclear blackmail and to counter the communist strategy for world rule.

Although there are serious differences between Red China and the Soviet Union, these are basically more of a procedural than policy nature. The immediate Red objective is the destruction of Capitalism. According to Communist theory, as world communism is established there should be a gradual synthesis of all divergent Communist groups. On this one point, however, the Red logic falls apart. While they can rationally project a course for complete subjection of the world and proceed on an orderly plan, as they are doing — they cannot understand or control their own nature. Unless something of a counter-revolution develops in the U.S., and a policy to break up the Red bloc in initiated, it should be expected that increasing tensions will develop within the Communist areas as the two Red super powers are extending their spheres of influence through Asia and Africa. Appendix A logically projects a collision course in which a nuclear holocaust is precipitated — a holocaust triggered by the sort of action which the Communists are unable to grasp. This projection is based on: the continuation of the muddled, dolsc-influenced American foreign policy, decline of American strategic power, the breakup of NATO, and the key military, political and geographical factors involved.

On the other hand, given an alarmed America, although time is fleeting, the course of the Ship of State could still be turned away from the shoals ahead. However, at this late date, great effort is required. Only a policy designed to bring down the Communist empire can be effective. But this is not to call for a policy of military destruction of communism, but rather one logically *designed* to cause internal collapse within the Red bloc. How should this noble but seemingly impossible undertaking be started?

First, a policy of *information warfare* should be initiated by recasting the government sponsored networks: Voice of America, Radio Free Europe and Radio Liberty. The effectiveness of the broadcasts can be measured by the intensity of the efforts to jam them with interfering broadcasts. Before the invasion of Czechoslovakia, only Radio Liberty was jammed; but since, newscasts from each of the three networks have been jammed. Of course, some broadcasts will always get through. Next, a policy of *Economic Warfare,* or economic non-action in support of Communism, should be initiated. Free World trade with the Red bloc should be halted, to stop building up the communist industrial system.

Either the provisions of the Internal Security Act of 1950 must be enforced or comparable legislation be provided which can be enforced to control internal subversion, "student" rioting, and tutorial propagandizing by college professors. Long range development programs should be established for advanced weapon systems, especially in the area of space systems. A crash effort is needed to allow recovery from the abortive McNamara years. The work on the ABM system should be pushed and expanded to protect the entire country. Associated with the need for the ABM, is that of a comprehensive bomb shelter system. A national countermeasures laboratory should be established to support strategic weapon systems.

Such a sweeping change in policy could only be initiated as a result of massive grass roots demands. A continuous wave of voter demands would be required on the Congress and the White House. But more important still, would be a constant deluge of letters, telegrams and phone calls to the press and various news media. The gentle portrayal of courageous protesters and glorifying obituaries to the demise of "grand old men of Asiatic Communism" must be switched to brief mentions of sniveling outcasts, victimized by propaganda from ruthless Communist villians. Further, the press must be brought around to covering such items as the road from Ankara to Saigon, and to editorializing about such situations as the effect of the leftward movement in Europe on NATO. An organized campaign is needed, of course, which even includes protests to media advertisers. Unethical– hardly! Brutal – yes! But consider Figure 1 and consider the fate of the citizens of Hue, or of the 50-75 million helpless people estimated to have been slaughtered in the Red bloc one way or another since 1919. The Reds consider these atrocities necessary to cower the people after a revolution.

From a military viewpoint, the best way to prevent an Armageddon is to be prepared to emerge from an attack as a still powerful nation. The Communists expect that the U.S.

will succumb to internal subversion and/or nuclear blackmail, but failing that, they are preparing to emerge from an "accidental" nuclear exchange as the dominant power bloc. Though this be a form of madness, in this sort of situation it is the madmen who have the advantage — being willing to losing all. Providing an effective counter-strategy should be considered as the major national objective for the 1970's.

Will the overwhelming superiority of American space technology—which alone could neutralize Red ICBMs and make them obsolete—continue to be denied to military strategists in the Pentagon? Will the knowledge of widespread networks of deep bomb shelters in all of the major cities in the USSR and Red China continue to be denied to the U.S. public?

If a national awakening in the United States is not forthcoming in the next few years the critical point in U.S. history will have passed. A nation who's economic-industrial power could have been positively used to dominate the course of world history, by breaking down the Red bloc, will be unable to resist Communist demands for further American disarmament and more trade-tribute.

Yet if the average American is not informed of the dire course of events, there can be no national awakening. And he has not been allowed to become aware of the true portent of his daily news, and of the real significance of the temporizing activity by his "representatives" in Washington.

But regardless of the fine spirit of the "Majority American," the demands of the present day are imperative: resolute action is essential for survival, and time is fleeting.

APPENDICES AND REFERENCES

tor. This was accomplished with patrol boats equipped with anti-shipping missiles and with aircraft based in southern India and Ceylon. This situation considerably negated the Russian influence in the Far East. After 1975, the major Sino-Soviet competition was for the control of Africa.

So went the capsule reviews presented over the American TV stations on that fateful Sunday of May 15, 1977. It almost seemed that the confrontation had been anticipated, so complete and clinically matter-of-fact were the news presentations given. All that was lacking was some inkling of a possible solution — and Washington had been unable to provide meaningful assistance.

It was pointed out that the presence of the UN Police Force, which the USSR had insisted upon in the Middle East (actually to prevent infiltration of Chinese units westward through Iran and Iraq) was really logical. And the fact that the Arab states had refused admittance to more of the Soviet military was also justified. However, the unified European Economic Community, which dominated the predominantly socialist governments of the major West European nations, could be called on to provide the desired military police force. This was then provided under the guise of a UN peacekeeping border patrol — made up largely of German and French troops. This police force was spread out along the northern border of Israel, in Syria and Jordan.

Following the initial Egyptian-African-Chinese attack on Sunday morning, using small rockets tipped with mini-nukes, and the sudden rout resulting from the use of Hiroshima-size land mines by the Israelis, all over the world, normal trade and business had quickly come to a halt. Only the most necessary services were provided and these were obtained generally by much prodding from harried officials. People were: anxiously monitoring newscasts; seeking shelter in rural areas; or engaging in final revelries before the impending holocaust. In Europe most of the cities had been evacuated to about one-half of their normal population by individual action, and there were rumors that both the USSR and Red China were evacuating all major cities, but no verification of this was available. China had cut all outgoing communications and their occasional radio broadcasts carried only music. The United States, which had launched a crash shelter program a year previously, was busy testing the shelter alarm system — the only portion then completed — so that a sense of irritation was added to that of futility, since little benefit could be seen from alert exercises without shelters.

On Monday morning, May 16th, the USSR had issued an ultimatum to Israel; either to surrender all nuclear weapons to the northern UN border patrols or to prepare for an invasion-occupation by the (largely European) U.N. forces to allow the confiscation of all nuclear weapons and the taking over of control of all atomic reactors and other nuclear production facilities.

The U.S. had withdrawn from the U.N. in 1975, following the destruction of the Panama Canal and exposure of a massive spy ring in the U.S. Government, which had been working closely with the Reds in the U.N. to subject the U.S. to U.N. control. Several thousand Communists had been identified in the employ of the Federal Government

and summarily fired, following the apparent defenestration of th
President. He had unsuccessfully tried to moderate public opinion fo
lowing the "accident" at the Panama Canal. It had developed that a
Albanian freighter was transporting a shipment of mini-nukes fror
China to Cuba when the cargo detonated while passing through th
canal. The only obvious explanation was that of an accident, sinc
Castro's revolutionary movement in South America had reached
highly successful stage and there could have been little cause to prc
voke the increasingly passive attitude of the United States.

After failing to quiet the general uproar, the American Presiden
had several hundred of the leaders of movements like the Students fo
Violent Overthrow and the Black Vanguard arrested and held incorr
municado. He also started to launch a thorough investigation of Corr
munist penetration into various branches of the government. It wa
thought that a cabinet officer was involved in the President's death. O
the next morning when the President's body was discovered it wa
found that the last person known to have been with him was a cabine
member who had flown to Moscow via Montreal, immediately afte
leaving the President. Although the Vice President succeeding had mad
an all-out effort to purge the Federal Government staff, and ha
mobilized the entire National Guard to suppress the open guerilla wai
fare which broke out in the cities, there was a general feeling of uneas
ness and hopelessness. There were many rumors to the effect that ther
were many more Communists in the government and that only a part o
their lower eschelon had been exposed by the top Reds to assuage publi
opinion. And, as several of the major cities and many smaller ones hae
been burned out to shells from the guerilla action, America was in ne
position to support resistance to Communist aggression abroad. Also
the news services were still able to mollify public opinion and thereb
controll mass response which might have otherwise developed.

Russia had given Israel only 24 hours to reply to the ultimatum
but at the end of this time, on 8:00 A.M. Tuesday, May 17th, had ag
reed to a 24 hour extension. Two more 24 hour extensions were subse
quently agreed upon, to allow continuation of the frenzied around-the
clock diplomatic negotiations. In the meantime, military forces all ove
the world were mobilizing and cities were being evacuated.

As the talks continued at the new U.N. headquarters in Nicosia
Cyprus, more and more U.N. (Socialist) forces were being air-transporte
to Syria and Jordan. Russian forces were being rushed to Kurdistan
which had been set up in 1976 as an "independent" Communist natiou
under the followers of Mullah Mustata El-Barazoni, a former Lieutenan
general in the Soviet Army, and his deputy, Jelal Talabani. Actuall
Kurdistan had been established as a robber-baron fiefdom in the north
ern part of Iraq in 1961, but when its existence was formalized durin;
the last year, the Russians had forced Turkey and Iran to cede a narrov
strip of land to the new nation. This provided a common border betwee
Kurdistan and the U.S.S.R.

But as the talks continued, and several divisions of U.N. ane
Soviet troops were brought into position in the surrounding areas, i

252

was suddenly noticed that the Israeli Air Force had largely disappeared. What had been thought to be Israeli aircraft, dispersed in the vicinity of the military and civilian airports, turned out to be mostly well-built dummies. The Israelis, knowing that their airfields were being zeroed in by missile launchers both from Alexandria and Kurdistan, as well as from mobile launchers in Syria and possibly from IRBM bases in the USSR, had quietly removed two hundred of their best fighter-bombers to a secret base or bases, two or three at a time, at night, and had substituted dummy aircraft at the Israeli airports.

Although the United States had no representation at these negotiations, no longer being a member of the U.N., it was generally known that the Israelis were secretly coordinating the whole situation with the U.S. True, the American fleet had been withdrawn from the Mediterranean to counter the presence of the Soviet Caribbean fleet, based at Havana. Also, U.S. submarines were still operating in the Atlantic but had been withdrawn from the Mediterranean, after it was discovered that the Russians generally tracked their course in the clear water there from special Algerian-based patrol aircraft equipped with high power green laser radars designed specially for anti-submarine operations. Also there were high speed patrol boats equipped with an underwater green laser for sub-tracking which would follow the subs, once they were detected by the Soviet planes. Another factor compelling the withdrawal of the American fleet from European waters was the licensing of Red privateers by the Communist government of Chile. As all U.S. shipping between the East and West coasts was now forced to sail around South America, the U.S. Navy had to convoy American shipping to provide protection against the Red raiders.

Upon discovering the absence of the best Israeli fighter-bombers, on Thursday, May 19th, the Russians immediately added the surrender of all Israeli aircraft to the ultimatum for control of all nuclear facilities and the corridor through Israel to Egypt. What the Russians feared was that these planes had been flown to South Africa to assist that country in holding out against their obviously inevitable conquest — whether by Chinese or Russian forces — in return for sanctuary for such principal members of the Israeli government and leading citizens as could be evacuated by air.

There was not the least suspicion that the 200 Israeli pilots, each personally selected by the Premier himself, had flown their planes on two hundred different routes, at dangerous ground-hopping levels (to avoid detection by U.N. and Soviet radars) to meet at two secret landing strips in Turkey and Iran. These impacted-earth runways had been specially prepared for such an occasion by the Israeli civil engineering staff which had previously worked in the vicinities on dam construction and irrigation projects. Once safely landed, the planes were serviced and the two 20-kiloton nuclear bombs they each carried given a final readiness check while the pilots rested for what each expected to be his last flight — but one that was apparently inevitable. For these 200 brave men were to undertake a mission perhaps without parallel since David faced Goliath — although unlike David they had no chance for personal survival.

Their assignment was to attack 200 key targets in U.S.S.R., selected on a priority basis designed to blast the industrial system of that Red empire as far back into the 19th century as possible. Flight plans had been painstakingly prepared for this contingency. Take-off times for each plane had been worked out to coordinate the various time-over-targets to one minute.

The Russians had moved many of their anti-aircraft defenses from the Ukraine north to face the trans-polar American threat, following the withdrawal of the U.S. fleet from the Mediterranean and the Soviet take-over of the series of former American Air Bases in Italy and North Africa. Also they had moved some of the anti-aircraft missile defenses to eastern Siberia to face the growing Chinese threat in that sector. Since the Israeli planes were equipped with highly advanced electronic counter measures equipment, to defeat tracking by ground-based missile defense radars, the probability of success of their mission was high, following their undetected arrivals at the two secret bases.

As the pilots rested, the service crews, who had been flown in by air transport, carefully serviced the airplanes and their superiors desperately continued the negotiations on Cyprus, hoping against hope that this horrible mission, now only hours away, could somehow be cancelled. It was not only the fate of these brave pilots and that of the millions of people in Israel, but also the lives of those living in many other nations, that was hanging in the balance.

The United States was at last equipped with a nationwide ABM system, and Europe was now seemingly safe as a peripheral part of the socialist bloc. Rationally, retribution by the Russians would be localized to the Middle East. But the iron-handed rule which had been established from the Kremlin was most rational when uncontested. Marshal Yakovlevich, who had reestablished a Stalin-like control over the U.S.S.R., had shown rare genius in managing the bloodless "conquest" of Europe and in meeting ploy with counter ploy in dealing with the Chinese. But his superlative strategy could only excite admiration from unconcerned observers – if there were such.

Because of the ancient prejudice which the Russians bore against the Chinese and the superiority they felt over the yellow race – so it had been carefully debated in many Israeli strategy meetings the last few years – an initial blow from the Israeli air force would most likely trigger a Sino-Soviet conflict. If the Soviets then attacked the Americans, both would be annihilated and the Chinese would be left to assume world rule, but if they attacked the Chinese, the yellow race could be returned to a rice and pork economy. And the continuation and ascendancy of white-rule communism might be possible through: rebuilding the surviving sectors of the Russian industry; from solidifying the loose control of Western Europe (if China did not strike against the Europeans also); and, from continuation of the still-effective subversion in the United States. But if a badly crippled Soviet Union, so the Israeli analysts concluded, did not attack China, the U.S.S.R. could only expect to slowly recover under the supervision of the Chinese. This analysis had also been supported by reports from a Shinbet (Israeli CIA) agent, placed high in the Soviet Government, to the effect that in the event of an U.S.–U.S.S.R. exchange, Russia had contingency plans to insure that China would in no case survive intact.

The major complication anticipated by the Israeli planners was that following a Russian attack, the Chinese might launch ICBM's against the United States in an attempt to involve the U.S. and the U.S.S.R. in conflict. It would be difficult to determine, from radars located in the United States, whether the missiles coming toward the U.S. over the north pole region had been launched in China or Siberia. However, a few months previously the United States had deployed two special radar tracking ships in Japanese waters, which had the capability of tracking ICBM launchers from the China-Siberian area. Hopefully, the presence of these tracking ships would discourage the Chinese from attempting to simulate a Russian attack on the United States.

As hope died in the hearts of the Israeli diplomatic team negotiations at Nicosia, the last minute preparations were made at the secret air bases in Turkey and Iran. As the zero hour arrived at 2:00 A.M. on Saturday, May 21, the coded affirmative command was received by radio, and the planes started taking off over a one and one-half hour interval — calculated to place each plane over the selected targets simultaneously at dawn.

Five minutes before zero-time, the Israeli Prime Minister stepped to a microphone, deep in a mountain bomb shelter. Solemnly he started reading his short, carefully timed, address, his voice so heavy with emotion that only his great will power enabled him to speak at all. Simultaneously, over many radio stations, instant translations were beamed, to reach all nations with the fateful message.

THE GERMAN VOLKS-ATOMBOMBEN
AND CHINESE 'ATOM CRACKERS'

Since the outbreak of the war, interest in uranium has intensified in Germany. I have now learned that research there is being carried out in great secrecy and that it has been extended to another of the Kaiser-Wilhelm Institutes, the Institute of Physics. The latter has been taken over by the Government and a group of physicists is. . .

So wrote Albert Einstein to President Roosevelt on March 7, 1940. But this letter merely supported the large amount of intelligence data already reaching the U.S., much through British sources, which conclusively indicated that the Germans had launched a large nuclear research program. Subsequently, as a result, the U.S. Manhattan Project was established and the development of the American atom bomb had a major effect on the course of subsequent world history.*

The initial American effort was a parallel one to that of the British, with each of the five possible methods of bomb manufacture being investigated simultaneously. The five methods were: the graphite reactor, heavy-water reactor, gaseous-diffusion, electromagnetic, and gas centrifuge processes. The first two involved production of a plutonium bomb and the last three a uranium-235 (U-235) type of bomb. In the U.S. the heavy water method was abandoned in favor of the simpler graphite reactor process, which led to the successful test of the first plutomium bomb on July 16, 1945.

The work on the gas centrifuge process was stopped early in the war by the Manhattan Project director, General Leslie R. Groves, because of the lackadaisical efforts by the university-industry team involved. [1] The significance of this decision will soon become apparent.

In the course of time, in parallel with the work on the plutonium bomb, the U.S. was able to also perfect the electromagnetic and gaseous diffusion methods for separation of U-235 and develop a U-235 bomb.

Although the explosive power of plutonium and U-235 bombs are comparable, the essential factor is that a U-235 bomb is required as a trigger for the hydrogen, or H-bomb. The much cheaper plutonium bomb cannot be used as an H-bomb trigger, and it is only the H-bomb which produces multi-megaton explosions.

Although the American bomb project quickly became a massive all out, maximum priority effort, the German activity was never centralized but remained divided into small projects at several universities and

---

* The story of the American effort is interestingly told in Stephane Groueff's *Manhattan Project,* Bantam Q 3643.

laboratories which tended to duplicate each others work. By 1942, they had worked out most of the background theory but were concerned not to let Hitler know that a bomb was feasible. There was some vague talk about explosives, but most discussions centered on the use of atomic energy for electrical power after the war. Nevertheless the gas centrifuge, or *ultracentrifuge* as they called it, method for production of U-235 had been successfully tested on a laboratory scale and production facilities were being established when the war ended. [2] The merit of the gas centrifuge process is that it was (is) a much cheaper process relative to the gaseous diffusion method developed in the United States. It is interesting to review the comment on the German effort by Dr. Samuel A. Goudsmit, chief American investigator of the German nuclear activity after the war:

> On the whole, we gained the definite impression that the German scientists did not support their country in the war effort. The principal thing was to obtain money from the government for their own researches, pretending that they might be of value to the war effort. One genuine selling point which they used extensively was that pure research in Germany in many fields was far behind the United States. [3]

It is significant to note that when the Russians invaded Germany they apparently had been fully informed on the German activity as they picked up the key atomic scientists and induced them to go to Russia by attractive contracts. However, it may be assumed that the Russians would have proceeded with the development of the gaseous diffusion facility, rather than the gas centrifuge, inasmuch as they unquestionably had extensive detail on the construction of the U.S. plants from Klaus Fuchs and other Soviet spies working in the inner circles of the U.S. atomic projects.

In June 1955, the Russians agreed to help the Red Chinese on a nuclear reactor and in a nuclear weapons program. With the Russian help, the first Red Chinese reactor was put into service on June 13, 1958. However, in late 1958, the U.S.S.R. became concerned about the belligerent attitude of the Chinese and put forth demands to bring Communist China under the control of the Soviet military. These demands were rejected by Mao Tse-tung and the Chinese proceeded independently in the development and production of their nuclear weapons and reactors.

The advent of the first Chinese nuclear explosion on October 16, 1964 created a shock throughout the Free World scientific community, because the radioactivity from the tests showed that the bomb was made from uranium-235 instead of plutonium. A reactor-bred plutonium bomb could have been produced as a by-product of a power reactor — but the U-235 bomb required either a massive industrial facility similar to the gaseous diffusion plant at Oak Ridge, Tennessee, or the perfection of the gas centrifuge process. And the latter would have been a great engineering achievement in the West. The significance is partially shown by the relative costs: a power reactor capable of producing plutonium for bomb manufacture, $50 million; a gas centrifuge facility separation of U-235, $200 million; a gaseous diffusion plant for separation of U-235, $1-2 billion dollars.

Not only would the selection of the gas centrifuge plant have been desirable from an economic viewpoint, but in operation the centrifuge process requires only about one-tenth of the amount of electrical power that the gaseous diffusion process does. This was also quite important as it has been estimated that a gaseous diffusion plant similar to the U.S. plant at Oak Ridge would have consumed about a tenth of the electrical power produced in China. But even more significantly, the gas centrifuge is better suited for production of a small quantity of the highly enriched U-235 required for the manufacture of H-bombs; the gaseous diffusion process is more effective in the production of a larger quantity of lower grade U-235 required for reactors used to generate electrical power. [4]

Since the Chinese had managed to employ a number of West German scientists to support their nuclear projects they were no doubt fully aware of the potential of the gas centrifuge. Very likely as they claim they built a gas diffusion plant, like the U.S. plant at Oak Ridge, Tennessee but much smaller. Then the output of the gas diffusion plant would be coupled to the gas centrifuge for final processing of the uranium-235 for weapons grade concentration. This combination would have reduced the size of both plants to a small fraction of what would have been required otherwise and give them the most advanced nuclear facility in the world.

But not only does the gas centrifuge appear to provide by far the most effective process for separating uranium-235 from uranium-238, but it has another, and perhaps more sinister application. *Nuclear Engineering International*, published in Europe, comments:

What then is the significance of the gas centrifuge? The principles are not new but, because centrifuge work in America has been classified as top secret, one must assume that this now has some military significance. In other words, it is thought to have the potential (even if this stage has not yet been reached) of providing a poor man's back-yard bomb factory. . .

There may also be some hidden subtleties in the use of gas centrifuges for separating plutonium isotopes. . .*The International Atomic Energy Authority Stockholm Symposium at the beginning of November on criticality control was fascinated by the information that plutonium-238 (which is not produced in any great quantity in a reactor) has a critical mass much smaller than plutonium 239. . .*America would be the first country to worry if the centrifuge succeeds. Her admirable doctrine of non-proliferation would be in danger. [5] (italics added)

What this means, when translated from the carefully guarded wording used by the editor of *Nuclear Engineering International* is that once that the centrifuge process has evolved into use in large scale commercial plants it can be adapted to separate the plutonium-238 isotope from the plutonium-239 isotope. Heretofore it has not been possible to separate these two isotopes. *And when this separation is successfully achieved it will be possible to make atomic bombs with much lower yield than the 20 kiloton weapons used at Hiroshima and Nagasaki. In other words, the next creation of science will be 'mini-nukes' for use in local wars which are 'just a little bit nuclear.'*

Following the first Chinese atomic blast on October 16, 1964 when it became known from radiation tests that the Chinese bomb had used uranium-235 instead of plutonium, the interest in the gas centrifuge was heightened. And the British, for example, initiated efforts to perfect a centrifuge for production of low cost uranium for nuclear explosives. [6] However, at this time, work on the gas centrifuge was already underway in Germany, Holland and France. Although formal acknowledgement of German nuclear research was not made until 1955, practical acceptance of the cold realities of the continuing international power struggle between the comfort-seeking Free World and the Spartan and (during the 1950's) monolithic Red bloc dictated to the NATO members that this sub-rosa activity be tolerated. Following the establishment of their formal nuclear program for the generation of electrical power in 1955, the developing German nuclear industry expanded quite rapidly.

As a logical part of the background research for their power reactor program the Germans resumed work on the gas centrifuge, or *ultracentrifuge* as they called it. Logical, because it is necessary to supply reactors for electrical power with uranium-235 which has been enriched over the natural-state ratio with uranium-238 to a concentration of a few percent, as a 'fuel.' Although the U.S. gaseous diffusion plant at Oak Ridge can accommodate the Free World market for reactor grade uranium 235 until sometime in the 1980's, projections indicate the need for additional enrichment plants to process natural uranium to obtain reactor grade U-235.

The gas centrifuge is also attractive for production of reactor grade uranium since it requires only one-tenth of the electrical power used by the U.S. diffusion method. Moreover, the development of such a facility could be expected to produce reactor-uranium at a lower cost than that available from the U.S. plant in Tennessee. To obtain the uranium ore to supply a processing plant, the Germans are preparing to mine the sizable deposits in the Black Forest in Germany and have made certain arrangements for purchase of uranium ore from Spain and South Africa.

By 1968, over two hundred West German firms were engaged in various phases of the nuclear industry and the scope of their efforts had reached what the Germans proudly termed "American proportions." Not only had the gas centrifuge process been advanced, but it was reported that they had perfected the essential technique for a neutron bomb* and methods of producing nuclear explosions which require no testing. [7]

---

* See note, page 97.

Probably to establish a European supply for enriched uranium-235 for power reactors without incurring American censure, Germany entered into a *tri-parte* agreement with England and Holland to build two centrifuge uranium enrichment plants — one in Holland and the other in the United Kingdom. Administrative headquarters will be located in Germany. [8]

Although these agreements are held to comply with the requirements of the Non-Proliferation treaty, the clear lesson of history is that deviations from strict procedures could allow a portion of the production to be secretly set aside for weapon production. As an example of the difficulty of maintaining adequate control for this sort of thing, in 1966 it was discovered that one U.S. contractor to the Atomic Energy Commission had, over the preceding six years, lost some 100 kilograms of uranium-235 — which is enough to make six of the Hiroshima size bombs. [9]

This is not to say that assembly of complete weapons would be undertaken, or even desirable from a security viewpoint, but merely to observe that it probably could be easily accomplished. However, it should also be allowed that some such program of semi-finished weapon fabrication is, or shortly will be, underway in Sweden, Italy, Switzerland, India and Japan. By the 1975-80 period the smaller countries such as Cuba should be expected to have manufactured, or traded for, a small nuclear arsenal of some type.*

A further, apparently unavoidable, complexity to emerge from the "nuclear Pandora's Box" will be the inspection of the gas centrifuge facilities in Holland. Although the British installations would be exempt from the U.N. inspectors enforcing the pending Non-Proliferation Treaty, those in Holland would not. Thus, the Soviet members of the Non-Proliferation Inspection teams would have full access to "inspect" all equipment and review related technical reports and drawings. However, if the Soviets were not able to arrange inspection of the Dutch centrifuge installations under the Treaty authority, they no doubt could easily do so under the Communist controlled** International Atomic Energy Agency (IAEA).

---

*There are credible reports that some of the Russian missiles armed with nuclear warheads are still in Cuba. [10] But aside from this, Russia and the Eastern European satellites have a staff of nearly 1,000 scientists in Cuba to supplement the training being given to Cuban students at the best scientific schools in the U.S.S.R. — including nuclear physics institutes (1969). The Soviets have also set up a small nuclear reactor in Cuba. [11]

**The U.S. Senate ratified the IAEA Charter on June 18, 1957 and the Agency was formally operating by the end of July. By the end of October 1957, the Communist-bloc nations had gained control of the IAEA. The State Department was really quite embarrassed since they had assured the Senate and the public that such an event could *never* happen. [12]

In short, it should be expected that in Europe, the U.S.S.R., Red China, and even perhaps elsewhere in the world, in addition to the manufacture of the large nuclear weapons with which the public is familiar, *that a new class of "mini-nukes," or "atom crackers" will be produced on a voluminous scale in the next decade.*

What should be considered is, that in the case of Europe, the secret production of nuclear weapons, both mini-bombs for the support of field armies and the multi-megaton H-bombs, may be rationalized on a plausable basis – especially because of the relative decline of U.S. strategic military power and because of the isolationist trend in American Diplomacy.

On the other hand, if the strong trend for socialization of Europe continues throughout the next decade – without one of those reverse movements which are so rare in history – the contrast between Western Europe and the Soviet bloc will be trivial. It is not unreasonable to suppose that the Russians could establish control over most of the countries in Western Europe by continued penetration of the governments, further shifts leftward at the polls, and continued subversion. The West German government has let their prominent scientists assist Red China on their nuclear weapons program so that they could get experience in weapons testing. [13]   As discussed in Chapter 9 it will be fortuitous if the Germans too are not enmeshed into the Socialist world within a decade.

REFERENCES

CHAPTER 1, Prologue.

1. Cottrell, Leonard; *The Tiger of Ch'in;* Holt Rinehart & Winston, N.Y., N.Y., 1962; p 147-50.
2. Creel, H.G.; *Chinese Thoughts From Confucius to Mao Tse-Tung;* Mentor Book MD 269, The New American Library, 501 Madison Ave., N.Y.; p 137.
3. Graham, William Cole; "The Meaning of Sex in Christian Life"; Publication of the United Youth Movement of the National Council of Churches; 1961; (out of print).
4. Holt, Bishop Ivan Lee; (Ed. by John Clover Monsma); *Science and Religion* ; G.P. Putnam and Sons, N.Y.; p 91.

CHAPTER 2, 'He Kept Us Out Of War.'

1. Link, Arthur S.; *Woodrow Wilson and the Progressive Era 1910-1917;* Harper & Bros., N.Y., N.Y., 1954; p 9.
2. Millis, Walter; *Road to War;* Houghton Miffin & Co., N.Y., N.Y.; 1935; p 62.
3. Ibid; p 56.
4. Ibid; p 134, 213.
5. Link; op. cit.; p 157.
6. Ibid; p 165.
7. UPI; *Los Angeles Times;* May 2, 1965.
8. Lansing, Robert; *Diary of:* "The Mentality of Woodrow Wilson"; Library of Congress; Nov. 20, 1921.
9. Op. cit.; Link; p 215.
10. Op. cit.; Millis; p 99-100.
11. Op. cit.; Link; p 210-214.
12. Op. cit.; Millis; p 229, 268.
13. Ibid; p 271-272 .
14. Ibid; p 290.
15. Rostow, W.W.; *The United States in the World Arena;* Harper & Bros.; 1960; p 23.
16. Op. cit.; Link; p 267.
17. Ibid; p 275.
18. Vernadsky, George; *Lennin, Red Dictator;* Yale University Press, New Haven, Conn.; 1931; p 149.
19. Kerensky, Alexander; Interview; *U.S. News & World Report;* March 13, 1967.
20. Ludendorff, Erich; *Meine Kriegserinnerungen;* Sechste, Unneränderte Auflage, Berlin; Ernst Siegfried Miller & Sohn Verlogs-buchhandlung; 1920; p 407.
21. Hoffman; *Der Krieg der Versäumten Gelegenheiten;* p 174.
22. Nevius, Allen, and Henry S. Commager; *A Short History of the United States;* The Modern Library, N.Y.; 1956; p 408.
23. Keynes, John Maynard, C.B.; *The Economic Consequences of the Peace;* Harcourt, Brace & Howe; 1920; Chapter II.
24. Keynes, John Maynard, C.B.; *A Revision of the Treaty;* Harcourt, Brace & Co.; N.Y.; 1922; p 43.
25. Ibid; p 197.
26. Beard, Charles A., & Mary R.; *Basic History of the United States;* Doubleday & Co, Garden City, N.Y.; 1960; p 405.
27. Allen, F.A.; *Only Yesterday;* Bantam Books; 1959; p 24.
28. Ibid; p 25.

CHAPTER 3, Dawn At Pearl Harbor.

1. Allen, Frederick Lewis; *Since Yesterday;* Bantam Books, N.Y.; 1961; p 7.

CHAPTER 3 (continued)

2. Ibid; p 258.
3. *The Forrestal Diaries;* Edited by Walter Millis; Viking Press; 1959; p 121-2.
4. Whalen, Richard J.; *The Founding Father;* American Library.
5. Ibid.
6. Hoover, Herbert; "A Call to Reason"; (Delivered over NBC, June 29, 1941.) *Vital Speeches,* Vol. VII; p 583.
7. Crocker, George N.; *Roosevelt's Road to Russia;* Henry Regnery Co., Chicago; 1959; p 92.
8. Waller, George M.; *Pearl Harbor, Roosevelt and the Coming War;* D.C. Heath Co., Boston; 1953; p 11.
9. Op. cit.; Crocker; p 71.
10. Hearings of the Joint Congressional Committee on the Investigation of the Pearl Harbor Attack, Part 12; p 17.
11. Op. cit.; Waller; Charles A. Beard; "Pearl Harbor-Roosevelt and the Coming of the War"; p 77.
12. Hoehling, A.A.; *The Week Before Pearl Harbor;* W.W. Norton and Co.; 1963; p 29.
13. Theobald, Robert A., Rear Adm., USN (Ret.); *The Final Secret of Pearl Harbor;* Devin-Adair Co. N.Y., 1954; p 37.
14. Ibid.; p 110.
15. Ibid.; p 115.
16. Senate Document No. 244, 79th Congress, 2nd. Session, July 20, 1946; *Hearings Before the Joint Committee on the Investigation of the Pearl Harbor Attack,* 79th Congress, 2 sessions; "Conclusions and Recommendations"; Majority Report, page 266-T; Minority Report, page 266-W.
17. Fargo, Ladislas; *The Broken Seal;* Random House, N.Y.; 1967.
18. Barnes, Harry E. (Editor); *Perpetual War For Perpetual Peace;* Caxton Printers, Ltd., Caldwell, Idaho; 1953.

CHAPTER 4, They Can Only Be Stopped.

1. *Newsweek;* February 9, 1953; p 24 and 76.
2. Bullitt, William C.; "How We Won the War and Lost the Peace"; *Life;* August 30, 1948.
3. Ibid.
4. Budenz, Louis; *The Bolshevik Invasion of the West;* The Bookmailer, New York, N.Y.; 1966; p 91.
5. Clark, Gen Mark; *Calculated Risk;* Harper Bros, New York, N.Y.; 1950; p 34.
6. Ibid; p 368.
7. Bullitt, William C.; "How We Won the War and Lost the Peace", Part II; *Life;* September 6, 1948.
8. Ibid.
9. Barron, Bryton; *Inside the State Department;* Bookmailer, New York, N.Y.; p 24.
10. Ibid.
11. Eden, Sir Anthony; *The Reckoning;* Houghton Mifflin Co, Boston, Mass.; 1965; p 433.
12. Op. cit.; Bullitt.
13. Ibid.
14. Flynn, John T.; *While You Slept;* Devin Adair, New .k, N.Y.; 1958; Chapter 6.
15. Baldwin, Hanson; *Great Mistakes of the War;* Harper & Bros., New York, N.Y.; 1950; p 79.
16. Wedemeyer, Gen. Albert C.; *Wedemeyer Reports;* Henry Holt & Co. N.Y.; 1958; p 428.
17. Freed, Fred & Leonard Giovannitti; *The Decision to Drop the Bomb;* Coward-McCan, N.Y.; 1965.
18. Wheeler, John N.; "Would Not Have Used A-Bomb – Eisenhower"; *Los Angeles Times;* August 1, 1966.

CHAPTER 4 (continued)

19. "Oppenheimer Opposed Atom Tip to Japan"; *Los Angeles Times;* January 6, 1965.
20. Op. cit.; Flynn; Chapter 6.
21. Smoot, Dan; *The Invisible Government;* Western Islands, Belmont, Mass.; 1965.
22. Ibid.; p 4.
23. Lie, Trygve; *In the Cause of Peace;* MacMillan Co., N.Y.; 1954; p 58-60.
24. S.I.S.S. Hearings; September 24, 1953, Part 3; p 503.
25. *Newsweek;* March 18, 1946.
26. Chennault, Claire, Gen. U.S.A.F.; *Way of a Fighter;* G. P. Putnam's Sons, N.Y.; 1949, p *x.*
27. Op. cit.; Bullitt.
28. Ibid.
29. Kennedy, Hon. John F.; Address given in Salem, Mass. on January 30, 1949. Read into the *Congressional Record* by Hon. George J. Bates on February 21, 1949.
30. Vinacke, Harold M.; *A History of the Far East in Modern Times;* Appleton-Century-Crofts Inc., N.Y.; 1961; Sixth Ed.; p 671.
31. *China White Paper;* Department of State; 1949; p 64-65.
32. Op. cit.; Wedemeyer; p 403.
33. Budenz, Louis F.; *The Cry is Peace;* Henry Regnery Co., Chicago; 1952; p 26-27.
34. Utley, Freda; *The China Story;* Henry Regnery Co., Chicago; 1951; p 121.
35. Kubek, Anthony; *How the Far East Was Lost;* H. Regnery, Chicago; 1963.
36. Op. cit.; Utley.
37. Op. cit.; Flynn.
38. Ibid; Chapter 14.
39. Kluckholm, Frank L.; *Lyndon's Legacy;* Monarch Books, Derby, Conn.; 1964; p 52.
40. Op. cit.; Flynn; Chapter 10.
41. Ibid.; Chapter 8.
42. Ibid.; Chapter 15.
43. Op. cit.; Utley; p 150.
44. Ibid.; p 155-6.
45. Ibid.; Chapter 4.
46. White House Press Release; January 5, 1950.
47. Acheson, Dean; Address to the National Press Club, Washington, D.C.; January 12, 1950.
48. Op. cit.; Utley; p 94; (quoted from *U.S. News & World Report).*
49. Kim, James; "Korean War Recalled: Were There Lessons?"; *Los Angeles Times;* July 20, 1965.
50. MacArthur, Gen. Douglas; *Reminiscences;* McGraw Hill, N.Y.; 1964; p 375.
51. Morison, Samuel E.; *The Oxford History of the American People;* Oxford Press, N.Y.; 1965; p 1070.
52. Truman, Harry S.; *Memoirs, Vol. II, Years of Trial and Hope;* Doubleday & Co., N.Y.; 1955; p 374.
53. "Walker Tells GOP He Fears Rusk"; *The Commercial Appeal,* Memphis, Tenn.; November 16, 1965.
54. Alsop, Joseph; "Bombing N. Vietnam Vital to Hopes for Peace"; *Los Angeles Times;* April 28, 1966.
55. "Nuclear Threat Helped to End Korean War, Eisenhower Says"; *Los Angeles Times;* September 19, 1966.
56. Op. cit.; Vinache, p 716.
57. Op. cit.; Utley, p 96-7.
58. Op. cit.; Flynn, Chapter 5.
59. Buckley, William F., Jr. & L. Brent Boswell; *McCarthy and His Enemies;* Henry Regnery Co., Chicago; 1954; Chapter III.
60. Ibid.; p. 17.
61. Toledano, Ralph de; *Seeds of Treason;* Henry Regnery Co.; 1962.
62. Op. cit.; Utley, p 165.

CHAPTER 4 (continued)

53. Op. cit.; Miroson, p 1076.
54. McCarthy Joseph; *America's Retreat From Victory;* Devin Adair, N.Y.; 1951.

CHAPTER 5, Vietnam.

1. Lippman, Walter; "The U.S. Isn't Able and Shouldn't Try to Be Policeman to the World"; *Los Angeles Times;* July 28, 1965.
2. *Why Vietnam;* U.S. Government Printing Office; August 20, 1965.
3. "Why U.S. Fights IN Vietnam"; *U.S. News & World Report;* February 28, 1966, p 76-85.
4. Thrapp, Dan L.; "War Seen Judgement on Both U.S. and Reds"; *Los Angeles Times;* March 20, 1966.
5. Cook, Don; "The Lesson of Dien Bien Phu"; *Los Angeles Times;* March 13, 1966.
6. Blator, Victor; *Vietnam, A Diplomatic Tragedy;* Oceana Publishers, Dobbs Ferry, N.Y.; 1965; Chapter 7.
7. Ibid.; Chapter 6.
8. Means, Marianne; "Foes Of '54 Play New Roles"; *Commercial Appeal;* February 20, 1966.
9. Op. cit.; Blaton; p 95.
10. du Berrier, Hilaire; *Background to Betrayal;* Western Islands, Belmont, Mass.; 1965; Chapter 3.
11. Op. cit.; Blaton; p 180-181.
12. Mecklin, John; *Mission in Torment;* Doubleday & Co., Garden City, N.Y.; 1965; p 35.
13. Op. cit.; du Berrier; Chapter 20.
14. Dodd, Senator Thomas J.; "Vietnam & the New Isolationism"; Senate Speech; February 23, 1965. (page 31 of reprint No. 765-428-96923).
15. "New Light On Why U.S. Is In Vietnam"; *U.S. News & World Report;* January 31, 1966, p 16.
16. Op. cit.; Mecklin; p 162.
17. Op. cit.; Dodd; p 25.
18. Higgins, Margurite; *Our Vietnam Nightmare;* Harper & Rowe, New York; 1965; p 188.
19. Ibid.; p 207.
20. *Newsweek;* September 16, 1963; p 23.
21. *Newsweek;* September 23, 1963; p 23.
22. Halberstam, Daniel; *The Making of a Quagmire;* Random House, New York; 1964; p 287.
23. Op. cit.; Mecklin; p 231.
24. Labin, Suzanne; *Vietnam: An Eye-Witness Account;* Crestwood Books, Springfield, Va.; 1964; p 37-39.
25. "U.S. Admits Receiving '64 Hanoi Peace Feeler"; *Los Angeles Times;* November 16, 1965.
26. McGaffin, William; "Credibility Gap Plagues President's Campaign"; *Los Angeles Times;* September 22, 1966.
27. Krock, Arthur; "Impressions of Johnson, The Kennedys, and Today's Government"; *U.S. News & World Report;* Decem[...] 1966.
28. Alsop, Stewart; "Pity the Poor President"; *Saturday Evening Post;* July 2, 1966.
29. Alsop, Joseph; "What 'Wasn't' Said in the Latest Fulbright Oration"; *Los Angeles Times;* July 28, 1966.
30. Buckley, William F., Jr.; "Intellectuals' Protests of Vietnam War Analyzed"; *Los Angeles Times;* September 2, 1966.
31. "Peking Sees U.S. Torn Apart by War Protests"; *Los Angeles Times;* November 26, 1965.

CHAPTER 5 (continued)

32. Kahn, Herman; "Bigger Wars Ahead?", *U.S. News & World Report* June 7, 1965.
33. Alsop, Joseph; "Hanoi's Escalation of the War Has Many Distrubing Implications"; *Los Angeles Times;* November 10, 1965.
34. *Los Angeles Times;* March 30, 1968.
35. Randolph, John; "Mile-Wide Fortified Barrier Envisioned"; *Los Angeles Times;* April 2, 1967.
36. Sell, Ted; "McNamara's Wall; *Los Angeles Times* June 1, 1969.
37. Cary, James; "Hanoi Irked by Saigon's 'Secret War' ";*San Diego Union;* November 4, 1966.
38. Stanford, Nancy; "Judd Urges Hitting of Vital Targets"; *San Diego Union;* June 17, 1966.
39. Ot. Cit.; Dodd; p 29.
40. "Russia: The Enemy in Vietnam?"; *U.S. News & World Report;* January 30, 1967.
41. "British Reject U.S. Bid to Buy Rockets"; *Los Angeles Times;* June 24, 1966.
42. "Aid & Comfort – USA to USSR"; *Washington Observer Newsletter;* July 1, 1966.
43. Goldwater, Barry; "Should Boycott Street Be One-way?"; *Los Angeles Times;* December 3, 1966.
44. Chamberlain, Rep. Charles (Mich.); (Abstract of speech – "Trade with N. Vietnam"); *Life Lines;* February 21, 1966.
45. Danielopol, Dumitru; "Bridge-Building With Allies Is Best"; *San Diego Union;* June 6. 1966.
46. Taylor, Henry J.; " 'Inconsistent' Is Word for U.S. Stand on Red Trade"; *Los Angeles Times;* June 24, 1966.
47. Lyons, Eugene; "Workers Paradise Lost"; *Readers Digest;* November 1967; p. 264.
48. Danielopol, Dumitru; "Aid-For-Freedom Swap With Soviet Proposed"; *San Diego Union;* January 21, 1966.
49. *Newsweek;* December 25, 1967. p 30-32.
50. Editorial, "World Watching Rhodesia"; *San Diego Union;* December 23, 1966.
51. Ibid.
52. Allen, R. S. & P. Scott; "U.S. Exporting Strtegic Items To Poland, Russia"; *Santa Ana Register;* March 25, 1966.
53. Allen, R. S. & P. Scott; " 'Bridge Building' With Reds Already in Effect"; *San Diego Union;* May 17, 1966.
54. Taylor, Henry J.; "Here's How We Trade With The Reds"; *The Miami Herald;* November 1, 1966.
55. *Washington Observer;* May 1, 1969.
56. Thurmond, Sen. Strom; "Soviet Liberation"; April 29, 1968.
57. Gross, Martin L.; "Saigon & Tel Aviv"; *Los Angeles Times;* April 4, 1969.

CHAPTER 6, Red Power.

1. Waley, Arthur; *Three Ways of Thought in Ancient China,* "The Brigand and the Sage"; Doubleday & Co., Inc., Garden City, N.Y.; 1956.
2. See Reference 2 of Chapter 1, p 103.
3. Op. cit.; Waley.
4. Elegant, Robert S.; "There Is a Method of Red China's 'Madness' "; *Los Angeles Times;* June 22, 1966.
5. Dommen, Arthur J.; "Chow Hints at Eventual U.S.–Red China Thaw"; *Los Angeles Times;* June 5, 1966.

CHAPTER 6 (continued)

6. Murphy, Charles J.V.; "Khrushchev's Paper Bear"; *Fortune;* December, 1964.
7. "Red China Feeds Gore to Young"; *Los Angeles Herald-Examiner;* June 27, 1965.
8. Neilan, Edward; "Maothink Warping Minds of Children"; *San Diego Union;* August 6, 1967.
9. Elegant, Robert S.; "Mao Reveals Direction of 'Great Leap' "; *Los Angeles Times;* August 7, 1966.
10. Gutierrez, Carlos M.; "China Hankers for War With America"; *Los Angeles Times;* October 16, 1966.
11. Elegant, Robert S.; "Half-Work, Half-Study Plan Revived in China"; *Los Angeles Times;* December 19, 1965 and February 21, 1969.
12. Hsieh, Alice Langley; "China's Secret Military Papers: Military Doctrine and Strategy"; *The China Quarterly;* April-June, 1964; p. 91.
13. "China Preparations for Air Raids by U.S. Told"; *Los Angeles Times;* July 6, 1965.
14. Elegant, Robert S. "Uneasiness Drives Youth From China"; *Los Angeles Times;* December 8, 1965.
15. Cheng, J. Chester; *Politics of the Chinese Red Army;* Stanford University, Hoover Institution; 1966; p 197.
16. Rigg, Robert B., Lt. Col. U.S. Army; *Red China's Fighting Hordes;* The Military Service Publishing Co., Harrisburg, Pa. 1952; p. 48.
17. Lapp, Dr. Ralph E.; "The Nuclear Power of China"; *Life;* May 28, 1965.
18. Ibid.
19. Sell, Ted; "Pentagon May Press for Another Bomber"; *Los Angeles Times;* November 21, 1965.
20. Neilan, Edward; "The Bomb and Red China's Intentions"; *San Diego Union;* January 22, 1967.
21. Strausz-Hupe', Robert, et. al; *Protracted Conflict;* Harper & Brothers, N.Y.; 1959; p 143.
22. Cheng, Chu-yuan; *Economic Relations Between Peking & Moscow: 1949-63;* Frederick A. Praeger, N.Y.; 1964; Chapter 7.
23. Ogata, Sodako; "The Japanese Attitude Toward China"; *Survival;* December, 1965; p 328-333.
24. Ibid.
25. Dommen, Arthur J.; "Japan Trade With Asia Reds Grows"; *Los Angeles Times;* September 7, 1965.
26. Hartt, Julian; "America's Secret Strategy for 'Containing' Red China"; *Los Angeles Times;* July 11, 1965.
27. Mendelssohn, K.; "Science in China"; *Nature;* July 1, 1967; p 10-12.
28. Genko Uchida; "Technology in China"; *Scientific American;* Nov. 1966; p 37-45.
29. Heiman, Leo; "Red China Seen Overtaking Soviet Industry Before Long"; *San Diego Union;* Nov., 5, 1967.
30. Hadley, Arthur T.; *The Nation's Safety and Arms Control;* Viking Press, N.Y.; 1961.
31. *The Military Balance: 1964-65;* Institute for Strategic Studies, 18 Adams Street, London, WC 2.
32. "Bottling Up the Atom"; *Newsweek;* June 19, 1967.
33. *Washington Observer Newsletter;* P. O. Box 1306, Torrance, Calif., January 15, 1967.
34. "Cheap Bomb Project Set"; *San Diego Union;* October 7, 1965.
35. Abramson, Rudy; "AEC Reveals Figures on Nuclear Production"; *Los Angeles Times;* June 15, 1967.
36. Portisch, Hugo; "Eyewitness in Red China"; *Saturday Review;* April 30, 1966.
37. *H. du B. Reports;* Box 855, Huntington, Ind.; Vol. IX No. 2 May, 1966.
38. Editorial; "Time to Move on Nike-X"; *Los Angeles Times;* June 22, 1967.
39. Neilan, Edward, "U.S. Keeps Tabs On Peking"; *San Diego Union;* May 6, 1966.

CHAPTER 6 (continued)

40. Cheng, Chu-yuan; Interview; *U.S. News & World Report;* November 14, 1966.
41. "What China Can Hit With H-Bomb"; *U.S. News & World Report;* July 3, 1967.
42. Abramson, Rudy; "China Nuclear Threat Seen as Possible by Early 1970s"; *Los Angeles Times;* August 3, 1967.
43. Case, Frank B. Lt. Col., U.S.A.; "Red China's Seapower"; *Military Review;* December, 1965; p 3-10.
44. "Red China May Have Missile Subs"; *Missiles & Rockets;* October 10, 1960.
45. "Peoples Republic of China"; *Jane's Fighting Ships: '66-67;* p. 54.
46. Evans & Novak; "Early Chinese H-Bomb Could Affect U.S. Plans"; *Los Angeles Times;* June 17, 1966.
47. Axelbank, Albert; "Red Chinese Sub Threat Concerns U.S."; *Los Angeles Times;* February 26, 1967.
48. Lapp, Ralph E.; *Kill and Overkill;* Basic Books, N.Y.; 1962; p 116-117.
49. Hsieh, Alice L.; "Red China's Military Doctrine"; *Military Review;* February, 1965; p 23-30.
50. Lin Piao, "Long Live The Victory of the People's War"; Foreign Broadcast Information Service, Dept. of State, September 3, 1965; No. 171 (4S) – 1965; p 23-25.
51. Chen Yi; Press Conference, September 29, 1965; *Survival;* December 1965; p 322.
52. Cheng, Chu-yuan; Interview; *U.S. News & World Report;* July 3, 1967.
53. Periscope; *Newsweek;* April 10, 1967.
54. Brown, Rothwell H., Brig. Gen. (U.S.A.–Ret); "That We Could Spread Light in Peking is Absurd"; *The National Observer;* February 8, 1965.
55. Dommen, Arthur J.; "Japan Getting Political Fallout of China Test"; *Los Angeles Times;* May 16, 1966.
56. (AP), "Healing of Sino-Soviet Rift if Mao Dies"; *Los Angeles Times;* April 30, 1966.
57. McNamara, Robert S.; "McNamara on BMD"; *Survival;* April 1967. (Condensed from McNamara's statement to a Senate committee by editors of *Survival.)*
58. Whalen, Richard J.; "The Shifting Equation of Nuclear Defense"; *Fortune;* June 1, 1967.
59. "Is Russia Winning the Arms Race?"; *U.S. News and World Report;* February 6, 1967.
60. "The Changing Strategic Military Balance U.S.A. vs. U.S.S.R."; American Security Council; 123 N. Wacker Dr., Chicago, Ill.
61. Prina, L. Edgar; "Russian Arms Spending Put At $50 Billion"; *San Diego Union;* October 24, 1967.
62. Dodd, Senator Thomas J.; *Congressional Record,* 88th Congress, First Session; February 21, 1963; p 2803.
63. "The Neutron Bomb: Why Doesn't the U.S. Have One?"; *Washington Report;* November 6, 1961.
64. Murphy, Charles J.V.; "A Strategy for the Pacific"; *Survival;* March 1966.
65. "The Menace In the Mediterranean"; *Intelligence Digest;* No. 349; December 1967.
66. Editorial: "Soviet Infiltration Continues"; *San Diego Union;* January 21, 1968.
67. Weller, George; "Yemeni Warfare Entangles Russia"; *San Diego Union,* January 14, 1968.
68. *Intelligence Digest;* Cheltenham, Gloucestershire, England; No. 351; February 1968.
69. Kahn Herman; Interview, "Bigger Wars Ahead"; *U.S. News & World Report;* June 7, 1965.
70. "Secret Attack Seen by Disarm Chief"; *San Diego Union;* June 21, 1966.
71. "Intelligence Report"; *Parade, San Diego Union,* January 7, 1968.
72. Stone, Jeremy J.; *Containing the Arms Race;* MIT Press, Cambridge, Mass.; 1966.

CHAPTER 6 (continued)

73. *Jane's All The Worlds Aircraft, 1966-67.*
74. Murphy, Charles J.V.; "Now the President Will Decide on His Own"; *Life;* February 16, 1962. Also op. cit.; Lapp; p 37.
75. "Pro and Con of Test-Ban Treaty"; *U.S. News and World Report;* August 26, 1963.
76. "Worldgram"; *U.S. News and World Report;* January 8, 1968.
77. Morris, Joe Alex, Jr.; "Egyptians Examining Bases of '52 Revolution"; *Los Angeles Times;* February 22, 1968.
78. "Russia, Power Play on the Oceans"; *Time;* February 23, 1968.
79. Bell, Lester; "Russia Subs Training for Offense Duty"; *San Diego Union;* September 1, 1965.
80. Taylor, Henry J.; "Jane's Reveals Mightiest Sub Fleet of all-Red"; *Los Angeles Times;* May 9, 1966.
81. Neilan, Edward; "Indian Red Sub Bid Alarms British"; *San Diego Union;* August 12, 1965.
82. "SS-9 Seen Spurring Nixon ABM Effort"; *Aviation Week & Space Technology;* March 31, 1969.
83. Hittle, Brig. Gen. James D., USMC (Ret); "Russia May Seek United States' Burial at Sea"; *San Diego Union;* October 30, 1966.
84. Roosevelt, Edith Kermit; "Russia May Bury U.S. At Sea"; *San Diego Union;* June 26, 1966.
85. Prina, L. Edgar; "U.S. Sees Challenge In Soviet Shipbuilding"; *San Diego Union;* January 11, 1968.
86. Roosevelt, Edith Kermit; "Degrading Ourselves"; *The Wanderer;* February 16, 1967.
87. "Delays in U.S. Nuclear Ships"; *Los Angeles Times;* December 30, 1968.
88. Lawrence, David; "The 'Doves' Cry Peace But Prolong The War"; *U.S. News and World Report;* February 5, 1968.
89. Sell, Ted; "New Space Peril"; *Los Angeles Times;* November 4, 1967.
90. Eaker, Ira C., Lt. Gen. (Ret); "U.S. Must Not Minimize Red's Latest Weapon"; *San Diego Union;* November 27, 1967.
91. "Tipping the Balance of Terror?"; *Newsweek;* October 2, 1967.
92. "McNamara Explains 'Limited' Missile Defense For U.S."; *U.S. News and World Report;* October 2, 1967.
93. Diamond, Edwin; "The Grand Illusion"; *Newsweek;* October 2, 1967.
94. Libby, Ruthven E., Vice Adm., USN (Ret); "Sea-Based Missile Interceptor Could Be Escape Hatch For U.S."; *San Diego Union;* December 3, 1967.
95. Prina, L. Edgar; "Navy Pushes Sea-Based Missile Defense System"; *San Diego Union;* December 20, 1966.
96. "Washington Report"; *Electronic Design;* October 11, 1967.
97. "The Talk of the Town"; *The New Yorker;* September 30, 1967.

CHAPTER 7, The Holocaust.

1. Kahn, Herman; "Escalation as a Strategy"; *Fortune;* April, 1965.
2. Wolf, Thomas H.; *Soviet Strategy at the Crossroads;* Harvard University Press, Cambridge, Mass; 1964.
3. *Principles of Guided Missiles and Nuclear Weapons;* NAVPERS 10784; p 252.
4. "War and the Cities"; *Nuclear Information* (CNI, 6504 Delmar, St. Louis, Mo) Oct-Dec 1962; p 3.
5. Martin, Thomas L., and Donald C. Latham; *Strategy for Survival;* University of Arizona Press; 1963; p 177.
6. Ibid; p 183-190.
7. Ibid; Chapter 9.
8. Kent, Francis B; "Radioactivity is a Way of Life in Guarapari" *Los Angeles Times;* August 28, 1966.
9. Glasstone, Samuel (ed.); *The Effects of Nuclear Weapons;* Atomic Energy Commission; 1962; p 445.

CHAPTER 7 (continued)

10. Fowler, John M; *Fallout — A Study of Superbombs, Strontium-90 and Survival;* Basic Books Inc. N.Y. 1960; p 177.
11. *Prepare For Armageddon: Survival in the Nuclear Age,* first edition; Lee Press, Cardiff, Calif.; 1968; Chapters 7, 8 and 11.
12. Reitemeier, R.; "Soil and Plant Relationships of Fission Products"; US AEC Report TID 5558; May, 1959.
13. Op. cit.; Kahn; p 73.
14. *Civil Defense — Fallout Shelter Program;* Hearings before Sub-Committee No. 3, House of Representatives, 88th Congress, June-July, 1963; Part II, Vol. 1; p 4426.
15. *Intelligence Digest;* No. 340; March, 1967; p 11.
16. Op. cit.; Hearings, Part II, Vol. 1; p 4390.
17. Op. cit.; Hadley; p 100.
18. Bengelsdorf, Irving; "Physicist Sees Danger in Civil Defense Boost"; *Los Angeles Times;* December 28, 1965.
19. Twining, Gen. Nathan F. USAF (Ret); *Neither Liberty Nor Safety;* Holt Rinehart and Winston, N.Y., N.Y.; 1966; p 112.
20. Donovan, R.J.; "Stark Peril of A-War Plagues U.S. in Future", *Los Angeles Times;* February 2, 1965.
21. Op. cit.; *Intelligence Digest;* p12.

CHAPTER 8   The Ultimate Weapon.

1. Eaker, Ira C., Lt. Gen. USAF Ret.; Copley News Service; *San Diego Union;* Nov. 22, 1964.
2. Lao Tzu; *The Way of Life;* excerpt from XXXVIII, Degeneration; the R.B. Blakney translation; Mentor Book, M 129; The New American Library, N.Y., N.Y.; p 38.
3. Lao Tzu; LXIV, Beginning and End; the Lin Yutang anthology, *The Wisdom of China and India;* The Modern Library; N.Y., N.Y.; p 616.

CHAPTER 9 From Marx to Marcuse

1. Payne, Robert; *Marx;* Simon & Schuster, NYC; 1968; p 317.
2. Vogt, Karl; *Meine Prozess Gegen Die Allgemeine Zeitung,* Quoting the cited letter discussing Marz, by a German Socialist, Lt. Gustav Techow.
3. Roddy, Joseph; "The Vatican and the Kremlin Keep in Touch"; Look; April 16, 1968.
4. Hukari, Harvey H.; "So You Think It's Easy to Be a Conservative?"; *Human Events;* Jan. 4, 1969.
5. Buckley, William, F. J. ; "On the Right"; *Twin Circle;* December 29, 1968.
6. "Hoover Says New Left Is Financed by Wealthy"; *Los Angeles Times;* July 8, 1969.
7. "Reds Play Key British Labor Role"; *Los Angeles Times* June 5, 1966.
8. Gregory, Gene; "Soviet Car Output Expected to Double"; *San Diego Union* 4/20/69.
9. Taylor, Henry J. "Selling Rope to the Hangman"; *Los Angeles Times;* March 20, 1966.
10. Scott, Paul; "Kremlin Seeks to Solidify Red Bloc"; *Human Events;* January 4, 1969.

CHAPTER 9 (continued)

11. Mortimer, Lee; *Washington Confidential Today*; Paperback Library; N.Y., N.Y.; 1962; P 119.
12. Goldman, Eric F.; *The Tradegy of Lyndon Johnson;* Alfred A. Knopf; N.Y., N.Y.; 1969; p 500.
13. "N. Korea called a possible Asian 'Second Front' "; *San Diego Union;* April 21, 1968.

CHAPTER 10, Pre-Emptive Urban Evacuation.

1. Huntley, Chet; "America the Beautiful"; NBC-TV; Oct. 3, 1965.
2. "A Trillion Dollars To Save The Cities"; *U.S. News and World Report;* Oct 3, 1966.
3. Reston, James; "The Big City: Was Jefferson Right?"; *San Diego Union;* Oct. 31, 1965.
4. Brinkley, David; "Brinkley Predicts End of State Rule"; UPI; July 17, 1965.
5. Shirer, William, L.; *The Rise an Fall of the Third Reich;* Simon and Schuster, N.Y.; 1960; p 200.
6. Bordman, George; "Workable? Our Hirlings Will Decide for You"; *The Santa Anna Register;* Jan. 17, 1966.
7. Smith, Clyde V.; "Weaver Envisions Future Restrictions on Land, Car Use"; *San Diego Union;* Nov. 16, 1967.
8. "New Trend for Factories: Go West! Go South!" *U.S. News & World Report;* Nov. 1, 1965.
9. Watson, Russell; "Taking No Chances"; *The Wall Street Journal;* Jan. 12, 1966.
10. Friedlander, Gordon D; *Birth of the 'New City'.*
11. Friedlander, Gordon D.; "Birth of the 'New City' an exciting Creation"; *IEEE Spectrum;* April 1967; p 70-82.
12. Langewiesche, Wolfgang; "Look at America's 'New Towns'!" *Readers Digest;* March 1967.
13. Eckardt, Wolf Von; " 'Creative Federalism' Gets Setback at Reston"; *Los Angeles Times;* Dec. 14, 1967.
14. "Assembly Line Cities"; *Los Angeles Herald Examiner;* Aug. 17, 1966.
15. Kristol, Irving; "Common Sense and the 'Urban Crisis' "; *Fortune;* Oct. 1967; p 233.
16. "Science & Space"; *Newsweek;* Jan. 8, 1968.
17. "Gallup Poll: Small Town Still Appeals"; *Los Angeles Times;* March 23, 1966.
18. "External Financing Needs Grow for U.S. Companies"; *Los Angeles Times;* Sept. 15, 1965.
19. "Open Spaces Get Wider, Cities Grow Denser"; *U.S. News & World Report;* Dec. 18, 1967.

CHAPTER 11, Design for Civil Defense.

1. Martin, Thomas L., Jr., & Donald C. Latham; *Strategy For Survival;* University of Arizona Press; 1963; p 262.
2. Gouré, Leon; *Civil Defense in the Soviet Union;* University of California Press; 1962; p 37.
3. Ibid; Chapter 4.
4. Salisbury, Harrison E.; *New York Times;* Sept. 30, 1954; p L33.
5. Op. cit.; Gouré; Chapter 6.
6. Ibid; p 109.
7. Op. cit.; Gouré condensed from several chapters.
8. UPI; "Fallout Shelters in Soviet Union Reported"; *New York Times;* May 16, 1961; p 30L.
9. Turpin, Dick; "Unique School is all Underground"; *Los Angeles Times;* Nov. 29, 1965.

CHAPTER 11 (continued)

10. "New Buildings With Fallout Protection"; DOD-OCD Pub. TR27; Government Printing Office; Jan. 1965.
11. Lewis, Fulton, Jr.; "Urban Renewal is a Hoax"; *San Diego Union;* Apr. 30, 1966.
12. Lewis, Fulton, Jr.; "More Cities Refuse Federal Urban Renewal 'Help' "; *San Diego Union;* October 15, 1965.
13. Op. cit.; Gouré; p 83-85.
14. "Fire Storms Not Likely in the United States"; Bulletin of the International Civil Defense Organization; July-Aug. 1965; No. 121-122.
15. Oehman, Gunnar, Lt. Co.; "Linus Pauling and Nuclear Weapons"; Bulletin of the International Civil Defense Organization; September, 1965. No. 123.
16. Lindgren, Nilo; "Electric Cars — Hope Springs Eternal"; *IEEE Spectrum;* April 1967; p 49-61.
17. Lessing, Lawrence; "The Revolt Against the Internal Combustion Engine;" *Fortune;* July 1967.
18. Miller, J.N.; "We Must Stop Choking Our Cities"; *Readers Digest;* August, 1966.
19. "Subways Don't Have to Be Miserable"; *Fortune;* April, 1967; p 177-184.
20. Michaels, Edward L.; "Today's Need For Balanced Urban Transit Systems"; *IEEE Spectrum;* Dec. 1967; p 87-91.
21. "A Tax Incentive That's Coming Under Fire;" *U.S. News & World Report,* June 12, 1967.
22. "Radioactive Fallout on the Farm"; Farmers Bulletin No. 2107, Department of Agriculture; Washington, D.C.
23. Op. cit.; Martin; p 242.
24. Ibid; p 263.
25. "Project Harbor Summary"; *Scientist and Citizen;* May-June 1965; p 16.
26. Ibid.
27. Carleton, Don E. (Brig. Gen. USA Ret.); "Civil Defense at the Local Government Level"; Industrial College of the Armed Forces; Publication L60-154; 1959-1960; Astia No. AD 249 066.
28. "State Population Disaster Seen"; *San Diego Union;* San Diego, Calif.; July 19, 1966.
29. Kastrup, Allan; "Rock Excavations for Total Defense and Peaceful Uses"; E.45; Swedish Institute; Stockholm 3, Sweden; 1962.
30. "Shelter Construction in Sweden"; The Royal Civil Defense Administration; 1961.
31. Winchester, James H.; "Inside Sweden"; *Science & Mechanics;* January 1968.
32. Greene, W.N., et. al.; "Evaluation of Fallout Contamination of Water Supplies"; Office of Civil Defense Contract to Merrimack College; OCD-PS-64-62, OCD Subtask 3131B; Final Technical Report for period of 1 Oct. 63 to 15 May 65.
33. Hearings Before the Subcommittee on Research, Development & Radiation of the Joint Committee on Atomic Energy; Eight-Eighth Congress, First Session; On Fallout, Radiation Standards, & Countermeasures; June 3, 4 & 6, 1963; Part I, Appendices 4, 5, & 6.

CHAPTER 12, The Defense Dilemma — A Muted Trumpet

1. McNamara: Why Is He Leaving?; Newsweek; December 11, 1967.
2. "Operation Candor Needed"; *Aviation Week & Space Technology;* May 26, 1969.

CHAPTER 12 (continued)

3. Arrow, Raymond; *TheGreatDebate: Theories of Nuclear Strategy;* Doubleday & Co. Inc., Garden City, N.Y.; 1965; pps 49, 53, 61 & 62, in sequence.

4. Cook, Don; "Pentagon Semantics Can't Cover McNamara's NATO Policy Shift"; *Los Angeles Times;* May 8, 1966.

5. Twining, Gen. Nathan F., USAF (Ret); *Neither Liberty Nor Safety;* Holt Rinehart and Winston, N.Y., N.Y.; 1966; p 83.

6. Op. cit.; Cook.

7. Ibid.

8. Strother, Claude; "Consideration of Comparative ECM Relationships in Weapons Systems Synthesis; *IEEE Transactions on Aerospace and Electronic Systems;* Correspondence; September 196?.

9. Cromley, Ray; "U.S. Eyes Possible Soviet Breakthrough"; *San Diego Evening Tribune;* Nov. 10, 1964.

10. *Liberty Letter;* No. 62; March, 1966 (Published by Liberty Lobby, Washington, D.C.).

11. *Washington Observer;* No. 73; February 1969.

12. "Teller Criticizes DOD Handling of LASV"; *Aviation Week & Space Technology;* August 17, 196? p 65, 68.

13. "Is Russia Winning the Arms Race?"; *U.S. News & World Report;* February 6, 1967.

14. Libby, Vice Adm. Ruthoon E. (USN Ret.); "Can We Retaliate Now If We Are Attacked?"; *San Diego Union;* March 13, 1966.

15. Pay, Rex; "New Effort Aimed at X-Ray Protection"; *Technology Week;* Jan. 2, 1967.

16. "U.S. Missile Defense to Use X-Ray Bursts"; *San Diego Union;* May 10, 1967.

17. *Op. cit;* Reference 13.

18. "U.S. Reported Developing Anti-missile X-Ray Bomb"; *San Diego Union;* November 17, 1967.

19. "AEC Tells Advances in Nuclear Warhead Power"; *Los Angeles Times;* February 1, 1966.

20. Pearson & Anderson; "ABM Effect Tested in Nevada"; *Los Angeles Times;* June 26, 1969.

21. Kennedy, Edward M., Sen. et al; *ABM; An Evaluation of the Decision to Deploy an Antiballistic Missile System;* Harper & Row, New York, 1969.

22. "Soviet Missile Threat Stirs Changes in Air Defense"; *San Diego Union;* April 23, 1966.

23. "Senate Group Defies McNamara on Nike-X"; *Los Angeles Times;* April 27, 1966.

24. "Installation of Soviet Missile Defense Seen"; *Los Angeles Times;* March 20, 1966.

25. "A Blunt Warning"; *Aviation Week & Space Technology;* September 8, 1969.

26. Goldwater, Barry M., Sen.; "Soviet Arms Spending Leads U.S."; *Los Angeles Times,* June 1, 1969.

27. "Jane's Reports 12 Tests of Soviet 'Space Bomb'"; *Los Angeles Times;* October 31, 1969.

28. "Digging In On ABM"; *Time;* March 28, 1969.

29. Andrews, Stanley M.; *Liberty Letter;* September 1969.

30. Leary, Frank; "Antisatellite Defense"; *Space/Aeronautics;* June 1969.

CHAPTER 13, The Supreme Court vs National Security.

1. "Report of the Committee on Federal-State Relations as Affected by Judicial Decisions"; Issued August 1958.
2. Eastland, Sen. James O.; Remarks to the U.S. Senate; *Congressional Record;* July 10, 1958.
3. Dennis v. U.S., 341 U.S. 494 (1951).
4. Schenck v. U.S., 249 U.S. 47 (1919).
5. Yates v. U.S., 345 U.S. 298 (1957).
6. Utt, Cong. James B.; "Washington Report"; August 10, 1961.
7. McAdoo, Bill; *Spark;* May 1966.
8. Toth, Robert C.; "Supreme Court Ruling on Red Party Reflects New Mood in U.S."; *Los Angeles Times;* November 21, 1965.
9. Ibid.
10. S.A.C.B. 367 USI.
11. Graham, Fred P.; "High Court Limits Law to Register Individual Reds"; *New York Times;* November 16, 1965.
12. Goldwater, Barry; "Laws Alone Can't Block Reds"; *Los Angeles Times;* November 28, 1965.
13. Coates, Paul "Commies Missed Out"; *Los Angeles Times:* June 12, 1966.
14. Op. cit.; To
15. "U.S. Court Throws Out Red Party Connection"; *Los Angeles Times;* March 4, 1967.
16. Watkins v. U.S., 345 U.S. 178 (1957).
17. S.2646, 85th Congress, Section 2.
18. Barenblatt v. U.S., 360 U.S. 109 (1958).
19. Sweezy v. Newhampshire 354 U.S. 234 (1957).
20. Pritchett, C. Herman; *Congress Versus The Supreme Court 1957-1960;* University of Minnesota Press, Minneapolis; 1961; Chapter 4.
21. Slochower v. Board of Higher Education, 350 U.S. 551 (1956).
22. Nelson & Globe v. Los Angeles, 362 U.S. 1 (1960).
23. Jenks v. U.S., 353 U.S. 657 (1957).
24. Pennsylvania v. Nelson, 350 U.S. 497 (1956).
25. Pfeffer, Leo; *This Honorable Court;* Beacon Press, Boston; 1965; p 396.
26. "In the 13th Year of the Warren Revolution"; *U.S. News & World Report;* June 20, 1966.
27. Kent v. Dulles, 357 U.S. 116 (1958).
28. *Congressional Record-House;* February 2, 1966; p 1732.
29. Lamont v. Postmaster General (1965), 14 L. ed. 2d 392.
30. Ostrow, Ronald J.; "Supreme Court Holds Arizona Loyalty Oath Unconstitutional"; *Los Angeles Times;* April 19, 1966.
31. "High Court Gets Tough With Loyalty Pledges";*Los Angeles Times;* December 3, 1967.
32. Graham, Fred P.; "High Court Voids Laws on Loyalty in State Schools"; *New York Times;* Jan 24, 1967.
33. Burder, Leonard; " '49 Feinberg Law Set Off Inquiries"; *New York Times;* January 24, 1967.
34. "Suit Filed to Challenge California Loyalty Oath"; *Los Angeles Times;* April 21, 1967.
35. Schware v. Board of Bar Examiners of New Mexico, 353 U.S. 232 (1957).
36. Konigsberg v. State Bar of California, 353 U.S. 252 (1957).
37. Pritchett, Charles H. and Alan F. Westin; *The Third Branch of Government;* Harcourt Brace & Co.; 1963; p 203.
38. Cole v. Young, 351 U.S. 536 (1956).
39. Young, Anthony; "High Court Limits Ouster of Risks to Security Sensitive Jobs"; *New York Times;* June 12, 1956.
40. Service v. Dulles, 354 U.S. 363 (1957).
41. Kenworthy, E.W.; "J.S. Service Wins"; *New York Times;*June 18, 1957.
42. Green v. McElroy, 360 U.S. 471 (1959).
43. Lewis, Anthony; "High Court Voids Check on Risks in Arms Industry"; *New York Times;* June 30, 1959.
44. Ostrow, Ronald J., "Ruling Due on Reds in War Work"; *Los Angeles Times;* May 17, 1966.

CHAPTER 13 (continued)

45.   Public Law 90-237; 90th Congress; S 2171; Jan. 2, 1968.
46.   Schneider v. Smith, 196 (1967).
47.   Editorial: Walk Right Aboard, Comrades; *New York Daily News;* January 18, 1965.
48.   Gordon, Rosalie M.; *Nine Men Against America;* Devin-Adair; N.Y.C.; 1958, Chapter 19.
49.   Webster, John A.; "A General Study of the Department of Defense Industrial Security Program" Masters Thesis; John W. Donner Pub. No. 18; School of Public Administration, University of S. California; August 1960.
50.   Edwards, Willard; *Chicago Tribune;* September 25, 1964.
51.   Congressmen August E. Johansen & James B. Utt; Statement, Oct. 2, 1964.

CHAPTER 14, Disarmament and Grandeur Control.

1.   Simons, Howard; "Now We're Accused of Imperial Technology"; *Los Angeles Times;* December 27, 1965.
2.   "Communism – Facing a Clouded Future"; *U.S. News & World Report;* January 3, 1966; p 34-37.
3.   *Hearings Before a Subcommittee of the Committee on Government Operations;* House of Representatives; 86th Congress, Second Session, March 28-31, 1960; p 101-103.
4.   Orwell, George; *Nineteen-Eighty-Four;* Harcourt Brace & Co.; 1949; p 33-35.
5.   *U.S. News & World Report;* June 11 & June 25, 1954; p 82 & 79-80.
6.   Sheply, James R. & Clair Blair Jr.; *The Hydrogen Bomb;* Daniel McKay Co., Inc.; N.Y., N.Y.; 1954.
7.   Ibid; p 24.
8.   Brown, Allen & Edward Teller; *The Legacy of Hiroshima;* Doubleday & Co., Inc., Garden City, N.Y.; p 46.
9.   Op. cit.; Sheply; p 210.
10.   Morris, Robert; *Disarmament; Weapon of Conquest;* The Bookmailer, N.Y., N.Y.; 1963; p 112.
11.   "Pro & Con of Test Ban Treaty"; *U.S. News & World Report;* August 20, 1963.
12.   "No Army, No Navy, No Air Force"; Department of State publication 7277; released September, 1961, by the Government Printing Office. Now "out of print". Copies available from the Bookmailer, 30 W. Price St., Linden, N.J.
13.   Cook, Con; "U.S. will Bar Aid For Some Atom Vessels;" *Los Angeles Times;* March 14, 1968.
14.   Manahan, W.A.; "1976 A Study in Disarmament"; *Christian Crusade;* November, 1965; p 36-39.
15.   Allen Scott Report; "Rostow Believed 'Father' of Commission Proposal"; *San Diego Union;* March 23, 1968.
16.   Edwards, Willard; "Rostow Backs Education on Soft Red Line"; *Chicago Daily Tribune;* June 18, 1962.
17.   Widener, Alice; "All in the Name of Peace"; U.S.A. Report; Nov. 29, Dec. 13, 27, 1963; U.S.A. Publishing Co., 530 E. 72nd Street, N.Y., N.Y.
18.   Widener, Alice; "More on the Phoenix Study – The 22 Recommendations"; U.S.A. Report; April 17-May 1, 1964.
19.   Elegant, Robert S.; "Why America Can't Turn Back on Asia". *Los Angeles Times;* August 28, 1966.

CHAPTER 14 (continued)

20. *Encylopaedia Britannica;* V16; p 92-95.
21. Ibid.; V15; p 1099-1101.
22. Rauchning, Herman;*The voice of Destruction;* G. P. Putnam's Sons, New York; 1940; p 191.
23. "Focus on Asia"; *Christian Science Monitor;* July 28, 1967.
24. "An Anniversary Talk With Huntley-Brinkley"; *McCalls;* Oct., 1966.
25. Hayek, Frederich A., "The Road to Serfdom"; *Reader's Digest;* April 1945.
26. "Radical Think Tank, The IPS"; *Human Events;* October 25, 1969.
27. Alsop, Joseph; "Sacrifice to the New Left"; *Los Angeles Times;* October 23, 1969.

CHAPTER 15, Epilogue.

1. Alsop, Stewart; "The New Snobbism"; *Newsweek;* September 8, 1969.
2. "Kuznetsov's Revelations Worry U.S. Intelligence"; *Human Events;* September 27, 1969.
3. "The Sino Soviet War"; *Los Angeles Times;* September 19, 1969.

APPENDIX B

1. Groueff, Stephane; *Manhattan Project;* Bantam Books Inc. N.Y.; 1967; p 17.
2. Irving, David; *The German Atom Bomb;* Simon & Schuster, New York; 1967; p 265.
3. Groves, Leslie R.; *Now It Can Be Told;* Harper Brothers, New York; 1962; p 230.
4. "Enrichment in the Seventies"; *Nuclear Engineering International;* March 1968.
5. "Swords and Plowshares"; *Nuclear Engineering International;* December 1965.
6. "Cheap Bomb Project Set"; *San Diego Union;* October 7, 1965.
7. *Zurcher Woche;* March 10 & 31, 1967. *Bild Zeitung;* January 16, 1966.
8. *Nuclear News;* May 1969. p3.
9. "Uranium Loss Discovered"; *The Louisville Courier-Journal;* September 18, 1966.
10. Marara, Luis V.; *Betrayal Opened The Door to Russian Missiles in Red Cuba;* The Truth About Cuba Committee, Miami, Fla.; 1968.
11. "The Cuban Nuclear Threat"; *Human Events;* March 19, 1969.
12. Allen, Robert S.; "Reds Grab Key Jobs in World Atom Agency"; *The Brooklyn Tablet;* November 2, 1957. Freiden, Seymour; "Expensive Bargin"; *New York Post Magazine;* January 22, 1961. Editorial; *New York Daily News;* October 7, 1961.
13. *Intelligence Digest;* May 1969.